PERSPECTIVES IN
CLINICAL PSYCHOLOGY

THE UNIVERSITY SERIES IN PSYCHOLOGY

Editor

DAVID C. McCLELLAND

Harvard University

ATKINSON, JOHN W.—*An Introduction to Motivation*

ATKINSON, JOHN W. (Editor)—*Motives in Fantasy, Action, and Society: A Method of Assessment and Study*

BAKAN, DAVID—*Sigmund Freud and the Jewish Mystical Tradition*

BASS, BERNARD M. and BERG, IRWIN A. (Editors)—*Objective Approaches to Personality Assessment*

BEARDSLEE, DAVID C. and WERTHEIMER, MICHAEL (Editors)— *Readings in Perception*

DANA, RICHARD H.—*Foundations of Clinical Psychology: Problems of Personality and Adjustment*

FLAVELL, JOHN H.—*The Developmental Psychology of Jean Piaget*

GUILFORD, J. P. (Editor)—*Fields of Psychology,* 3rd Ed.

GUIORA, ALEXANDER Z. and BRANDWIN, MARVIN A. (Editors)— *Perspectives in Clinical Psychology*

HELSON, HARRY and BEVAN, WILLIAM (Editors)—*Contemporary Approaches to Psychology*

HSU, FRANCIS S. K.—*Clan, Caste, and Club*

McCLELLAND, DAVID C.—*The Achieving Society*

McCLELLAND, DAVID C., BALDWIN, ALFRED L., BRONFENBRENNER, URIE, and STRODTBECK, FRED L.—*Talent and Society*

PEREZ, JOSEPH F., SPRINTHALL, RICHARD C., GROSSER, GEORGE S., and ANASTASIOU, PAUL J. (Editors)—*General Psychology: Selected Readings*

PETTIGREW, THOMAS F.—*A Profile of the Negro American*

QUAY, H. C. (Editor)—*Juvenile Delinquency: Research and Theory*

SARASON, I. G. (Editor)—*Contemporary Research in Personality*

STERN, PAUL J.—*The Abnormal Person and His World: An Introduction to Psychopathology*

SWARTZ, PAUL—*Psychology: The Study of Behavior*

Perspectives in Clinical Psychology

Edited by
ALEXANDER Z. GUIORA
and
MARVIN A. BRANDWIN
University of Michigan

D. VAN NOSTRAND COMPANY, INC.
PRINCETON, NEW JERSEY

TORONTO   LONDON   MELBOURNE

Preface

THIS BOOK IS a reflection of and a response to the increasing awareness that clinical psychology is in a transitional state. Its traditional conceptualizations and orientations have been challenged by the profound and accelerating social and technological changes of recent years. At this crossroads of its development, after two decades of rapid growth, clinical psychology faces the necessity of re-evaluating its underlying structure of beliefs, functions, and role identifications. It is evident that there are many salient and controversial issues confronting clinical psychology as it turns to this task. By drawing upon the writings of colleagues whose perspectives have taken shape through serious reflection and extensive clinical experience, the editors hope to direct attention to representative contemporary currents of thought bearing influentially upon some of these issues. As our primary aim is to provoke consideration of significant problems, rather than to provide reassuring but premature resolutions, the selections offered include several pairings of contrasting positions.

The content of the book is presented under three headings: (Part One) Clinical Interaction and Judgment; (Part Two) Conceptual Context and Perspective; (Part Three) Professional Identity and Direction. This differentiation serves mainly as a convenience of organization and is not assumed to derive from the intrinsic nature of the field of clinical psychology. Each of the three Parts is preceded by introductory commentary which, in addition to the initial Introduction, expresses the editors' viewpoints with regard both to the individual selections and the general areas of concern under consideration.

The material presented is perhaps of special pertinence to those who have but recently committed their professional lives to the responsibilities and prerogatives of clinical psychology—new Ph.D.s and advanced graduate students in clinical training programs. Such emphasis is justified not because they have the most to gain but because, in essence, they have the most to offer. For whatever value or potential is inherent in the ideas advanced by the contributing authors can find fruition only through these younger clinicians. The book is not intended, however, to be directed solely to a specific group of readers already committed to a particular professional position. Many facets of the issues here dealt with are not unique to clinical psychology, as even a cursory glance at the history of science will attest. If the clinician's striving can be characterized as a reaching toward a greater breadth of knowledge about human behavior and a deeper comprehension of the implications of its application, then the presented selections are germane to the broad and diverse audience which shares such a striving. The book is addressed, therefore, to all students of psychology, in the fullest sense of the term: colleagues in clinical psychology and related professional disciplines, graduate and undergraduate students in the entire range of the behavioral and social sciences, and, in sum, anyone open to the challenge and ferment of new ideas.

ALEXANDER Z. GUIORA
MARVIN A. BRANDWIN

Contents

Contributors

DAVID P. AUSUBEL, M.D., PH.D.
Professor of Psychology and Education, The Ontario Institute for Studies in Education, Toronto, Ontario, Canada
Professor of Educational Theory, University of Toronto

DAVID BAKAN, PH.D.
Professor of Psychology, University of Chicago

JAMES BUGENTAL, PH.D.
Partner, Psychological Service Associates, Los Angeles, California

H. J. EYSENCK, PH.D.
Professor of Psychology, University of London
Director of the Psychological Laboratories, Institute of Psychiatry, Bethlehem-Royal and Maudsley Hospitals

SOL L. GARFIELD, PH.D.
Professor of Psychology and Director of the Clinical Psychology Program, Teachers College, Columbia University

STARKE R. HATHAWAY, PH.D., L.H.D.
Professor and Director, Division of Clinical Psychology, University of Minnesota Medical Center

PERRY LONDON, PH.D.
Professor of Psychology and Psychiatry, University of Southern California

PAUL E. MEEHL, PH.D.
Professor of Psychology and Adjunct Professor of Law, University of Minnesota
Professor, Division of Clinical Psychology, University of Minnesota Medical School

SAMUEL MESSICK, PH.D.
Executive Director of Research Programs, Educational Testing Service, Princeton, New Jersey

CARL R. ROGERS, PH.D.
Resident Fellow, Western Behavioral Sciences Institute, La Jolla, California

JOSEPH F. RYCHLAK, PH.D.
Professor of Clinical Psychology, Saint Louis University

NEVITT SANFORD, PH.D.
Professor of Psychology and Education and Director of the Institute for the Study of Human Problems, Stanford University

ROY SCHAFER, PH.D.
Clinical Professor of Psychology, Department of Psychiatry, Yale University School of Medicine
Senior Staff Psychologist, Division of Student Mental Hygiene, Department of University Health, Yale University

HANS H. STRUPP, PH.D.
Professor of Psychology, Vanderbilt University

THOMAS S. SZASZ, M.D.
Professor of Psychiatry, Upstate Medical Center, State University of New York

FREDERICK WYATT, PH.D.
Professor of Psychology and Director of the Psychological Clinic, University of Michigan

PERSPECTIVES IN
CLINICAL PSYCHOLOGY

Introduction

IT HAS BECOME a truism to say that the profession of clinical psychology is in transition. Indeed one may justifiably say that it has been in a continuing state of transition since it first emerged as the unplanned and occasionally unwanted offspring of an oftentimes not too harmonious union of academic psychology and clinical psychiatry. Thrust into early pseudo-maturity by the exigencies of the war years, American clinical psychology was spared the painful necessity of renouncing childhood narcissism through that combination of experience and self-scrutiny by which other older professions have gradually shaped a realistic, differentiated, and viable identity. The new breed of psychologist, in the satisfying reciprocity of enthusiastic practical endeavor and public acceptance, could easily dissociate himself from more subtle and disquieting reflections about his origin, identity, values, and purpose. Most clinicians who were swept up in the initial tide of growth learned to get along nicely in the "professional swim" without needing to wonder where the current flowed. In the past decade it has become an increasingly eddied current.

The sobering effect of the realities of its service responsibilities and an increasing public and professional sophistication have gradually imposed upon clinical psychology the awareness that some of the traditional conceptions and expectations that had sustained its early growth are no longer sufficient to ensure its continued advance. This realization promises to have a profound impact on the future of our field. Already one perceives a considerable broadening of the ever present undercurrent of concerned critical reflection toward a more comprehensive re-evaluation of the fundamental premises of the profession. To the resurgence of previously unresolved problems and ambiguities is added the leaven of the skeptical, searching orientation of graduate students and younger clinicians, not fully committed to the role adaptations of their teachers and older colleagues

1

and seeking a more certain, satisfying, and cogent identity commitment for themselves.

The turbulence of this reassessment process is reflected in the disparate attitudes noticeable in recent thinking in clinical psychology. A shifting emulation of one or the other of clinical psychology's progenitors vies with alternate tendencies to reject both areas in an effort to define a new, separate role image. Expressions of doubt and anxiety at giving up prior adjustments are countered by a welcome of the challenge of and opportunity for creating other adaptations. In both clinical and organizational activity there are contrasting strivings toward synthesis or compartmentalization of function. The increasing number of articles and conferences devoted to aspects of these concerns attests to their vitality in the present consciousness of clinicians. It is evident that the questions have now become more relevant and insistent, the ambivalence more acute, and the need for resolution more compelling.

There are undoubtedly many psychologists who would perceive the introspective turmoil of contemporary clinical psychology as a transition period analogous to an adolescent identity crisis out of which, hopefully, can evolve a realistically mature "self" with appropriate integration of inherent capacities. Others may prefer to view this transition period as a passage from a spoiled childhood to inevitable demise under the rigors of the "real world" of hard facts, cold statistics, and impassive "cookbooks."

The editors cannot ascribe to the latter point of view. It is our firm conviction that the course of transition is toward enhancement, rather than diminishment, of the unique contribution that the clinical psychologist can offer as scholar and healer. The skills which clinical psychology brings to the search for understanding of human behavior and *the human* behaving will remain resonant to meaningful and significant dimensions of human experience. More precise definition and attunement of our available skills is obviously needed, as well as continued development of new conceptualizations and methods. But it would be deceptive to equate progress with only the degree of "realness" conferred on clinical data by inclusion in a notational model, whether of theoretical or mathematical form.

Most professions have managed in the course of their development to evolve a sufficiently explicit and traditionally accepted image to permit young people motivated toward a career in that profession to gain a relatively early and reasonably close identification with the role which that profession has defined for itself. Because of the relative newness of clinical psychology, the young clinician generally brings to his choice of career a more diffuse and variable orientation than his counterparts in other professions. He is unable to draw from a strong fund of tradition to ease the insecurity which he may experience upon undertaking his duties. His course work and practicum experience have probably provided him with a fairly comprehensive core of relevant knowledge and a sufficiently adequate competence in clinical techniques to permit at least a superficially smooth assumption of the professional stance. But the resolution of the problem of identity corresponds to no set curriculum.

Most supervisors are undoubtedly familiar with the varied manner in which the identity problem is expressed through the content brought to the supervisory sessions. Nor need we remind the young clinician of what he himself often senses so acutely. The persistent thread of anxiety woven into the fabric of his daily activities is of no little consequence to the efficacy of his clinical interactions or to the quality of intellectual and emotional satisfaction gained in the learning process. Whether this anxiety acts as a stimulant or a deterrent to potential growth may depend in large measure on his opportunity to become cognizant of and to explore the wellsprings of his uncertainties.

Although individually elaborated, the anxiety we refer to is an essential concomitant of the contemporary state of clinical psychology and, as such, cannot remain incidental to the overall concern of the pre-doctoral training program. Much of what is learned in the classroom may remain sterile in the clinical situation if it has not become assimilated through emotionally meaningful self-appraisal and related to the broader context of attitudes and values within which one's professional identity takes shape. To a considerable extent this process of assimilation takes place via the extracurricular "bull session," that vital if unhonored supplement to the official course catalog. A more directed focus within the training program is warranted.

We have been impressed at the receptivity of students to discussion of areas of ambiguity and controversy associated with the material they are learning—at their willingness to direct intellectual curiosity toward more than the comforting certainties of familiar, conceptually isolated, or measurable but peripheral bits of clinical data. It may well be that the most important long-range contribution of any teaching program is the fostering of a disposition to probe beyond reassuring certitudes—for tolerance to ambiguity and tolerance to knowledge are, in a sense, two sides of the same coin. At this point in its progress clinical psychology cannot afford rigid crystallization of attitudes into comfortable, detached preoccupation with narrow segments of clinical content or practice. This would serve mainly to avoid anxiety and, in so doing, would block the possibility or realistic assessment and resolution of issues that promise to confront us with increasing insistence.

The views of the editors are admittedly biased (as any perspective that derives from strong personal commitment is apt to be) and this book is intended to reflect that bias. This collection of readings, however, is offered more as a stimulus to reflection than as the presentation of a wholly consistent, comprehensive, or conclusive position. These selections, grouped under the three general area headings of "Clinical Interaction and Judgment," "Conceptual Context and Perspective," and "Professional Identity and Direction," are intended to highlight some representative contemporary issues and, hopefully, to stimulate critical examination of the conceptual fabric underlying both existing diversity and congruence of opinion. It will soon become evident that questions posed with regard to any one of these areas may also be applicable to the other areas. For example, inquiry into the transactional implications of the test situation, such as asking whether the tester's personality and the role he assumes are important determinants of the reactions elicited by a test instrument, n raises related questions about the psychotherapy relationship and the research process—and even about society's evolving definition of what clinical psychology is.

The three area headings, therefore, should be viewed as arbitrary distinctions (for the sake of convenience) in what are really multiple expressions of the same basic concerns. To what extent do our current conceptual frames of reference—or the various modes of interaction between the clinical psychologist and those with whom he relates, or the "findings" emerging from such interaction—have relevance to the problems with which we are seeking to cope? Are our traditional methods of investigation fruitful, or even appropriate, in our search for knowledge about the human condition? What are our goals? What should be the clinician's identity, his expectations, his obligations? What are the essential ingredients, emotional and cognitive, which the clinical psychologist brings to his task, and how do these affect what he believes and what he does?

The presented selections provide a spectrum of opinion bearing on these and other questions, rather than definitive answers or easy resolutions. We hope these writings will contribute toward a more general and informed awareness of some exigent areas of concern and the viewpoints expressed can serve the reader as a context against which to orient his own reflections. The opportunity to engage in honest intra-professional dialogue must be pursued if genuine progress is to be gained. The willingness to pose questions and to explore the implications of such inquiry may well be the determining factor as to which of the two transition analogies mentioned previously will prove more apt. To do less than attend fully and openly to the dilemmas, inherent or apparent, which are perhaps the inevitable concomitants of any progressive unfolding of knowledge, is to risk by default the maturity of our profession.

A.Z.G.

M.A.B.

·····································

PART ONE

Clinical Interaction
and Judgment

ONE OF THE essential premises underlying the clinical psychologist's activities is that human behavior requires comprehension both in terms of its systematic regularities and its individual variations. This is so whether the primary focus be on diagnostic testing, psychotherapy, or research. It applies whether the immediate concern be the advancement of knowledge or its application to specific purposes, such as helping another individual to deal more adequately with the world he experiences. Because clinical psychology does concern itself intimately with the uniqueness of events, it is appropriate that special attention be directed to the clinical tools by which understanding is gained.

It is now generally recognized that the investigative process per se distorts the "reality" of any observed domain of events. Distortions of this nature are usually viewed as irrelevant, random occurrences whose effects may be cancelled out by appropriate statistical means. The emphasis on individual variation which characterizes clinical psychology, however, includes the assumption that distortions related to interaction effects between person and clinical instrument are themselves of crucial import and cannot implicitly be considered either as random or irrelevant. Much of our current effort to improve our clinical tools reflects this position. We are less prone to profess complete objectivity of our test instruments in the light of considerable evidence pointing to subtle and not so subtle influences of situational variables on response patterns. Nevertheless we still go about our daily business with more than a reasonable amount of denial and self-deception with respect to the clinical engagement. Although the inanimate tools of our profession are subjected to conscientious scrutiny in the search for improved reliability, validity, and sensitivity the role of the psychologist himself as a clinical instrument receives surprisingly little consideration. Of relevance here are differences in the way we comprehend the activities of the psychologist. There are some who prefer to view him as an independent observer and recorder of behavioral data to which objective principles of analysis and interpretation can later be applied. Consistent with this position would be a minimizing of subjective aspects of clinical judgment in the effort to improve the reliability of prediction.

There are, however, others who conceive of the psychologist's role in the clinical situation in a somewhat different manner and, consequently, place different emphases in considering the nature of the clinical judgment process. They would at times question whether undue preoccupation with inanimate instruments, theoretical models, technical procedures, and sophisticated statistical methods of avoiding subjective effects has tended to obscure potential insights into human behavior which would be gained by closer observation and use of the clinical interaction per se. According to this position the psychologist in any clinical situation is implicitly an active agent with an impact and an influence upon the stimulus configuration to which the patient responds. The ongoing act of participation necessarily affects the *what* and *how* of eliciting, recording, analyzing, and interpreting data. Therefore, commensurate attention need be directed in all clinical activities toward comprehension of the subjective factors, not merely in order to discount them but to make use of them to better understand the total ongoing process.

From the standpoint of this latter perspective the clinician is indeed a clinical instrument, perhaps the most crucial one. More importantly, he is an instrument whose potential for self-observation and regulation makes possible a controlled yet creative examination of significant individual differences in patient behavior. For example, in the test situation the tester's awareness of his own contribution to the dynamic interplay of variables associated with the test stimuli, the patient, and himself can be a fruitful source of hypotheses to which the test data can be meaningfully related. Similarly, tentative hypotheses which are suggested by test data derived at a particular point in the testing process can be rejected or elaborated on the basis of careful manipulation of relevant parameters of the patient-examiner interaction. The interpersonal dynamics of the test situation can either enhance or impede our understanding of clinical data, depending on whether or not it is adequately comprehended and effectively used. The same may be said with regard to situational variables in other areas of clinical function, e.g. transference and countertransference reactions in psychotherapy or examiner influences in research. Clinical judgment in this sense is intimately related to a selective search for comprehension of an immediate and changing pattern of events as well as to the goal of predictive power of a more general nature.

The first three papers presented in this section focus on some implications of the psychologist's personality attributes for the clinical engagement, in both the positive and negative aspects. But their larger view is toward the complex interweaving of reactions which pattern the behavior of all participants in the clinical situation. Schafer's searching examination of the examiner's contribution to the situational context of diagnostic testing impressively counters the notion that diagnostic testing is a standardized procedure or that limitation of attention only to actual test responses safeguards objectivity of interpretation. One might note that even a posture of detachment on the part of the examiner is a communicable attitude carrying stimulus value which may have considerable subjective significance for both the examiner and the patient. By highlighting some of its possibilities, pitfalls, and values Schafer's insights into the interpersonal structure of the testing situation provides a perspective against which the clinician may profitably re-examine his own style and conceptions. For a fuller discussion of the interpersonal context of diagnostic testing the reader is directed to the remainder of Chapter II in Schafer's *Psychoanalytic Interpretation in Rorschach Testing,* from which the presented selection is taken. Bugental's paper directs the awareness of the psychologist, this time in his role as therapist, to some aspects of his own humanness as they affect the authenticity and outcome of the therapeutic encounter. Of related nature is London's intensive exploration of the implications of the therapist's moral attitudes and commitments for the treatment interaction. His probing discussion highlights a number of questions and dilemmas confronting the clinician. Though easy resolution of the issues raised may not be forthcoming, it is essential to our role as therapists that they be candidly acknowledged and dealt with.

The remaining three papers in this section relate more directly to the issue of clinical judgment. They discuss, from sharply different perspectives, the nature and proper domain of the clinician's cognitive activities. Meehl speaks for those who consider predictive efficiency the dominant criterion of clinical success, and who find clinical methods of inference sorely wanting in this respect. He discusses evidence supporting his belief in the predictive superiority of a more empirically minded, statistically oriented methodology and urges acceptance and further advancement of efforts in this direction. In contrast, the papers by Bakan and Rychlak argue the legitimacy, relevance, and value of subjective elements in the clinical judgment process. They present theoretical considerations which define a view of the psychologist's cognitive activity from a rather different frame of reference than does Meehl. Neither of these positions is intended to totally exclude the other. What is essential is that the premises of each be carefully considered so that their appropriate contexts, values, and applications be clearly grasped. Granted that bias is inevitable; however, whether one prefers to believe that the clinician's awareness of his own cognitive processes holds the key to comprehension of human behavior or that, as Meehl has stated, "the clinical interpreter is a costly middleman who might better be eliminated," one's biases should not be based on acts of faith but exposed to constant and candid examination and evaluation.

A.Z.G.

M.A.B.

Interpersonal Dynamics in the Test Situation*

ROY SCHAFER

THE CLINICAL TESTING situation has a complex psychological struc-ture. It is not an impersonal getting-together of two people in order that one, with the help of a little "rapport," may obtain some "objec-tive" test responses from the other. The psychiatric patient is in some acute or chronic life crisis. He cannot but bring many hopes, fears, assumptions, demands and expectations into the test situation. He cannot but respond intensely to certain real as well as fantasied at-tributes of that situation. Being human and having to make a living— facts often ignored—the tester too brings hopes, fears, assumptions, demands and expectations into the test situation. He too responds per-sonally and often intensely to what goes on—in reality and in fantasy —in that situation, however well he may conceal his personal response from the patient, from himself and from his colleagues.

In short, an intricate interpersonal relationship, with realistic and unrealistic aspects, exists during the testing. This is not an evil. It should not be striven against. As in psychoanalytic technique, this re-lationship must be regarded as inevitable, as a potentially significant influence on the patient's productions, and as a possible gold mine of material for interpretation.

Analyzing the interpersonal relationship and the real test situation may take us out to, or beyond, the borders of "objective" test inter-pretation—in the narrow and, I believe, superficial sense of "objec-tive" test interpretation. But if we mean, as we should, to track down the origins and vicissitudes of the patient's test responses, we must deal with the total situation in which the responses occur. The inkblot alone, the digit span sequence alone, the picture of a boy and a violin alone, do not totally define the stimulus situation existing at any mo-

* From Roy Schafer, *Psychoanalytic Interpretation in Rorschach Testing.* New York: Grune & Stratton, 1954, pp. 6–32. Reprinted by permission.

ment. There are many other more or less uncontrolled but more or less identifiable stimuli in the situation. There are larger situational and interpersonal meanings that surround and invade the simple test stimuli. It is with these meanings that we shall be concerned in this chapter.

First to be considered will be the needs and problems of the tester as these are defined by his professional and personal position and by the realities of the testing situation and relationship. Afterwards the psychological situation of the patient being tested will be considered, and then the implications of the preceding analyses for interpretation of test results.

A. THE DYNAMICS OF TESTING

The needs and problems of the tester in the testing situation are defined by his historical and social position as a particular type of professional man, by his spontaneous and imposed assumptions as to his professional and scientific responsibilities, by the additional responsibilities he assumes and gratifications he seeks because of his personality make-up, and by the behavior of the patient and the particular conflicts in the tester this behavior stimulates. The tester's needs and problems will be sensed by the patient, the more so the more sensitive, paranoid, overcompliant and/or negativistic the patient is. These needs will, as they impinge on the patient's own needs and assumptions, influence the patient's definition of the testing situation.

As evidenced by the relatively recent papers by Gitelson (5) and Berman (1) among others, it being acknowledged more and more, regarding countertransference in psychotherapy and psychoanalysis, that it is not only futile but psychologically meaningless to set up an ideal of complete therapeutic impartiality or objectivity. Inevitably there are personal reasons why someone chooses to practice psychotherapy. As Fromm-Reichman has described, there are certain gratifications and securities the therapist seeks through his job and through his relationship with patients (4). The same may be said of the tester. The tester's responsibility, like the therapist's, is not to try to eliminate these needs; it is his responsibility to acknowledge their presence, understand them, keep them relatively unobtrusive, and try to ascertain how they have influenced the patient's productions and his own interpretations of these productions. The last two of these responsibilities are capable of very incomplete fulfillment at best. In psychotherapy, for example, the therapist often discovers only long afterwards that a look, a word, a gesture, made a difference in the patient's definition of the relationship. It would therefore be too much to ask a tester to be altogether clear about his influence on the testing situation. So far as major disruptions of test performance are concerned, however, the tester often can come to tentative conclusions.

In what follows the needs and problems of the tester will be discussed from three points of view—that of his professional situation, that of his role in the test relationship and that of his own personality. It should become progressively clearer as we go on that these three points of view are not really separable. Professional, technical and personal problems are inextricably intertwined.

1. The Tester's Professional Problems and the Test Relationship

The following discussion will concentrate on the psychological situation of a tester in a psychiatric hospital or clinic—the situation with which I am most familiar. It seems, however, that a good deal of what will be said is transposable, with appropriate modifications, to most situations in which clinically oriented testing is done. In the end, the reader will have to analyze his own work situation and decide which of the factors discussed here apply and to what extent; he will also have to determine which other factors, not mentioned here, also apply.

The emphasis in what follows will be on difficulties. This should not be taken to mean that the tester's relationships with colleagues and patients are always and inevitably miserable, conflict-laden affairs. They are very often cooperative, secure and gratifying. Therapists and testers can and do work together in the spirit of pooling their approximations in order to understand the patient better, and with an individualized relationship that takes account of the assets, limits and liabilities of each. Similarly, patients usually do have a strong enough wish to get well, a good enough sense of reality, or at least sufficient desire to be liked or to receive attention, that they cooperate adequately throughout the testing.

In the background of the professional problems to be considered are a number of historical and social sources of confusion and anxiety. For one thing, the status and boundaries of clinical psychology as a profession are still unsettled. There is no binding consensus on what is "good practice." There is a lack of firm, professional tradition in clinical psychology. There is, for example, little standardization of basic examination and treatment practices, and it is only recently that any code of ethics has been proposed (6). Then, there is much leeway left to the psychologist's temperament in defining his "style" of practice. In addition, the relation between theory and practice is often unclear, even though theory in this field usually greatly and immediately influences practice. And very important is the extremely rapid growth of the profession of clinical psychology during and after World War II. Swift growth of a profession inevitably means—for many, if not all—sketchy or inadequate training, and premature assumption of responsibility and status as the "expert" professor, supervisor or private practitioner. Finally, there is the "hot potato" of lay psychotherapy and psychoanalysis; the tensions between psychologists and psychiatrists, and also among psychologists, are constantly felt these days.

Because of its rapid growth, a boom town excitement has characterized clinical psychology until very recently. News of a "good" test, like news of striking oil, has brought a rush of diagnostic drillers from the old wells to the new and has quickly led to the formation of a new elite. The same has been true for new statistical techniques. Checking the claims made for new tests and new statistical techniques has provided many graduate students with dissertation projects, the reports of which have tended to crowd the psychological journals. And the handbooks and source books have been pouring out like maps of the countryside that are sure to lead one to riches.

Almost all that has been said about clinical psychology is true for psychiatry as well. While an older profession by far than clinical psychology, psychiatry has grown rapidly in recent years and has also been having its booms and busts. New treatment techniques (both physical and psychological), new theoretical emphases (particularly the variants of Freudian psychoanalysis), and new personalities and "splinter" groups have appeared rapidly during and after World War II. Being in its own quick flux, psychiatry imposes special burdens and uncertainties on its practitioners. These burdens and uncertainties inevitably intrude into—and to some extent disrupt—the psychiatrist's smooth working relationships with members of other professions, such as psychologists and social workers, who make claims, demand equal status and privileges, and create uncertainties themselves.

All of these social and historical factors combined have kept the tester's professional setting—and his self-concept as a professional—anxiety-arousing, obscure, fluid, doubt-laden and open to opportunistic manipulation. But in addition, these factors have been challenging, exciting and stimulating to exploration and growth. In this uncertain, hectic atmosphere works the tester—whose professional, individual and interpersonal problems we shall now consider.

Ordinarily the tester has a service function. The patient is referred to him for testing by someone—psychiatrist, judge, teacher, social worker or psychologist—who has therapeutic or administrative responsibility for the case. The tester must produce a report that contributes in various measures to diagnosis, comprehension of dynamics, prognosis, and plans for therapy or disposition. Whether he be in private or group practice, the tester's economic and professional status and his self-esteem depend on the value of his reports to the sources of referral. There is therefore every reason to assume that the tester's needs for security and gratification will be intimately involved in each of his testing relationships. Since, as will be discussed later, there is also every reason to assume more or less resistance to the testing in many patients, and therefore more or less apparent threat to the tester's "success," the tester must be on the alert for a significant degree of anxiety, demand and resentment between himself and the patient in the course of the testing.

If the tester is in group psychiatric practice, he often both is put and puts himself on the defensive. As a rule, he tests patients who, for the time being at least, are in the care of or being worked up by psychiatric residents. The residents themselves are often professionally insecure and anxious—not only about their comprehension and handling of their cases, but about their relationships to senior staff members as well. In addition, they are usually essentially unfamiliar with tests and principles of test interpretation. They do not know what to expect from the tester and are unprepared to evaluate what they do get. To them testing may well appear as some strange hocus-pocus or at least as something not immediately comprehensible and therefore to be on guard against. Often, therefore, the psychiatric residents fall in with the attitude toward testing displayed by the chief of their psychiatric section or clinic or by other senior staff members. They assume, not always correctly, that the chief's attitude is informed and trustworthy. If this attitude is hostile and disparaging, as will soon be discussed, the tester is certainly in a difficult position.

But if the prevailing psychiatric attitude is favorable, difficulties do not end; other problems arise. To some extent, and not always subtly, the residents ambivalently transfer to the tester major or full responsibility for clarification of diagnostic, dynamic, prognostic, therapeutic or dispositional problems in the case. It becomes the tester's "job" to settle the problematical issues. This difficulty becomes especially acute when cases are not routinely tested but are referred for testing only where major confusions or uncertainties exist in the psychiatrist's mind. A heavy and therefore inevitably anxiety-arousing responsibility is thereby imposed on the tester. His way of coping with this anxiety may significantly influence his personal approach to the patient and his interpretive approach to the test results.

Since the tester is, as it were, ambivalently glorified by these high expectations, the combination of glorification and reactive anxiety may facilitate his falling back on the implicitly megalomanic defense of being a know-all. Defensive loss of sight of one's personal and professional limitations—if it works at all—does no more, of course, than afford some relief from *conscious* anxiety; the tester remains fundamentally anxious but now has the added burden of maintaining an especially vulnerable grandiose self-concept. Under these conditions, the patient becomes, in fact, more of a threat than before and is met by the tester with more anxiety, resentment, and demand.

Further unfortunate consequences are possible. The test responses may be overinterpreted. Any new test with a colorful set of interpretive principles may be seized on, especially if seemingly deep or complex interpretations may be arrived at simply or mechanically— as in the case of the Szondi test (2, 9). The formulation of interpretations may be dramatized by pseudo-literary and pseudo-philosophical metaphor—as is so often evident in Rorschach interpretation. Test jargon may be resorted to more and more. And, in the end, the tester's denial of personal anxiety over inadequacy means denial both of the complexity of human problems and of the uncertainty of human understanding.

"Omniscience," with or without literary and philosophical trimmings, is not the only way out, however. A common alternative solu-

tion to the demands and anxieties imposed by the psychiatrist's glorification of the tester is the hedging solution. The hedging does not
have to be explicit hedging of the could-be-this, could-be-that variety.
More commonly the hedging is obscured in a buckshot barrage of
interpretations. Almost every variety of psychopathology is mentioned somewhere in what is likely to be an overly long report. No
hierarchy of importance of the variables mentioned is established.
In the end the tester will always be able to say—autistically—that
the test results reveal the specific problems of the patient. The un-
sophisticated or insecure psychiatric resident—also autistically—may
agree. And a good but profitless time will be had by all.

A further aspect of the ambivalent glorification problem is that
the psychiatric resident, in the negative part of his ambivalence, may
also fear and resent being "shown up" or at least having his life
"unnecessarily complicated" by test findings at variance with his
own. The resident may then uncritically accept confirmatory reports
or confirmatory parts of reports, and blithely or critically disregard
the tester's nonconfirmatory contributions. This internally contradictory position is not infrequently taken by senior psychiatrists who
have remained significantly insecure and pretentious. Think what
this does to the morale of the tester. He cannot be sure he will be
esteemed or appreciated for even his best work. He is naturally
tempted to play along with the psychiatrist's impressions in order
to protect his job (or referrals), his professional relationships and
status, and his self-esteem. By playing along he also may avoid facing
the fact that his is actually a "lower" professional status. Or the
tester may be driven to rebel, to fight the psychiatrist arrogantly
with as many interpretations as possible that clash with or show up
the psychiatrist. Then again, he may withdraw his emotional investment in testing, feeling that the condition of his professional acceptance and survival is that he be a yes-man.

More likely than not, the tester will not be characterized by any
one attitude, but will shift about among these submissive, rebellious
and withdrawn positions, especially during his younger, less secure
years. These shifts will often be implicit and covert, but will emerge
at times of crisis in professional relationships.

The overvalued tester may—it is common enough these days—be
inadequately experienced, trained or supervised. He may then naively
or fearfully retreat from human complexity and desperately avoid
saying "I don't know" and "I'm not sure." He may manufacture

"experience" by recalling previous interpretations as previous interpretive successes; that is, having handled an interpretive problem a
certain way one or more times in the past, he may believe that
that is *the* way to handle it. An error or a hunch repeated enough
times easily gets to feel like a confirmed principle.[1] And this pre-
maturely independent tester may be driven into all the other misconceptions and misrepresentations discussed above—hedging, etc.

Such pushes and pulls as these—toward grandiosity, hedging, pro-
pitiation, rebellion and withdrawal—play on the tester all the time
in settings where he is consistently overvalued or inconsistently and
opportunistically overvalued. These pushes and pulls are more or
less part of the context in which clinical testing is done, and help
determine how it is done, how the patient is regarded and related to,
and how the results are interpreted and presented.

Of course, the tester usually is not simply the passive victim of the
psychiatrist's misconceptions. He may actively contribute to these
misconceptions and to the resulting conflicts and anxieties. He may,
for example, oversell himself, appearing on the scene like a fortune
teller with his Rorschach crystal ball, acting and writing reports as
if his tests do say the last word about the patient and, in effect,
according the psychiatrist no status at all. This pretentious approach
is certain to provoke retaliation, very often in the form of the ambivalent overvaluation just discussed. The tester may also contribute
to conflict by writing far-fetched, jargonistic or hedging reports;
these may provoke justified skepticism and indifference. Frequently
incorrect diagnoses or poorly integrated personality sketches may
well lead to a decrease in referrals or to the psychiatrist's filing the
test reports without reading them. It is incorrect, therefore, to view
either the psychiatrist or the psychologist as the "villain of the
piece." The complexities of the professional relationship are such
that frequently, in spite of genuine good will between them, both the
psychiatrist and the tester may unnecessarily and unwittingly provoke each other and then retaliate.

Of course, consistent or inconsistent overvaluation of the tester
represents only one type of difficulty in the tester's professional re-

[1] Instead of repeating one's own errors, one may repeat errors or cling to
prejudices of one's teachers. Positive identification with teachers—despite its
strengthening aspects—will also limit both one's own capacity to think critically about all aspects of one's work and one's flexibility; negative identifications will be equally—though differently—self-limiting.

lationships. This difficulty is mentioned first because, as clinical testing is more and more accepted as part of psychiatry, it is coming to
be more typical. A much older but still lively set of problems centers
around undervaluation of the psychologist—real and fantasied. It is,
for example, difficult for the tester to accept the fact that a nonmedical psychologist may be and usually is a second-class citizen in
a psychiatric setting. It is additionally difficult because his scientific
and psychological training, even if superficial, exceeds that ordinarily
encountered in psychiatric residents. The tester can hardly avoid
resentment, rebelliousness, withdrawal and the like, when faced with
the status of subordinate or technician that is frequently imposed,
explicitly or implicitly, by psychiatrists and, to an extent, *implied
in the realities of the situation*. He is, after all, performing an auxiliary function.

Matters get still worse when the tester, as he often does, secretly
regrets not having an M.D., that is, all the authority, prestige, mo-
bility, responsibility, income-potential and opportunity for therapeutic and psychoanalytic training that in reality go with the M.D.
degree in this field, and all the omniscience, omnipotence, and solid
living that are associated with this symbol in our magical thinking.
The craving for the M.D. may underlie, accompany, or be displaced
by the desire to do therapy. Very often testing is regarded as—and
in fact is, to an extent—the back door into doing therapy. The
tester then submits himself to what he regards as the debasement of
his clinical novitiate in hopes of ultimately being appointed a high
priest of therapy. In all this, on the side of the physician-therapist
and on the side of the psychologist-tester, there are great potentialities for reenactment of sibling rivalries and propitiations and also
father-child rivalries and propitiations.

Another type of devaluation of testing is that common in large
hospitals. The tester sends out his report and, because few cases are
presented at staff conference, because few detailed case histories are
prepared, because the tester is relativly isolated from many of the
psychiatrists, and because relatively few, if any, patients enter
psychotherapy, he may never know whether the report was read or
used or how well it "fit" the case, and he may feel that his work
makes little or no difference to anyone. Morale, professional self-
esteem, cannot be sustained very well under these conditions.

The feelings of occupational and therefore personal inferiority, of
being, so to speak, a clinical eunuch, may provoke the tester to over-

compensate. He may feel impelled to "show up" the psychiatrist by proving him "wrong," or to outdo him in depth and breadth of interpretation. Inevitably this solution suffuses his work with further anxiety—about success and failure—and with burdensome, compulsive demands for powers and achievements that are not easily to be had, if at all. The quality of test reports may suffer. In the end the patient may suffer too, because the tester passes the buck to him, and demands of him what he, the patient, may not be eager or able to provide—maximal cooperation and self-revelation.

Thus, undervaluation as well as overvaluation of his work, on the part of both his psychiatric colleagues and himself, may well impose extra, unrealistic demands on the tester, and through the tester on the patient. This conclusion raises two questions: In what ways will these demands be made on the patient, that is, with what ultimately disruptive assumptions may the tester, under the pressure of these professional problems, approach the patient? And what unfortunate consequences are possible? Five such assumptions or demands will now be considered, along with the complications they create.

a. The tester wants responses. He needs them to render service. It is rare that a patient yields no test responses. It is not at all rare, however, that the patient, because of a repressive, depressive, negativistic, or paranoid orientation, or because of psychological deficit, yields minimal responses, that is, responses few in number, brief in extent, and barren in content. This is particularly likely to occur in the Rorschach and Thematic Apperception tests. To the insecure tester, who will regard minimal response as little better than nothing, this may mean defeat at the hands of the patient. As the testing proceeds, anxiety-driven resentment against the "thwarting" patient, and intolerant demand for output, may readily increase. In consequence, the patient's anxiety, resentment and unproductivity may also increase.

In this and in other contexts, each tester will deal with his and the patient's anxiety and resentment in his own way. His "own way" will, of course, be influenced by the type of patient and by his own current personal and professional life circumstances. The tester may become bored and possibly even sleepy; he may become irritable and impatient; his helpfulness may become condescending; his friendliness may break the rhythm and continuity of the total test; his inquiry may become perplexing or humiliating.

A good part of the minimal response problem may reside in the tester's assumption that only *content* really matters. This assumption may be taken over from the psychiatrist who has already been thwarted by the patient's rigidly concealing defensive structure and who has turned to tests as "royal roads to the unconscious." Sometimes the tests do clarify some of the underlying dynamics of these resistant patients, but often they don't. The fact they *do* or *don't* may then itself be more significant than any particular content they may elicit. That is to say, granted that the tester has tried hard but not too hard to break through the patient's resistant attitude, the test results may then offer an independent assessment of the depth and rigidity of the patient's defensive structure. A secure and sophisticated psychiatrist may accept this; an insecure and naive psychiatrist, overwhelmed by his brief acquaintance with the id, may not. In such a way, the competence and personalities of his colleagues may play a large part in the tester's security in his own work.

The rigidly defensive or otherwise psychopathological basis of paucity of responses itself constitutes a finding of the foremost importance in any psychological appraisal. Appreciating the value of analysis of defenses helps avoid the pitfalls of this situation. The desperate alternative of trying by arbitrary, far-fetched, symbolic alchemy to turn leaden test responses into golden content interpretations is hardly satisfactory, though common enough these days. Similarly desperate and arbitrary is the solution of falling back on tests, such as the Szondi (2) and Draw-A-Person (7) tests, with a set of *mechanical* interpretive principles that allow seemingly deep and broad interpretations to be made under any and all circumstances. The Draw-A-Person test is of demonstrated value as a projective technique, but it is no substitute for a psychoanalysis.

On the other hand, while the tester wants responses, he does not want to be swamped by them. Detailed, elaborate and abundant responses require a great deal of time and effort to record, sift, analyze and synthesize. The tester may often justifiably feel, therefore, that the burdens of a long, "rich" record represent hostile demands and subtle obfuscation by the patient. For example, some patients, particularly some obsessional patients, do assault the tester through a relentless "compliance" with the Rorschach test instruction to give all their impressions of each inkblot. The resentment felt by the overwhelmed tester, with developing writer's cramp and a cramped time schedule, can be *used* by him to increase his understanding of the patient's motives and defenses. This resentment may, however, be *abused* by him if he takes revenge on this maliciously "sincere" patient. Very often, the tester's suppressed and obliquely expressed resentment is sensed by the patient, increases the patient's anxiety, and only spurs him on to greater "cooperation."

Much of the difficulty here begins with the tester's assumption that every response is to be valued, and that a patient should never be stopped in the midst of a stream of responses. "Who knows," he may wonder and hope, "the twenty-third response to this Rorschach card may express something of basic significance that was avoided in the twenty-two that came before?" This is, of course, a vain hope. An average of ten responses per card provides more than enough material for description of the major personality characteristics and problems of the patient. Of fine trends there is no end anyway, whether they are seen in the test results or not.

It is important, however, to know whether the patient, if left to his own devices, will run on seemingly endlessly. This may be established in the course of the first two or three Rorschach cards. But beyond that point the problem often becomes one of unrealistic, inhibiting fear on the part of the tester that he will hurt, depress, anger or otherwise disturb the patient—in short, the tester's fear of asserting his authority and responsibility in the testing situation. As in rearing, teaching or testing children, it seems that this *laissez-faire* attitude may well stimulate rather than avoid increased anxiety and distress in the patient. The *laissez-faire* attitude may be wrongly supported or rationalized by a naive attitude toward standardization of test administration (see section *e* below).

Thus, because he wants responses, that is, because he wants the patient to tell important things about himself, the tester may be at once plunged into a morass of mutual anxiety, demand and resentment.

b. The tester wants not only responses but, wherever scoring is called for, scorable responses. But he often receives vague, evasive, fluid or overabundant material to score. This may apply to the spontaneous responses and to responses to inquiry. *Vagueness* and *evasiveness* are encountered, for example, in patients with low anxiety tolerance and little capacity for reflection and self-confrontation;

fluidity in schizophrenic settings, where inquiry often leads only to greater confusion than that caused by the patient's spontaneous inadequate communications; *overabundance* in obsessional, pedantic settings, where qualifications, doubts, alternatives, exceptions, and negations thrive.[2] In this respect too, as in the demand for responses in general, the patient's defensive policy and the tester's "service" needs may easily clash and cause disruption of the testing relationship. It helps to remember that evasiveness, vagueness, fluidity and pedantic outpourings may express character trends and psychopathology of primary significance.

c. The tester wants frankness. The patient may, however, be compelled to withhold some responses. The tester, especially if he is naively content-oriented, may then feel he is losing vital material, and may try, by persistent, challenging inquiry, to force the patient to be frank. Here too the defensive aspects of the withholding, particularly its paranoid or obsessional aspects, should be recognized as test findings of major significance. No more pressure should be put on the patient than that necessary to test the rigidity of this defensiveness.

The withholding of responses may, however, be threatening to the tester on another basis. That is when the differential diagnostic problem involves psychosis, and when the tester suspects that the withheld responses are autistic. This problem is not unusual in paranoid disorders and in patients showing remission or "sealing over" of psychotic breaks. In these cases, the tester may at least safely conclude that reality testing is sufficiently well preserved or restored to force self-critical rejection of bizarre reaction tendencies. This conclusion itself will be of the greatest significance for prognosis and therapy. Diagnostically, it will raise the question whether the patient ought not be regarded as a "borderline" or "sealed-over" case rather than fully psychotic; at the same time, it will call attention to possible paranoid trends of significance. In short, fluctuations in frankness should be made objects of diagnostic study in themselves, and should not be regarded—as nowadays, in psychoanalysis, resistance is no longer regarded—as an unfortunate interruption of "real" communication.

[2] Vagueness, unreflectiveness and fluidity are also often encountered in organic cases and in children.

d. The tester wants a verbatim recording. Careful analysis of verbalization is often crucial in understanding the patient. But many patients, despite all reminders of this need of the tester, talk too fast or too long at a stretch for verbatim recording to be possible. If this volubility is persistent, *despite the tester's intervention,* it expresses considerable narcissism, negativism, provocativeness and demandingness on the part of the patient. The patient's "sympathetic" suggestions that a dictaphone would make life easier for the tester only underscore his weak or hampered adaptiveness.

It is never easy to handle this type of situation. There are few situations in testing that are equally exhausting. One great temptation is to retaliate passively, avoiding open conflict, by beginning to abstract the patient's verbalizations or by simply recording, "etc., etc." Some valuable material may, however, be lost this way, particularly material that clarifies the inner structure of responses and the patient's attitudes toward his responses. The loss of such material is against the interests of both the tester and the patient, and this will inevitably cause some anxiety and resentment in the tester. Another great temptation is to comply passively, again avoiding open conflict, by scribbling as fast as one can in order to "get it all down"; although this solution may be successful, disruptive resentment at being rushed so is inevitable. Even if the situation is handled by persistent interruptions of the patient, to allow time to catch up, an unpleasant social demand may still be felt and resented. Unfortunately, the intellectual, professional satisfaction of being able to observe and interpret this *quite significant* narcissistic, demanding, provocative verbal display lessens the tester's tension only a little usually.

In part, it is perhaps wisest to find a position between these three methods of handling the problem—abstracting, writing faster, and reining in the patient. In addition, however, the tester should always feel free to interrupt the testing with open discussion of the problem of the patient's too rapid verbalization. This, reinforced by mild scolding perhaps, often affords a very good release of the tester's tension. Of all solutions, this one is the most likely to pay off. As in the case of overproductiveness, it is safe to assume that the patient will only be made more anxious and be stimulated to increased provocativeness by the tester's passive retreat into *laissez-faire.* True, in response to explicit pressure by the tester, the patient may alter his form of provocativeness, either by then saying very little, in which case the tester will have to intervene again and prod the patient toward a middle position, or by rendering exaggerated, mocking obeisance to the tester's recording needs, in which case the tester has what he asked for and need only note the switch in aggressive and defensive policy.

The patient's talking in a low voice, mumbling and trailing off present similar problems regarding verbatim recording. In interpretation, the aggressively demanding aspects of these types of verbalization should not be ignored in favor of the pathetic manner in which they are frequently expressed.

e. The tester wants to sustain the "standardized" administration of the test. This is a worthy ideal and certainly to be pursued with reasonably cooperative patients. Standardized administration is desirable as a way of maintaining a relatively set baseline for the interpersonal comparisons which are so vital in the interpretation of test results. It is also desirable if the tester intends to use his test records in a research project. But it is naive to think that standardization may be maintained by the tester alone. It takes two to keep things standardized. A patient is called "cooperative" when he accepts the tester's assumptions about the testing situation. When the patient rejects these assumptions, the tester will be painfully and unproductively rigid if he does not move away from the routine test procedures, and does not attempt thereby to engage the patient and find some acceptable ground on which the testing may proceed.

One patient, for example, for clearly emotional reasons, may say, "I don't know," in response to intelligence test questions he may safely be expected to know. Another patient may require much help in constructing TAT stories, and may even produce no more than descriptions of the pictures and "guesses" at possible situations depicted therein. A third patient may attempt to reject all or nearly all of the Rorschach cards without producing interpretations, or may, as described above, produce far more than is necessary and convenient. There is no end of these exceptional, unstandardized modes of response on the part of patients. Intervention by the tester is obviously called for in these situations. Insofar as he intervenes, he does alter the test situation, but he gains the important advantages that come with maintaining control over the test situation and with decreasing anxiety and tension stirred up by the test situation itself. The tester's responsibility in these instances is always to be sure of what he gets under standardized conditions before modifying his administration, to record his interventions and to attempt to establish their consequences.

He must ask himself, for example, "Did help with that fourth block design encourage or discourage the patient? Was it appreciated or resented? Could the patient catch on with help and use the help on later problems, or was the help wasted?" "Did special reassurance about the acceptability of certain Rorschach interpretations ease the patient's tension and free the flow of responses? Did it evoke only greater demands for reassurance? Were these demands oblique, as in constant self-disparagement, or childish, as in direct pleas to be told that the answers are 'right' or 'acceptable?' " Similarly, "Did encouraging the patient to give at least one (or more than one) response to each Rorschach card actually increase productivity? If it did, was the result instructive or was it empty? If it did not, was it in spite of real effort on the patient's part or did it only elicit a little token compliance?" These and similar questions are often grossly answerable. The answers, and thereby the deviations in administrative technique, ultimately enrich and clarify rather than impoverish and obscure the test findings.

The preceding analysis has not been exhaustive. It has touched on only some of the common needs and problems that confront the tester as a service-oriented psychologist. It should be clear by now, however, that in reaction to the various stresses existing within his professional context and as a manifestation of his own way of coping with these stresses, the tester may enter the testing situation with quite a number of burdensome assumptions, anxieties, oversensitivities and demands. The manner and extent of the patient's acceptance or rejection of these assumptions and demands, and the manner and extent of the tester's coping with the problems that ensue, together significantly influence the smoothness and instructiveness of the testing and the accuracy and effectiveness of the final test report.

The professional problems just considered constitute only one segment of the tester's psychological situation. There are, in addition, problems inherent in the test relationship itself and problems created by the individual adjustment patterns and difficulties of the tester. We shall now consider these two sets of problems in turn.

2. *Psychological Constants in the Tester's Role*

On the surface it seems adequate to define the clinical tester's role as follows: the tester is a person trained in certain techniques of observation and in certain ways of thinking about behavior, who attempts to perform a helpful, socially useful, auxiliary service to other persons—patients—troubled by adjustment problems. The patient, insofar as he wants help and is in contact with reality, perceives and accepts this role of the tester.

This definition, though valid, is superficial and incomplete. Testers, like patients, have unconscious reaction tendencies. They think and feel irrationally as well as rationally. They respond to certain aspects of their life work and relationships in terms of primitive, magical, dramatized conceptions. However much "ego autonomy" may obtain in the tester's work, that is, however free his work may be from the vicissitudes of unconscious personal conflicts and primitive conceptions, the autonomy or the freedom is always *relative*. We have already seen how problems of professional training, competence, status and role definition decrease the tester's relative "ego autonomy" and foster disruptive behavior in relation to the patient and the psychiatrist.

The channels of communication between daily behavior and deep conflict are never entirely closed. The channels may be more open in some testers than others. Also, in any one tester, these channels may be more open at one time than another. But the unconscious, primitive, more or less rejected tendencies and conceptions are ever present and ever ready to find an opening through which they may gain expression. The play of irrational tendencies and conceptions that underlies and sometimes invades the tester's professional functioning may support and promote his work, undermine and limit his work, or both, depending on the strength of these tendencies and the tester's style and effectiveness of coping with them.

It therefore seems worthwhile to explore some of the implicit, primitive, not so "socially acceptable" aspects of the tester's role. Some of these originate primarily in the tester's personality, that is, they reflect his way of structuring most or all situations he gets into. Others, however, derive largely from certain constants in the situation or role in which the tester functions. Situations and roles play on us, as well as we on them. Situations and roles bring one or another of our partial trends to the fore and obscure others. It is necessary to emphasize this because our growing acquaintance with character analysis and projective test theory tends to intrigue us too much with how we structure situations and to blind us to how much situations structure us. Ultimately, and as usual, the most enlightening approach to the problem is to view it as a matter of interaction, of mutual influence between the demands and implications of the role and situation on the one hand and the specific personality on the other.

It may seem to the reader that what follows confuses the individual psychopathology of testers with the general psychology of testing. This criticism would hold that most testers are essentially normal, objective, professionally detached participant-observers, and are not volatile, childish, erratic and irrational. This criticism ignores the restraining, modulating, buffering influence the defensive and adaptive ego functions exert on volatile, childish, erratic and irrational reaction tendencies. There is no internal contradiction in saying that the most primitively conceived and experienced reactions may occur in the tester without spilling over into his behavior as a tester and utterly disrupting it. Ego barriers and controls stand between these primitive reactions and conceptions on the one hand and conscious experience and behavior on the other. Exploring the primitive aspects of the tester's experience adds depth to our understanding of the tester and the test results and does not devalue the tester as a psychological participant-observer.

At least four constants in the tester's role may be singled out for purposes of this analysis: the role is voyeuristic, autocratic, oracular and saintly. These are constants in the sense that they appear to be present regardless of the personal needs and circumstances of fate that brought the tester to begin with to his professional role, and regardless of the tester's individual response to particular patients or patients in general.

a. The voyeuristic aspect of the tester's role. The tester is in the position of a psychological voyeur. He peeps into the interiors of many individuals and never once commits himself, as would be required under normal social conditions, to a relationship. His desk and writing board, his pictures, blots, blocks and stopwatch are doors and windows between him and the patient. All is observed from the safety of psychological distance and transiency of relationship. The tester's human obligations in the testing situation are temporary and usually shallow. Maintenance of sufficient superficial good will to complete the tests is often all that is required. In return for both his deliberate and his unwitting—but sensed—revelations about himself, the patient receives a bare minimum of information about the tester. Equally important, the tester ordinarily need not return any interpretations in exchange for the patient's self-exposures; he leaves that part of the job to the therapist. The tester finds out but tells nothing.

As will be discussed below, this peeping may be used by the tester in various hostile ways. It may also significantly increase the anxiety of the patient. The hostile and anxiety-arousing aspects of the peeping may, in turn, stimulate in the tester anxiety, guilt and desire to atone, or rigid denials of these. There is no clear line between keeping the patient reasonably comfortable during the testing and being ingratiating and overindulgent. There is also no clear line between being reasonably firm with and detached from the patient and being coldly indifferent to his trials and tribulations. The tester's anxious or guilty response to the voyeuristic aspect of his role may further obscure these two lines; it may lead him, depending on his character make-up, his life circumstances, and his response to the particular patient, to feel and behave too close to the patient, too distant from the patient, or in an inconsistent way, both too close and too distant. These excesses may then impair the effectiveness of the testing and the adequacy of the final test report.

Going further, our knowledge of primitive, affect-laden levels of thinking suggests that psychological voyeurism may be unconsciously elaborated as an act of hostile, sexual intrusion. That is to say, even if the tester did not, to begin with, choose testing in part as a more or less sublimated outlet for his infantile voyeuristic inclinations, these inclinations may well seize on the looking-in-secret aspects of testing and thus may invade the professional role. When this occurs in force, further anxiety and guilt about testing may result. This anxiety and guilt may then be manifest in awkward or avoided inquiry into fantasy material and emotional reactions, in atonement through ingratiation or superfluous reassurance, or in rigid maintenance of distance from the patient. On the other hand, the opportunity for voyeuristic intrusion afforded by testing may stimulate too much inquiry, too eager pursuit of "suggestive" details of responses and verbalizations. This will inevitably put the patient on guard and increase the tension in the test relationship. More about the patient's reactions to this psychological and sexual peeping aspect of the tester's role and to the other aspects to be discussed next will be found in Section B of this chapter.*

b. The autocratic aspect. The tester not only looks surreptitiously; he also dominates. The autocratic, dominating aspect of his role is implied in the fact that there is little sharing of control in the relationship. Even though inactive for long periods during the testing, the tester is the controlling one in the relationship. The tester tells the patient what to do, when to do it and when to stop, sometimes how to do it. He often demands to know why the patient did what he did, when he did, and the way he did. He brings out anxiety, inadequacy, compliance, rebellion and a host of other reaction tendencies. The tester is, in this respect, a psychological ringmaster. True, patients often fight hard and with more or less success to keep control of the situation themselves, but even then they are still oriented toward the tester's whip. The tester implicitly remains the dominant one. This is so even if he simply tells the patient during the Rorschach test, for example, "It's up to you," every time the patient asks for rules or guidance. In this regard, the situation is reminiscent of the cartoon showing a child in a progressive school desperately asking the teacher, "Do I have to do what I want to do?"

In a keenly insightful paper—a paper we shall return to frequently—Schachtel has discussed varieties of response to the freedom or lack of rules in the Rorschach situation (*8*). However, Schachtel equates complete permissiveness with freedom, and ignores the fact that complete permissiveness and lack of rules is just another kind of demand or control and not an absence of it. This point will be amplified later.

The tester's conflicts over and guilt concerning domination and manipulation of others—on a more primitive level, his conflicts over sadistic impulses—may therefore easily intrude into the test relationship. This is particularly likely when the patient expresses considerable anguish in the course of and in response to the testing. One tester may well need and enjoy his autocratic powers. He may be unduly threatened, resentful and retaliatively "strict" if the patient resists his domination. Another tester may play down or relinquish his control in order to lighten his guilt or blunt the overt, implicit or potential resentment of the patient. He may even fall back to a masochistic attitude of despair over how "impossible" it is "to han-

* Not included here.—EDS.

dle" this patient. But it is always a reality of the testing relationship that control or dominance is ultimately in the hands of the
tester. His way of using, abusing or hiding the ringmaster's whip in
his hands may have much to do with the quality and quantity of
the patient's productions and his own interpretation of them.

c. The oracular aspect. The oracular aspect, like the voyeuristic
and dominating aspects, is also a constant in the clinical tester's role.
After all, the tester does draw momentous and portentous inferences
from signs and symbols. He "sees into" hidden meanings, predicts
turns of events, implicitly or explicitly advises. This oracular position may be reinforced if the tester is overvalued by the psychiatrist,
as has been already pointed out. It may be further reinforced by the
fact that the prescription of tests is often explained to the patient
by the psychiatrist as a way of obtaining "objective" evidence as to
the type and extent of problems or personality changes. In part, this
explanation may imply to the patient *and to the tester* that the
psychiatrist or therapist is a fallible, ordinary human being, while
the tester cannot possibly be fooled, misled, confused or otherwise
troubled by the possibility of error. The tester, it is promised, will
come up with *the* answer. Still another contribution to the tester's
oracular conception of his role may be made by the patient: patients
commonly ascribe magically insightful and influential powers to doctors, therapists and their agents.

The tester, when he chose clinical psychology as his life work, may
have been seeking just such an oracular role. Testing—or therapy—
may be to him a royal road to omniscience—short, broad, smooth
and well-marked. One sees this conception in blatant form in many
young graduate students of clinical psychology for whom there is
no response they cannot interpret, no contradiction they cannot resolve, no obscurity they cannot penetrate, no integration they cannot achieve. One sees it too in the grandiose claims made about many
of the newer projective tests, not to speak of the Rorschach test
itself. To those who anxiously lose distance from and cling to this
oracular fantasy, the confusing patient—not a rare bird—is a serious
threat and is resented. But in all of us, even if well repressed or well
controlled, there is this longing for omniscience, for oracular powers,
and as testers we must cope with constant stimulation of this longing.

It must also be pointed out that it is easy enough for any tester
to feel in instances of clear-cut disagreement between his test report

and the psychiatrist's or therapist's opinion that he is right "really," and that his colleague is being misled by superficial appearances or by misconceptions. The line between sticking to one's guns with realistic justification and remaining defensively, megalomanically aloof from contradiction or correction is not a clear one, especially since it often enough does happen that the combination of tests and tester penetrate deeper or more accurately into the patient's problems and present status, or certain aspects of these, than the combination of clinical interviews and psychiatrist.

The tester may, on the other hand, beat a hasty retreat from the oracular implications of his role, responding more to its burdens than to its apparent blessings. He may minimize to the psychiatrist and to the patient the importance of his contribution. He may write reports full of pseudo-objective references to specific intelligence test scores, to specific numbers of *Whole* responses or *Human Movement* responses in the Rorschach test, and the like. He may write reports full of anxious doubts disguised as careful weighing of each point. In the end, he may refuse to take a stand on major points even when the available material is adequate for a strong stand. He will thereby dump all the responsibility for understanding the patient back into the lap of the psychiatrist.

d. The saintly aspect. By definition, the tester's role is a helpful one, even if only in an indirect and auxiliary way. The patient comes to the psychiatrist for help and the psychiatrist sends the patient to the tester with the assurance that the tester's report will more or less increase the effectiveness of treatment or the correctness of disposition.

Now, we have seen how, on a primitive level of experience, examining the patient takes on voyeuristic connotations, how instructing and questioning the patient takes on autocratic connotations, and how understanding the patient takes on oracular connotations. In the same primitively conceived way, helping the patient takes on saintly connotations. Is it not so that the tester does his best to help, no matter how provocative or "ungrateful" the patient? Does not the tester give out with all he has so long as he believes it is for the patient's good? Does he not implicitly promise psychological salvation? Will he not subdue his own needs and resentments and selflessly try to understand and feel the tragedy of the patient? Is not this code like that of a saint with a sinner, a slave or a leper?

It certainly is—as it is in the case of the therapist too—once we get below the level of objective, logical appreciation of reality and confront some of our magical thoughts and wishes. Often patients tend to cast us in just this saintly role and they find us not altogether unprepared for it.

The obligations of saintly restraint and warmth and of the power of salvation are heavy burdens to bear. Testers will be driven in various directions by these primitively conceived constants of their social and professional role. One way of "coping" with burdens is to drop them and flee. The tester may then be crisp with and overly detached from the patient. He may maintain to himself that his is only a research or theoretical interest in the patient or that the ultimate fate of the patient is no concern of his. He will then steadfastly refuse to exert himself to get a reasonably full record from the patient with a reasonable minimum of pain. If the patient does not spontaneously "come across," the tester will contend, "It's his problem, not mine!" And if the patient makes a move to put himself in the tester's hands psychologically, the tester will take cover behind "standardized administration" more quickly than he needs to. There will be no room in this test relationship for even the little bit of mutuality that is possible.

In contrast, the tester may be seduced rather than repelled by the saintly aspect of his role. As we shall see later, this is particularly likely if his reaction formations against dependent and hostile impulses are rigid and pervasive. He then may go all out to comfort the patient and sell him on the Promised Land benefits of taking the tests. He will go to inappropriate lengths to get the fullest possible record with the least possible pain. At all times, this tester will need to have it perfectly clear to the patient that he is being helpful. But his saintly advances may be spurned by the patient, that is, his reassurances brushed aside, his instructions and explanations ignored, his kindnesses unappreciated, and his urgings ineffective. In this case, he may redouble his saintliness in what will now be a clearly hostile, guilt-provoking maneuver, or he may become impatient, irritable, cold, bored or otherwise unsaintly.

These have been caricatures of reactions to the saintly aspect of testing. Their purpose has been to highlight its most disruptive consequences. No tester plays "saint," but all testers are tempted by their role—and by the patient—to feel saintly and to act accordingly.

The voyeuristic, autocratic, oracular and saintly constants in the test situation must be coped with by every tester, each in his own way. Some of these ways of coping have already been touched on; others will be discussed below. What has not been pointed out so far, and what must certainly be remembered, is that the tester can more or less come to terms with (not escape) these constants in a primarily adaptive manner. He need not invariably be driven to extreme acceptance or rejection of the irrational implications of these constants. He may be relatively free to look searchingly, control flexibly, interpret both imaginatively and soundly, and help out with realistic restraint and self-assertion. He is more likely to do so if he is aware of the complex psychological implications of his job and of his relationships with colleagues and patients. A sense of professional security and self-esteem, based on experience and competence, also helps greatly. With the help of insight, security and self-esteem, the tester is also more likely to find his way again, if, as not rarely happens, he loses it in overreacting to particular patients or to problems in test administration. The tester's competence and humility, his powers of reality testing, his genuine interest in helping others, and his understanding and acceptance of himself will powerfully counteract the irrational conceptions and temptations. And, it must be stressed, the irrational tendencies may not only hinder but also promote testing skills; up to a point they may increase alertness, strength, insightfulness and responsiveness.

3. The Tester's Personality in the Test Relationship

Having considered some of the major ways in which the situation and his role play on the tester, we may now round out our analysis of the tester by considering ways in which he, in accordance with trends dominant in his personality make-up, may actively play on or structure the test situation.

Eight types of testers will be discussed: those with an uncertain sense of their own identity; the socially inhibited or withdrawn; the dependent; those with rigid defenses against dependent needs; the rigidly intellectualistic; the sadistic; those with rigid defenses against hostility; and the masochistic. Admittedly, these are "types." They are oversimplified characterizations which will be helpful for purposes of discussion. These eight types are not exhaustive, mutually exclusive or otherwise systematically selected and described. They merely summarize frequent and conspicuous problems of testing and are discussed only to open up the study of the individual aspects of the tester at work. *Ultimately, these types should be thought of as aspects of each tester's personality, one or more of which might usually be dominant, but any of which might become dominant at certain times of crisis in the tester's total life situation or in the tester's relationship with a particular patient.* An effort will be made to point out how each of these major tendencies may facilitate as well as hamper effective testing.

a. The tester with an uncertain sense of personal identity. The study of clinical psychology is probably particularly attractive to persons with a chronically diffuse self-concept, persons who are unsure what sort of individuals they want to be, what kinds of relationships to cultivate, which of their impulses and feelings to accept and express and how to express those they can accept, which of their assets to develop and which traditions and values to adhere to. These individuals may be described as having an uncertain sense of personal identity, following Erik Erikson's use of the concept of identity (*3*). Psychology may seem to them to offer help in working out their personal solutions to this problem. *Clinical* psychology particularly may have this appeal because it deals with such problems as these all the time, and because, at first acquaintance, it seems to offer all the answers.

To a tester beset by identity problems, testing becomes a means of observing a wide variety of personal identity solutions. By "discrediting" other solutions—often easy enough to do in a clinical setting—the tester may employ his observations to reassure himself either as to his "normality" or as to the acceptability of his "abnormality." He may also use his test observations to pick up such fragments from the total personality pictures of various patients as seem usable in his personal integrative efforts. We do, after all, observe traits in our patients which we admire or envy, such as charm, wit, verbal facility, forcefulness and imaginativeness. As a way of finding out how other persons manage or mismanage, testing is therefore relatively safe and inexpensive, even though not too personally rewarding in actuality. Insofar as this identity orientation involves direct or indirect self-confrontation, it may imbue testing with considerable anxiety. Insofar as the identity orientation exists within a predominantly narcissistic setting, it may lead the tester to demand richly self-expressive material from patients incapable of giving it, and to manifest excessive favoritism in his dealing with patients—love flowing to the instructive or admired ones, for example, and boredom and disgust to the barren, obscure, or challenging ones. This identity orientation may also lead the tester to lose himself in his case material, and weaken or obscure whatever sense of identity he has to begin with.

On the positive side, the tester's search for an identity may increase his perceptiveness of just how the patient is trying to solve his problems, just how the patient does try to conceive of himself. Uncertainty about one's self may contribute significantly to a capacity to see the great variety of solutions available to others and the subtler aspects of the way others flounder around among these solutions. It may thereby foster a feel for uniqueness and a tolerance for and constructive use of ambiguity and apparent contradiction in the implications of test findings. Also, insofar as it involves self-confrontation, this orientation may contribute to the personal and professional growth of the tester.

b. The socially inhibited or withdrawn tester. To this tester, testing may become an avenue toward human contact, and in some respects toward interpersonal intimacy. At the same time, however, testing offers this tester the defensive advantage of reassurance against the dangers and the pain of ambivalence in relationships; it does this by guaranteeing that there is nothing binding in these moments of intimacy, that there is little danger of control of the relationship slipping out of his hands, and that the flow of intimacies will be in one direction only—towards him. The controlled, temporary, one-way intimacies in the tester's professional life will have appeal to the extent that the tester's personal relationships are fraught with compulsive, schizoid or paranoid anxieties and inhibitions.

Under these conditions, difficulties may develop in the test relationship if the patient vigorously attempts to wrest control of the situation from the tester, and to move in on him in a "too personal" way, demanding more human response and involvement than the tester is prepared to give. Considerable anxiety may ensue in the tester. This anxiety may lead him to become cold, brusque, irritable or more withdrawn. Ultimately the testing may become a painful and unprofitable experience for both participants.

On the positive side, social inhibition is often accompanied by hypersensitivity to emotional nuances in relationships. This hypersensitivity may add to the tester's perceptiveness—provided that the tester is not overly paranoid or arbitrary in his perceptions to begin with.

c. The dependent tester. As an expression of a dependent orientation, testing may be viewed as a means of obtaining receptive gratifications. These receptive gratifications are of the sort that are implied in esteem and appreciation the patient expresses to the tester as a professional helper, and in the major share of the work of personal communication assumed by or imposed on the patient in the course of testing. The tester asks, the patient gives. In this respect, the tester's looking and controlling become a kind of feeding on the patient. The demanding or ungiving patient—another common bird—may easily stir up disruptive resentment in such a tester. To the extent that his own passivity leads the tester to misconstrue (and mishandle) the testing situation as one in which he may regularly enjoy free receptive gratifications, to that extent will his testing relationships be tense, cold, hostile, and frustrating.

This tester may, for example, fear displeasure or resentment in the patient. He will want to stay on the patient's good side, i.e., his generous, indulgent, supportive side. In response to discomfort in the patient, the dependent tester may not press inquiries or demand for continued effort even though such pressure is clearly indicated. He may defensively rationalize this gingerly policy by asserting the necessity of maintaining good rapport. That this is a defensive rationalization is attested to by the unnecessary sacrifice of dynamically or diagnostically significant material that may have been entailed by his kid-gloves approach. Good rapport is not, after all, an end in itself; it is a way at getting at the material we need to write worthwhile reports and thereby help the patient. To a degree, rapport must often be sacrificed in order to clarify crucial problems in the course of administration and inquiry. (Here again is a parallel to therapy.) One may easily hesitate, for example, before inquiring into a possible contamination in the Rorschach record of a suspicious, hostile patient. It is easy to feel, "What a mess I'll get into if I inquire into this! Is is really worth it?" When passivity and fear that the patient will withdraw his "supplies" are strong enough to interfere persistently with thorough test administration, some active self-confrontation on the tester's part is obviously in order.

d. The tester with rigid defenses against dependent needs. Defenses against dependent needs, perhaps particularly reaction formations, often play a vital part in the clinical psychologist's choice of profession. The psychologist tends to the needs of others and, in his professional role at least, denies his own. Unconsciously, through identification with the cared-for patient, the tester may derive some indirect gratification to balance his conscious "sacrifice." The repressions of and reaction formations against dependent needs may, however, be too rigid or too weak. If too weak, the type of behavior described under the heading "the dependent tester" may well occur. If too rigid, that is, if the tester's entire life is dominated by a defensive imperative always to give and never to receive, then the tester will in a too cold, too maternal, too saintly or too syrupy way try to force the patient into a passive receptive role. Patients long for this role but are typically terribly afraid of it. Consequently, the test relationship may suffer in response to the "all-giving" tester.

If the tester's defenses against dependent needs are neither too rigid nor too weak, that is, if dependent needs are well integrated into his character structure, then he will be a very good tester indeed. At least, his moderate and flexible defenses and his self-tolerance will limit the demands he makes on the patient and increase his empathy for the patient's needs and his tolerance of the patient's need-denying defensive tendencies.

e. The rigidly intellectualistic tester. To an extent an intellectualistic bent is necessary and probably present in all psychologists. So long as it remains under some control, this bent is, of course, an important asset. Insofar as it involves isolation of affect, intellectualizing makes it possible to deal with what is often very highly charged and potentially disturbing material in the patient's responses. It also helps to maintain due caution in interpretation, it supports reasonable skepticism, it opposes mechanical interpretation, and it increases alertness to the infinite variety of shifts in emphasis or meaning of responses in different configurations. The intellectualistic bent can be the driving force behind thoroughly exploring the implications of test results in daily clinical practice, and it can be the driving force behind using tests to refine and develop theoretical hypotheses.

Against the background of a rigidly intellectualistic character makeup, however, testing may tend to become too much of a detached, "logical," verbalistic, puzzle-solving affair. In his test report, the rigid intellectualizer may use his findings in a provocatively "informed" manner to complicate the case unnecessarily; he will interpret everything in sight, and substitute quantity for quality, doubt for responsibility, and overabstractions for descriptions. He may go blithely and pretentiously on and on about castration fears, incestuous wishes, sadistic fantasies, phallic mothers and what-not without the least twitch of personal anxiety and with absolutely no "feel" for the unique, emotionally tangible qualities of the specific patient. Insofar as the tester's intellectualizing is tainted by underlying grandiose aspirations, the tester may use his test reports to reassure himself that he indeed "sees all and knows all."

Something of this intellectualistic detachment and omniscient pose will certainly be communicated to the patient, who will understand it—in part, correctly so—as coldness and narcissistic self-absorption. Many of our gratifications as testers come from cases we find interesting and instructive, but there is hardly an easier way to irritate a patient than to convey to him the feeling that you view him as "an interesting case." Patients fear and resent being reduced to the level of laboratory specimens; they insist on being recognized as unique human beings.

f. The sadistic tester. Out of a sadistic social orientation, testing may become a means of ferreting out the "weak," "debasing," "humiliating" aspects of the lives of the hated Others. As has been described in connection with the autocratic aspects of the tester's role, testing does facilitate safe and socially sanctioned tyranny or domination of the relatively helpless "sick one." When, in addition, inner scorn and subtle humiliation of the patient are dominant tendencies, the test relationship may become clearly sadistic. Deeper transference implications of dominating, shaming and proving one's self superior to parents and siblings may easily find a place within this testing orientation. To the extent that the patient's illness itself constitutes a sadistic assault on others—and the intrusive tester will certainly be no exception to the patient's sadism—to that extent will the testing settle down to a war of attrition. The tester who, within this orientation, sets himself up as the Chief Inquisitor will tend to write one-sided reports that sound like exposés or denunciations; he will be insensitive to or ignore signs of strength, adaptability and appeal in the patient.

On the other hand, test reports often do have to deal with serious psychopathology and "base," unpleasant impulses and feelings. A capacity for forthrightness of description is required to write good test reports. In a test report, as anywhere else, it takes a certain aggressive freedom to call a spade a spade. If the tester can tolerate some awareness of inner, irrational hostility—even toward the patient he is testing and describing—and if he can get some pleasure out of competition and "overwhelming" his opponent, he will be freer to call a schizophrenic a schizophrenic and a psychopath a psychopath. It will be easier for him to see and handle the sadism in the patient's masochistic maneuvers and the burdensome mockery in the obsessional neurotic's conscientiousness and compliance. He will not be too eager to be taken in and manipulated by tears, smiles and groans. He will not have to undo every "malignant" interpretation with a benign one, and he certainly will not have to avoid "malignant" interpretations.

g. The tester with rigid defenses against hostility. Like defenses against dependent needs, defenses against hostility probably also play a vital part in the clinical psychologist's choice of profession. Conquering hatred and fear of others by devoting oneself to their welfare is an old and honored way of achieving adjustment and surviving in society. When repression of, reaction formation against, and undoing of hostility are crucial defensive aspects of the tester's personality, testing may easily signify atonement through good deeds. Through transference on the tester's part, testing may further signify forgiving or curing parents or siblings by whom the tester has felt abused or neglected. Like the therapist in the same dynamic position, the tester may then narcissistically hate patients when, by not exposing themselves to him, they resist his desperate efforts to be "good" to them.

If this tester's reaction formations are corrupted by unsuccessful warding off of hostility, he may behave much like the sadistic tester toward the patient, but with the difference that his manner and his inner feeling will be one of tender loving care. In this there will be a masked "return of the repressed"—a hallmark of weak reaction formation. A saintly attitude, as has already been discussed, will justifiably put the patient on guard in the test relationship and will very likely increase his sense of guilt. This too-benign tester conveys to the patient the guilt-provoking and irritating attitude, "I am being so patient, tolerant, understanding and helpful, and you ungratefully refuse to cooperate." In this way, saintliness can be a powerful sadistic weapon.

Finally, while rigid defenses against hostility may, on the one hand, blind the tester to malignant implications of the test results or lead him to minimize them or undo them by qualifications, they may, on the other hand, contribute to his perceptiveness of strengths, adaptive potential and constructive strivings in the patient.

h. The masochistic tester. In the setting of a passive masochistic social orientation and adjustment, a tester may thrive on the great portion of his daily life he spends arduously in contact with human beings whose capacity to give warmth and support and to tolerate anxiety and frustration is seriously limited. In other words, the tester may relish the patient's narcissistic demands, abuse and noncompliance. He may even do much to exacerbate such behavior. He may, for example, let control of the testing slip out of his hands and allow the entire situation to become relatively disorganized. His pleasure in testing may derive from the anxiety he unconsciously engenders in his patients and the resulting difficulties he creates for himself. Inasmuch as masochism has its accusing, hostile aspect, his pleasures in interpretation may consist in exposing just how "bad" people "really" are.

In one respect, the masochistic orientation may be a help to the tester, and that is in its making it bearable to spend a great part of his waking life with patients. A masochistic streak, especially if coated with humor, increases ability to take punishment.

Other orientations and their consequences could very well be added to the eight described above. Those that have been mentioned and others that may be conceived of should not be thought of as mutually exclusive by any means. Various combinations and layerings of these are likely to be the rule among testers, just as among any other group of human beings. It is worth repeating that these orientations might best be thought of as different facets of every tester's personality, any one or combination of which may stand out under the impact of different crises in the tester's life and of patients different in personality type.

Under favorable conditions, that is, with a cooperative patient, with no major crises in the tester's life, and with the tester reasonably well integrated, none of these orientations may become disruptively prominent or dominant. The entire testing may be carried out in the setting of well-sustained mutual good will and collaboration. This is often the way it is. The importance of this entire discussion does not lie in any contention that patients are consistently very difficult to test; it lies in the fact that where difficulties arise, the basic assumptions of the interpersonal test relationship are shaken up and rise to the surface. The psychological complexity of the test relationship must be recognized and clarified—generally, for a theory of testing, and specifically, for the successful administration and interpretation of tests.

REFERENCES

1. BERMAN, LEO. Countertransference and attitudes of the analyst in the therapeutic process. *Psychiatry:* 1949, *12,* 159–166.
2. DERI, S. *Introduction to the Szondi Test.* New York: Grune & Stratton, 1949.
3. ERIKSON, E. *Childhood and Society.* New York: Norton, 1950.
4. FROMM-REICHMAN, F. *Principles of Intensive Psychotherapy.* Chicago: University of Chicago Press, 1950.
5. GITELSON, M. The emotional position of the analyst in the psychoanalytic situation. *Int. J. Psychoanal.:* 1952, 33, 1–10.
6. HOBBS, N. *et al. Ethical Standards for Psychologists.* Washington, D.C.: American Psychological Association, 1953.
7. MACHOVER, K. *Personality Projection in the Drawing of the Human Figure.* Springfield, Ill.: C. C. Thomas, 1949.
8. SCHACHTEL, E. G. Subjective definitions of the Rorschach test situation and their effect on test performance. *Psychiatry:* 1945, *8,* 419–448.
9. SCHAFER, R. Review of *Introduction to the Szondi Test* by S. Deri in *J. abnorm. soc. Psychol.:* 1950, *45,* 184–188.

The Person Who Is the Therapist*

JAMES BUGENTAL

IT IS A familiar observation that the psychotherapist is the latest descendant of a line which traces back to prehistory. The psychotherapist's predecessors are the medicine man, the sorcerer, the priest, the family doctor. In every age man has needed to have some-one to turn to for help in contending with the awful unknownness of his fate. Inevitably, invariably, the one turned to has been invested by himself and by others with supranormal vision and potency. This has usually been both his greatest reward and his most terrifying burden. Certainly this is true for the psychotherapist today.

It can hardly be debated that there is a selective process, operating at both conscious and unconscious levels, which determines those of us who will come into the field of psychotherapeutic practice. We bear no mark of the caul, nor do we often experience a "call"; yet just as surely do we find ourselves making those choices in our development that lead us to this work. By no means do I imply that this is altogether a bad thing; nor do I mean to reassure that it is altogether a good thing either. For the moment let it rest that a great many psychotherapists, the present writer included, have sought through becoming psychotherapists to deal with their own anxieties, both existential and neurotic.[1]

GRATIFICATIONS IN BEING A THERAPIST

Therapeutic Addiction

Anyone who gets deeply involved in the practice of intensive psychotherapy is in grave risk of becoming "hooked." Exceptions to that generalization would be few indeed. I doubt that mescaline,

---

* From James Bugental, *The Search for Authenticity,* copyright © 1965 by Holt, Rinehart and Winston, Inc. Reprinted by permission.

[1] Indeed, let me append to this observation that one of the most frequent incentives to becoming identified with the existential viewpoint is the hope thereby to forestall existential anxiety, in other words, to deny the very viewpoint with which one affiliates.

marihuana, opium, or heroin can lastingly give the gratifications to the user that the practice of intensive psychotherapy makes available.

Now, what are these gratifications of being a psychotherapist?

One-way intimacy. Allen Wheelis (1958) has described what he feels is a powerful selective factor operating in determining who will become a psychoanalyst. This is a hunger for closeness, a great desire for affective intimacy, and a great fear of it. The practice of psychotherapy makes possible a kind of one-way closeness of great intimacy, quite frequently with more affective expression than is to be found in any other relationship, not excluding the marriage relationship (Warkentin, 1963). Yet it is in many ways "safer" to the therapist, in that he is supported by his ethics and training in withholding himself from the commingling which is potential. How beautifully, then, this practice fits the needs of those with a great affect hunger, a great desire for intimacy, and a great fear of affect in intimacy.

Omnipotence. Second, the practice of intensive psychotherapy provides rich nourishment for one's omnipotence and omniscience strivings. Many of us who feel frightened and impotent in living in general find in the practice of therapy a kind of splendid calm, which we and the patient conspire together to believe is the benign influence of our perspective.

THERAPIST'S LOVE. I would like to comment at greater length on a frequent, special instance of the omnipotence striving being acted out in the therapeutic relation. This is the myth of the curative effect of the therapist's love. A great many therapists at one time or another seem to pass through a phase where they become convinced that ample doses of unquestioning, undemanding love from the therapist for the patient is the curative agent which can produce profound changes. This seems to come about because many patients are emotionally deprived people who seek the kind of concern from their therapists that they feel they never received from their parents. The response of the patient to seeming to gain that caring from the therapist is often dramatic and pervasive, for a period. Only when the therapist has worked with a truly dependent personality over a period of years does he begin to recognize, if he is wise, that while the patient may indeed achieve remarkable reorganizations of his life through the benign influence of the therapist's love, these are all fragilely hung on the relationship. The patient resists with frightening ruthlessness any attempt by the therapist to reduce that dependence. It is not unusual for the work of months and years, all the hard-won gains in life effectiveness the patient and therapist have worked out, to be brought crashing down in a relatively short space of time when the therapist begins to try to free the patient of his dependence upon the sustenance of the therapist's concern.

Kathryn came to therapy because of tremendous depressive episodes that brought her several times to the brink of suicide and that seemed to be linked with her husband's drinking bouts. She found in me a person who gave her great warmth and acceptance. Her mother had been a rejecting household drudge who had evidently been afraid of close relationships and had been able to give only in terms of endless hours of work. Kathryn was a gifted woman of superior intelligence with tremendous ability to do a capable job in her semitechnical profession. When first seen, she was on the verge of being dismissed from her work because of the erratic quality of her performance. In eighteen months of therapy she effected a divorce from her husband, gained an advance in her position, was functioning at a level superior to any she had ever in her life known for an extended period. Her therapeutic sessions were characterized by exploration of very deep, primitive material, a great deal of emotional intensity, and her professions of great gratitude toward me.

Periodically throughout this period, though, when some life crisis would occur, Kathryn would call me day and night, and repeatedly. Distraught, disorganized, in danger of upsetting all the great improvements in her life, in lengthy telephone calls she made many, many bids for reassurance of my concern for and belief in her. The length and frequency of the phone calls would increase for a time, then the crisis would pass, and she would seemingly knit together and perform well again.

At length, when she achieved a degree of stability, though still punctuated with these crisis episodes, I began to withdraw some of my support, to insist that Kathryn limit the length and frequency of her phone calls. A tremendous battle ensued. Seemingly blind to her own interests, Kathryn jeopardized her position, began drinking heavily, and insisted on the need for more frequent contacts with me. Now she became badgering and demanding. She called for more and more evidences of closeness. She made threats upon her own life and eventually became threatening toward me. Wherever I had set limits, Kathryn was compelled to test, to try to overthrow those limits.

We can talk of Kathryn as a pseudo-neurotic schizophrenic, and this is probably accurate. We can speak of her tremendous passive-hostile character structure, which was unanalyzed or insufficiently analyzed, and this is probably true. We have only touched one half of the story when we characterize Kathryn in this fashion. My own neurotic needs are portrayed in my placing the main reliance on the curative effect of my concern. In a sense, I presented Kathryn with a world different from the world of contingency, choice, and tragedy. I presented her with what seemed to be a world of certainties, though those certainties hinged on me, the person. Together we created a symbiosis of the most malignant type. It could only end in the destruction of both of us if allowed to run its course. Kathryn's reality sense was adequate to present her unverbalized cues that the relationship could not continue and continue to be more and more supportive as she needed it to be. Thus she had to make more and more demands to try to quiet those cues and to reassure herself that this indeed was *the* unique relationship. On my part, committed to a course based on unstinted giving, I found myself called upon to give more and more until my own limits were severely threatened.

Let me be clear, I am not devaluing the significance, even the essential quality, of the therapist's concern for his patient. Psychotherapy is an intimate relationship. It does involve the feelings of both participants, but when this becomes an infantile acting-out then it is no longer psychotherapy; it is a *folie à deux*.

Contingency mastery. A third important gratification in the practice of psychotherapy is the opportunity the therapist has for a vicarious and seemingly safe way of dealing with contingency, with the basic realities of life. I have heard therapists say they found themselves using the patient as a guide dog to go through the mine field of certain threats first in order to reassure themselves that it can be negotiated. I respect the therapists who recognize this. Nearly all therapists do this in some measure, all too often without such candid recognition. We live in anxiety; we seek to become more self-trusting; we never achieve this fully. When, with full recognition of the patient's needs, we can encourage him to confront that which breeds anxiety within ourselves, we are heavily invested in the outcome.

Masculine tenderness. A fourth gratification in being a therapist is that it provides an opportunity to give tenderness, compassion, and love within a structure in which one's masculinity is not questioned.

A great many who are drawn into this field have fears of emotions, fears that they represent weakness and perhaps effeminacy within us. Often these fears are completely unconscious, and we may even be counterphobic in being overly expressive of our emotions. We document with research and learned papers the healthfulness of emotional expression and the disasters attendant upon emotional inhibition. And in the therapeutic hour, secure in our masculinity of being doctors and healers, we can dispense tenderness and love without arousing our own anxieties.[2]

Rebelliousness. A fifth, very frequent gratification in the practice of psychotherapy is that it gives us an opportunity to attack authority and tradition while armored in all the prerogatives of our own authoritative position. We have studied and observed how the needless inhibitions of society complicate the lives of all of us: the taboos about sexual talk and actions; the guilts about ambivalence toward parents, spouses, and others; the shame of death wishes and other hostile impulses. These, we have learned, are part of the influences that have made our patients suffer and—though we seldom verbalize this to the patients or to ourselves—have made us suffer. With the authority of being a therapist, we can strike back at these influences. Notice how often we psychotherapists, particularly in our earlier years of practice, become great users of the four-letter words (Feldman, 1955). Notice how often we are flagrant in our verbal expressions of sexual and hostile impulses. It seems quite clear that this is an acting-out, a counterphobic kind of behavior which represents the celebration of the license of being therapists. Thus we pay back society, hit back at authority. It is not a matter of chance, for example, that most therapists tend to be political and social liberals. We would like to think that this is chiefly because we have had an opportunity to see the crippling effect of social ills, and I am certain this is one significant reason. On the other hand, the person who is in some revolt against what he feels is social injustice may find in the practice of psychotherapy a relatively safe way to express his rebellion.

I have listed some of the ways in which the practice of intensive psychotherapy can provide powerful and unique gratifications to the

---

[2] Jourard, in an exceedingly provocative paper on "Some lethal aspects of the male role" (1962), has elaborated important significances of this observation.

therapist. It is inevitable that those of us who are most in need of these kinds of gratifications will be drawn to this practice. I want to make it clear that I do not feel these neurotic sorts of gratifications are by any means the only satisfactions in this work. I do think that these neurotic gratifications are much more frequently present than we generally recognize, that they are seldom completely removed by personal therapeutic experience, and that we have a responsibility to try to remain aware of their operation in our daily practice.

Synergic Gratifications

Having listed some important aspects of the practice of psychotherapy that provide addictive or neurotic gratifications, I would like to describe now some creative gratifications that are also realized in our work. Maslow's (1962a) term "synergy" best delineates the common property these have. In a truly synergic relation that which most contributes to the fulfillment of one of the participants is most fulfilling of the other also. It should be evident that I do not hold with the view that the psychotherapist has no needs seeking satisfaction in his work. On the contrary, the therapist must find important fulfillment if he is to be able to mobilize his total resources for the task, as he must frequently do. Some of the incentives to his doing so seem to be the following.

Participation. To the psychotherapist is offered the opportunity to participate with unique immediacy in the business of life itself. In psychotherapeutic practice one deals daily with the life *and* death of human personality and potential. I mean no play on words, and the melodrama implicit in this characterization is that of the human experience itself. As the therapist accompanies his patient in his efforts to confront the minor and the great issues of his life, to contend with the ever-present unknownness of choices and their consequences, to meet and live with the multiple emotional seekings and stresses of human relationships—as the psychotherapist visits the heights of elation and self-affirmation, the depths of confusion and madness, the brink of suicide, the bleakness of relinquishment, and on and on—then the therapist must know the limitedness of his gifts and how privileged his situation in viewing the human condition.

Personal growth. A good therapeutic relation is growth-inducing in both participants. Growth potential is infinite, and the therapist who is an authentic participant in his work with his patient has repeated stimulation and opportunity to increase his realization of his own potential. In a climate in which genuineness is requisite and yet always sought anew, that which is false and self-defeating in the therapist himself must ever and again be illuminated for the inauthentic self-deception it is. The therapist who has come to love the realization of human potential—and I am convinced this is a distinguishing characteristic of the dedicated therapist—will be continually renewed in his own growth (Whitaker and Malone, 1953).

Psychological processes. A high proportion of psychologist-psychotherapists entered their parent discipline of psychology because, among other reasons, of a fascination with psychological processes which may be likened to that some people show with mechanics, others with color and form in the arts, and still others with mathematics and quantitative processes. There is no other opportunity in all the world like that of intensive psychotherapy for a person with this orientation to immerse himself in the working of psychological processes in their natural condition. All our familiar psychological topics of learning, motivation, attitudes, emotions, attention, remembering, perception, and so on—all of these are displayed in endless variation and exquisite detail.

Patients' growth. Most patients who come to the psychotherapist show improvement. The doubters to the contrary, the psychotherapeutic experience is generally one in which there is a gain in human effectiveness and satisfaction (although, albeit, not the magical one frequently initially expected). It is for the therapist, once he has adjusted his own sights to realistic dimensions, a deeply meaningful experience to have participated in his patient's emergence. There are, of course, the failures, the disappointments, the questionable outcomes. However, with experience, constant self-development, and much learning just to wait, the proportion of favorable outcomes increases; the pervasiveness of the changes becomes more evident. It is, then, an enriching feeling to have been an intimate participant in this growth.

MATURITY OF THE PSYCHOTHERAPIST

I want to talk now about some observations on what it means to be a mature psychotherapist. In one sense I am going to be describing a goal never fully attained. In another sense I am going to be describing what it means to be a mature person generally. Here, however, we are particularly concerned with the person who is the psychotherapist and so will dwell especially on that aspect. As a preliminary, we will talk about some pseudo-maturity patterns.

Pseudo-Maturity Patterns

Pontificating. First, we can recognize a group of therapist behaviors that are rather clearly those of the immature personality. These include the therapist who pontificates, speaking as though the infallible intermediary between God and the patient: pronouncing judgments, giving instructions, and acting-out a certainty that is the therapist's own resistance to contingency. Whatever the patient says is the occasion for the therapist to give a lecturette. These sorts of behaviors are sometimes useful in short-term counseling and in handling emergency situations; and some use of very unequivocal pronouncements may be made by mature therapists. What is indicted here is someone who relies almost solely on this way of participating.

Acting-out giving. A more frequent sign of pseudo-maturity, one in which the therapist's own needs are more covert and unconscious, is that form of acting-out giving by the therapist which is actually a substitute for his genuine presence in the interview. The therapists who are caught up in the delusion of the curative power of unstinting love, which was described above, would be primary examples of this type of acting-out. Genuine presence with the patient, encounter and engagement with him, seldom will be expressed through continual and unilateral giving by the therapist. Perhaps that word "unilateral" needs emphasis. The therapist who genuinely engages with his patient demands bilateral exchange, not on a "bargaining basis" but on a basis of a mutual respect, a demand which the therapist who is acting-out in his giving could not afford to risk.

Enacted openness. A variation of this same pattern of acting-out giving as a substitute for genuine presence occurs in the kind of enacted openness which is really exhibitionism on the therapist's part. I had a patient who went to a psychotherapist who in the second session undressed himself completely as a demonstration of his openness and lack of pretense to the patient. This is clearly an acting-out designed to allay the therapist's fears of his own secretiveness and possibly to stimulate the patient to similar exhibitionism. Certainly a kind of enacted openness, which masks the lack of real presence, is often performed by therapists who are caught in the subject-object split and who treat themselves as things to be observed and manipulated for their patients' welfare, at least as they see it. They are very like the kind of martyr-mother who has so little belief in her own worth that she misuses herself, seemingly for the child's benefit. Such therapists and parents really teach a kind of alienation and a lack of presence that is highly pathogenic.

When working as a therapist to therapists, I often can get a useful clue as to the nature of the acting-out giving which is a substitute for genuine presence when the therapist is able to be giving only in his in-office life, while his extra-office life is often characterized by great loneliness and isolation. More than one therapist who is tremendously warm and giving in his relations with his patients is distant, awkward, and ungiving in relations with his children, his wife, and his colleagues.

Submergence in a theory. Another sort of pseudo-maturity that is often somewhat subtle and difficult to recognize is that in which a theory or system displaces the person of the therapist. Such a therapist becomes, as it were, an embodiment of a particular viewpoint, rather than a person in his own right. This can be true, and I think I have recognized it, in psychoanalytic, Adlerian, Rogerian, and existentially oriented therapists. "A good theory is the most practical thing," it is said, but a good theory is a tremendously effective way of avoiding contingency. Existential theory, let me assure you, is magnificent in its seeming power to offset existential reality. Writing a book or giving speeches about a theory often can be a good way to avoid being a person while wearing the mask of the theory.

Encouragement of impulsivity. A final kind of pseudo-maturity pattern has already been alluded to in speaking of the gratifications of being a therapist, but needs to be mentioned again here: the en-

couragement of the patient in his acting-out impulsivity and overthrow of the superego. This attempt to free the patient to be that
which he "naturally" is by raising no question of responsibility about
the patient's impulses is an all too frequent type of therapeutic
pseudo-maturity.

Genuine Maturity in the Therapist

Recognition of limited knowledge. Probably one of the first evidences of genuine maturing in the therapist comes when he expresses
and evidences his acceptance of the fact that he has but limited
knowledge of his patient. Since we, as therapists, get to know our
patients so much more thoroughly than we know any other human
beings in our lives, we often feel that we really know them fully.
This is a myth; this is our omniscience fantasy being enacted. Those
who have had an intensive psychotherapeutic experience will recognize how great the area is that they have never been able to transmit
to their therapists, how much of their living the therapists knew
little about as contrasted to the relatively smaller area in which the
therapists truly understood fully.

I am speaking here of the best relationships between therapists
and patients, even when continued over several years. As therapists
we never know all about our patients, only some aspects. These may
be terribly important aspects and certainly significant to know, but
we need to recognize they are but a part of what could conceivably
be known about our patients.

Selective participation. A second mark of the maturing therapist
is his selective use of his own participation. This is to say he is able
so to modulate when and how he intervenes that his participation is
maximally effective in a restricted area. The maturing therapist
speaks sparingly, but with precision. A very common fault of the
tyro-therapist is that he talks too much or too little or at the wrong
time.

Genuine encounter. A third characteristic of the maturing therapist
is his willingness genuinely to encounter his patient. This does not
mean a kind of exhibitionism or display of himself. It does mean a
willingness to "be there" with his patient, to confront his patient
directly when appropriate, to take responsibility for his (the thera-

pist's) own thinking, judgments, feelings, and to be authentic in his own person with the patient. All too often therapists who believe in this sort of authenticity portray in their own manner an avoidance of authenticity that can but present a contradictory message to the patient. Sidney Jourard (1964) has the idea that one of the main things which has a curative effect in the therapeutic relationship is the therapist's serving as a model of authenticity for the patient.

THERAPIST AUTHENTICITY. In the therapist's handling of limits and endings we have a clear example of one of the ways in which a therapist may not be authentic. The therapist who is repeatedly careless about starting appointments on time or terminating sessions on time or who, on the other hand, is too punctilious about time-limits demonstrates this. So does the therapist who cannot sort out when to make a statement in a declarative, simple, direct fashion and when to phrase it in conditional language. Far too many therapists seem to me to talk with the kinds of qualified phrasing more appropriate to the *Journal of Experimental Psychology* than to the needs of the therapeutic hour. They are apt to say to the patient, "It seems like you may be projecting the attitude that you apparently had toward your father onto me," rather than telling the patient directly, "You're reacting to me as you did to your father." The use of many qualifiers, the use of the third person instead of the first, the statement of an interpretation as a possibility rather than a clear perception (when it is that) may be indications of this same avoidance of presence. Again, the therapist who excuses a patient from paying for a missed appointment because the patient forgot or was held up in traffic is not being authentic in his relation with the patient but is acting-out his own need to give and probably to suffer. The therapist who cannot admit his mistakes but always has some explanation for them is another example.

Evolving concepts. A further evidence of growing maturity in the therapist is that he has an evolving set of constructions about himself, his world, the nature of psychotherapy, and what he means by the concept of personality. I am mistrustful of the therapist who believes he has reached final answers on any of these points. Recognition of the dynamic quality of knowledge, of the continuing learning experience of therapeutic work, demands that one be changing if one be dedicated and aware.

Therapeutic guilt. I have reserved for the last one of the most difficult aspects of therapeutic maturity, the acceptance of the guilt of being a therapist. Certainly all that has been said about the neurotic gratifications of being a therapist and about the kinds of patterns found in pseudo-maturity as a therapist will have indicated already that there is inevitably a load of guilt in being a therapist. I will not re-elaborate on these points. The point is this: there is a guilt for our failure to be all that we can be as therapists to these people who come and give us their lives and their trust.

The other day I saw Jack again for the first time in five years. I first saw Jack eleven years ago; that was for vocational guidance. He came back a year later because he was having trouble with his marriage, and I was able to be of some help in patching up a shaky relationship. Seven years ago when he came to me the marriage had collapsed at last, and he was readjusting his life to a new pattern of living. At that time we attempted intensive psychotherapy, and I saw him for several years. I think Jack was helped by the experience. However, I put it in this somewhat tentative fashion because I can see so many ways today that he could have been helped so much more.

I look at Jack in my office today, and I see a man with the gray coming in at his temples. I see in him also virtually a boy of twenty-nine as I first saw him eleven years ago. The prime years of his early maturity are embraced by our relationship. As I look at Jack, I think of Louis whom I am currently seeing and who is about the age Jack was when he first came to me. Louis is going to have a much fuller life than Jack has had because I am so much more able to meet him and to help him in becoming himself. To look at Jack is to look at my own guiltiness for not having been all that Jack needed. I comfort myself that I served him with sincerity with the best of my skill at that time. I comfort myself that many another therapist might have done no more for him than I did, but this does not give Jack back his lost years.

This is a story of the therapist's guilt. If I am to be a growing, evolving person, each old patient I see again is an accusation; each patient of former years will be in some measure someone who trusted me and whom I failed by today's standards. If I become despondent or self-punitive, I am acting out a neurotic type of guilt; but if I recognize the legitimate responsibility I had in this matter I am revitalized in my own growth.

CONTINUED GUILT. But there is yet one further way in which this guilt operates. When I recognize that I am continuing to try to grow, to increase my awareness, skill, competence in effectively being in the relationship with my patients, then I must look at my patients today and know that each one of them is getting less than I hope I will be giving his successor five years hence. There is guilt in this too.

You may protest, "This all sounds very masochistic and self-punishing. It's just the way things are. There's no need to expend guilt and regret it." In one sense you are very right; in another you are very wrong. Yes, this is the way things are, but the fact that a condition is so does not mean necessarily that it is unladen with emotional significance. It is so that I can only do so much for my patients now and that that seldom is all I potentially can do, even today. On the other hand, if the sense of guilt becomes an interference with my effective use of myself rather than part of a heightened sensitivity, then it is clearly becoming a neurotic guilt and an attempt to forestall other anxiety. The kind of guilt I am trying to characterize here is not forestalling of anxiety, nor yet laden with additional anxiety. It is an emotional fact of being.

Conclusion

I want to conclude by saying very briefly what it means to me to be a psychotherapist. I feel like one of the more fortunate people. The men and women who come to see me entrust me with that which is most deeply meaningful in all their experience. They offer me the awesome privilege of participating in the very essence of their lives. When I am most authentic, I am most humble in my appreciation of this opportunity.

As I started this, I called attention to the lineage from which we psychotherapists take our vocation: medicine man, wizard, priest, and family doctor. This is a proud line, and we may be proud to be part of it. These are the bearers of man's hope and man's faith. These are the personifications of man's courage and creativity in confronting the immensity of the unknown. We are for our brief time hoisted on the shoulders of our fellows that we may catch some glimpse of the yet untouched reaches of what it means to be truly man.

58   PERSPECTIVES IN CLINICAL PSYCHOLOGY

REFERENCES

FELDMAN, J. J. The use of obscene words in the therapeutic relationship. *Amer. J. Psychoanal.*, 1955, *15*, 45–48.

JOURARD, S. M. Some lethal aspects of the male role. *J. existent. Psychiat.*, 1962, *2*, 333–344.

JOURARD, S. M. *The Transparent Self: Self-disclosure and Well-being.* Princeton: Van Nostrand, 1964.

MASLOW, A. H. *Summer Notes* . . . Del Mar, Calif.: Non-Linear Systems, Inc., 1962.

WARKENTIN, J. The therapist's significant other. *Ann. Psychother.*, 1963, *4* (1), 54–59.

WHEELIS, A. *The Quest for Identity.* New York: Norton, 1958.

WHITAKER, C. A., & MALONE, T. P. *The Roots of Psychotherapy.* New York: Blakiston, 1953.

....

The Morals of Psychotherapy*

PERRY LONDON

INSOFAR AS HE is concerned with the diagnosis and treatment of illness, the modern psychotherapist has grown up in the tradition of
medicine. But the nature of the ailments he deals with and the
way he treats them set him apart from the physician and in some
ways make him function much like a clergyman. He deals with
sickness of the soul, as it were, which cannot be cultured in a laboratory, seen through a microscope, or cured by injection. And his
methods have little of the concreteness or obvious empiricism of
the physician's—he carries no needle, administers no pill, wraps no
bandages. He cures by talking and listening. The infections he seeks
to expose and destroy are neither bacterial nor viral—they are ideas,
memories of experiences, painful and untoward emotions that de-
bilitate the individual and prevent him from functioning effectively
and happily.

Our traditional understanding of the physician is that he relieves
men of their suffering regardless of their moral condition. Historically, the dedicated physician has treated the good and bad alike,
ministering to their physical needs as best he could.

He has done so for reasons that are both technically and theoretically sound. In his technical work, the physician rarely needs to
be concerned with the moral attributes of his patient, for they generally have no bearing on the diagnosis he will make or how he will
combat an illness. In theory, the physician is committed to the task
of saving and enhancing the life and physical well-being of his patients. So he treats them all, and treats them as they come—and
this is perhaps the noblest tradition within medicine.

Psychotherapists have been nobly moved to adapt this tradition
to their own practice. In so doing, they argue that the mental therapist is no moralist, that he has no business becoming involved in

the moral, religious, economic, or political beliefs of his client, and that he has no right, in the course of his practice, to make value judgments of his client, to moralize or preach at him, or to try to dictate to him some "good" way of life. His purpose is to alleviate the suffering, the mental anguish, the anxiety, the guilt, the neurosis or psychosis of the client, not to change his way of life along moralistic or ideological lines.

This argument has a great deal in its favor. It has served the historical purpose of permitting students of mental health and illness to investigate objectively the conditions that predispose people to mental troubles and the kinds of people who suffer from such difficulties. It has allowed therapists, free of metaphysical concerns, to develop a technical armamentarium that, though limited, can often be used much as the physician uses his store of pills and skills. It has been largely responsible for the creation of a new "helping" art, one that has not only demonstrated its usefulness, but has also been able to entertain legitimate pretensions to being a scientific discipline.

It is impossible to overstate the importance of freedom from metaphysics and morals to the conduct of scientific research, especially to the objective analysis and interpretation of data. But the psychotherapist, in his actual practice, does not usually function as a researcher. He is a clinician. And much of the material with which he deals is neither understandable nor usable outside the context of a system of human values. This fact is unfortunate and embarrassing to one who would like to see himself as an impartial scientist and unprejudiced helper. It is a fact none the less, and one which, for both technical and theoretical reasons, may be painfully important to students of human behavior in general and to psychotherapists in particular. Moral considerations may dictate, in large part, how the therapist defines his client's needs, how he operates in the therapeutic situation, how he defines "treatment," and "cure," and even "reality."

Many psychotherapists are poignantly aware of this. Students of mental health find that it is difficult even to *define* such terms as "health," "illness," and "normality," without some reference to morals; and worse still, they cannot discuss the proper treatment of what they have defined without recognizing and involving their own moral commitments.

The issue is the same whether the problem is a social one like prostitution or an apparently individual one like obsessional neu-roses. Neither can be called an illness on the grounds of invasion by a foreign body or of the malfunctioning of specific organs. Nor do people die directly from them. They may be abnormal in a statistical sense, but this is hardly a basis for worry. Living one hundred years or making a million dollars is also deviant in that sense. The objectionable feature of these problems concerns the vio-lation of the public moral code, in the one case, and the experience of apparently unnecessary personal anguish—which either presup-poses the virtue of comfort or abjures the discomfort of preoccupa-tion—in the other. In both, the assumption of a moral desideratum underlies the definition.

Yet psychotherapeutic training programs in psychiatry, psychol-ogy, social work—even in the ministry—often do not deal seriously with the problem of morals. Psychotherapeutic literature is full of formal principles of procedure and somewhat vague statements of goals, but it generally says little or nothing about the possible moral implications of those procedures and goals—indeed, it often fails even to mention that there are any moral, as opposed to scientific, implications to psychotherapy, though the objectives of the latter are rationalized by the former. It is as if therapists were themselves unconscious of some of the most profound difficulties in their own work. Or perhaps the opposite is true—that they are well aware but find that, as Marie Jahoda puts it, "[it] seems so difficult that one is almost tempted to claim the privilege of ignorance." Perhaps so, but ignorance can serve no useful purpose in this matter, and may even impair the uses of the craft.

At some level of abstraction, it is probably correct to declare that every aspect of psychotherapy presupposes some implicit moral doc-trine, but it is not necessary to seek this level in order to say why it is important for therapists to recognize the moral concomitants of patients' problems and the implied moral position of some of their solutions. Some problems are inevitably moral ones from the perspective of either client or therapist, and some can be viewed as strategic or technical ones and treated without reference to particular value systems. In the one case, the therapist must fulfill a moral agency in order to function at all, whereas in the other he may restrict himself to the impartial helping or contractual function with which he is usually identified. But if he does not know the difference, then his own moral commitments may influence his technical functioning so that he willy-nilly strives to mold men to his own image, or his technical acts may imply moral positions which he might himself abhor.

MORALS AS TECHNICALITIES

To be sure, there are many people and problems that clearly do not require much moralistic concern by therapist or patient. These are in fact purely technical problems and can be assessed, for the most part, on purely empirical grounds. An example might be the case of a phobia in a child. Such a condition will often succumb to fairly specific techniques without much thought to the value systems that may underlie their use. Similarly, many psychogenic physical symptoms in children and adults may be treated without seriously invading the patient's value system and without challenging his moral code or, for that matter, knowing anything about it. Some familial conflicts are resolved by fairly simple means—helping people to improve interpersonal communication, to discover that their feelings can be voiced without disastrous consequences, and so forth.

Such problems require few moral commitments from the therapist beyond the belief that children ought not have phobias, people should be free of allergies, members of families should not be in continuous conflict, and so on. It would be precious for most of us to labor these as moral issues, not because they are free of moral underpinnings, but because the consensus which exists about them almost everywhere is so great that it makes them virtual universals.

The technical problem that becomes a moral problem in psychotherapy, often in a critical way, might be stated like this: How does a psychotherapist properly deal with a client who reports that he has perpetrated a theft or been sexually delinquent? Or suppose a religiously devout patient reports that he is conflicted, guilty, and anxious about the use of birth control devices. What defines a therapeutic reply to a person who feels that his behavior, or thoughts, violate the word of God, or the Church, and that at the same time he cannot control them?

Suppose, for that matter, the converse—a patient reports particularly opprobrious behavior about which he does not experience guilt, anxiety, or conflict; suppose, in effect, he thereby violates the moral code of the therapist.

What should the therapist do? Avoid comment? Refer his comments to the ostensible code of the client without reference to his own? Should he circumvent the moral issue itself and attempt to penetrate the dynamic, or unconscious, or historical situations that may have "determined" the behavior?

A common technical objective of therapists of all schools is to help the client to be free of his unrealistic conflicts—but when conflicts revolve around moral issues, how is it possible to help without becoming directly involved in the moral issue? How is it even possible, for that matter, to decide whether a conflict is realistic without moral involvement? It is specious to argue, as some therapists do, that moral concerns are simply manifestations of "resistance" and that the underlying dynamics of the client's situation never relate to moral problems. It seems viciously irresponsible for the therapist to argue that, at such times, he must formally remove himself from the discussion by telling the client that the therapy session can be helpful for discussing "personal, emotional problems, not moral ones." The naive injunction that, regardless of what approach he *does* take, the therapist must *not* moralize at the client, has little value here—it is hard to imagine that the failure to moralize alone arranges things so that the client can then solve his own moral dilemmas.

Within the framework of technical therapeutic objectives, independent of his own scheme of values or his awareness of the relevance of the client's morality to the conflict situation, it is unclear what the therapist should do here. Most therapists, regardless of the particular psychological orthodoxy to which they adhere, would probably agree that there are a number of perfectly valid, even necessary, technical actions which may be considered in such a situation. The therapist might reflect, interpret, probe the origins of the symptom, or its intensity, or its continuities and discontinuities; he might ask the client to free-associate in general or in response to particular words or phrases. He might challenge him to explain clearly why he deprecates his own impulses, or to explore deeper underlying motives for his anxiety or his preoccupation, to describe this or think about that or understand a third thing. What unites all these technical operations in most actual cases, I believe, is first, the fact that the therapist *says something,* and second, the fact that he almost inevitably avoids expressing an opinion about the *moral issue as such.* Morality, religion, the oughts and shoulds of human behavior, are not his ostensible concern.

But these issues are surely the concern of the client; to the extent that he is in touch with reality, let alone has any care to serve his own best interests, he must necessarily be concerned with what he should and should not do. This kind of concern may be one of the things that brought him to a psychotherapist in the first place, and however independent a soul he may be, one of the main things that keeps him there is the hope that he can be helped to guide himself along lines of behavior that will make his life more meaningful and satisfying. It is largely this hope that may compel him to invest the therapist with greater importance than most other people and to view the therapist, more or less realistically, as the agent of the resolution of his conflicts. It is my contention that the force of this agency, in those conflict areas in which morality figures, propels the therapist into the practical position of moralist whether or not he wishes to assume it.

That he should not wish to assume such a role is understandable, but the studied attempt to avoid doing so sometimes leads therapists into logically untenable positions. A therapist of my acquaintance, for example, once offered her students as a cardinal rule of psychotherapy the dictum that one "does not get involved in the politics or religion of the patient." At the same time, she could not advise how to avoid doing so—once the client has made them explicit issues—except by declining to offer one's personal politics or religion as solutions to the client's problems. While this may be sound negative advice, it is of questionable use to either therapist or patient. The strategy itself requires some rationale—it seems unreasonable to propose a list of ideas, beliefs, and attitudes that are outside the scope of the therapist's function, without similarly defining relevant alternatives that are appropriate to his function. Such a task is, at best, very difficult to do, and still harder to justify. And considering only tactics, how does one explain to the patient that it is legitimate for him to talk about anything, but it would not be proper for the therapist to talk back about A, B, or C?

Another analyst of my acquaintance said to a patient, in response to queries about certain guilt-provoking behavior, "Why should I give a damn how you act?" but on another occasion, in relation to the same behavior, told him that therapy would have to terminate if the patient did not discontinue his "acting-out." In the first instance, the analyst was referring, albeit for technical reasons, to his own moral view of the patient's behavior, while in the second situation he was considering the behavior as a technical problem in the therapy. But the behavior was the same in both cases! It seems unrealistic to discuss the same behavior as a therapeutically irrelevant issue in the first instance and a therapeutically critical one in the second. Could one seriously expect the patient to honor the distinction?

The "neutralist" position is most clearly stated by a third analyst who says, "When I am working in the privacy of the analytic session, I don't care if the world is coming down around my patient's ears on the outside." He does not stipulate, incidentally, whether his attitude would be the same if the financial world of the patient were collapsing, indicating that he would no longer be paid, or if the patient were, on the outside, "acting-out" in a fashion which "interfered with the progress of the analysis."

It is obvious that, in most therapeutic situations, there are choice points at which the therapist must manifest some very real concern with the life the patient leads outside the therapy situation proper, and that some of that concern will be directed toward how the patient ought or ought not to act.

Morals as Generalities

Consideration of the foregoing as a purely technical problem also forces a more general issue into bold relief. This concerns what the therapist wishes ultimately to accomplish: the long-range goals of his therapy. The technical problem deals with immediate goals, but this asks what he wishes to see happen to this person, not merely in therapy, but in life. In what ways does he, as therapist, want his ministrations to alter the client's life?

Ultimately, I believe, this is a moral question that is always answered by the therapist in practice, whether or not it is ever posed in words; and the answer in fact is formed in terms of some superordinate, if unvoiced, moral code of his own. Sometimes the nature of the answer is masked by the impersonal scientistic language of mental health—but it is less subtly hidden in the words of the minister who counsels against premarital intercourse because of its "unfortunate psychological consequences"; of the Catholic caseworker who opposes his client's divorce because of its "mentally disrupting effect"; of the libertarian who helps his client accept the "psychological legitimacy" of extramarital affairs. Such therapeutic goals reflect personal morals and not scientifically validated conclusions.

Perhaps the most general, and accurate, answer that sensitive and self-conscious therapists could offer to the question of their goals could be put so: "I want to reshape this person's existence so that he will emulate values which I cherish for myself, aspire to what I wish humanity to be, fulfill my need for the best of all possible worlds and human conditions."

It is a truism that the therapist is himself a human being, that he lives in society, and that wisely or unknowingly, responsibly or casually, he has made moral commitments to himself and that society. But the present argument carries this platitude to its own logical, if unheeded, conclusion—that the very nature of his interaction with the people he serves involves a moral confrontation which, at the very least, renders communication of some part of his own moral commitments an inescapable part of his therapeutic work.

No one seriously doubts the validity of this argument in the case of the pastoral counselor, for he is almost always publicly committed to a religious-moral system whose content is usually well known to his clients before they ever approach him. No one believes, for example, that a priest will "accept" crime or sexual misconduct when confessed, as something less than sinful, regardless of the immediate response he makes to the confession. And while he may be understanding of the cause of this behavior and eager and able to temper judgment of its severity, and may deeply empathize with the guilt and anguish of its perpetrator—there is still little doubt that he looks upon the action as sinful and the behaver as a sinner, independent of the determinants which contributed to the act. For the priest, despite all else, is publicly committed to the notion that every individual is ultimately responsible for paying the price of his choice—and the person who confesses knows this all along.

The notion that the psychotherapist's situation differs much from the priest's is, I believe, a convenient fiction. To any given incident revealed by his client, the psychotherapist makes some kind of response, or so he is seen. He may carefully avoid making a very emphatic positive or negative response—he may manifest a studied, neutral attitude, and he may sincerely and devoutly feel neither censure nor approval of the situation at hand. But to regard this neutrality as an amoral position, to salve his own democratic, egalitarian, or relativistic conscience, to convince himself that he "is not imposing his own value system upon his client"—merely because he does not want to impose it—is ultimately to deceive both the client and himself. For this belief implicitly denies the essence of the psychotherapeutic relationship: that its most critical points are those involving the *interactions* between participants, not the private experiences of either of them. In other words, psychotherapy is a social, interpersonal action, characterized by an exchange of individual, personal ideas and feelings. The verbal content of the exchange differs with the respective roles of client and therapist, but the relationship is, in vital respects, a reciprocal one.

The very fact of the exchange relationship dictates, I believe, the inevitability of the therapist's functioning practically as a moral agent for three reasons:

1. He influences the moral decisions of the client because the client necessarily interprets the therapist's response to his moral concerns. If the therapist approves his behavior, he may reinforce it. If the therapist disapproves, he may change it. If the therapist appears neutral, he may interpret this as either tacit approval or tacit disapproval—and in many instances, it may be either one, complicated by the therapist's fears of upsetting the client or his reluctance to "dictate" ground rules of propriety. In any case, the very fact that the therapist permits discussion of these issues largely legitimizes any attempts on the client's part to interpret the therapist's reaction to his remarks.

2. Therapists are affiliated with professional societies. These societies have generally published codes of ethical conduct that dictate ground rules of propriety to the therapist, codes that attempt to establish minimal bounds to his conduct. Breach of these codes generally results in expulsion from the professional society. Whether or not he makes the binding limits of his code explicit to his client, the ethical therapist must act on these limits at critical points in therapy —and whenever he does so, he serves an explicit moral agency.

3. Therapists have personal value systems, and it is difficult to see how they could possibly form relationships with clients even for the sole purpose of understanding them, never mind helping them, without being cognizant of their own values and making implicit comparisons between themselves and their values and those of their clients. The failure to respond in any way to those comparisons, by some process of suspension of his own beliefs, may be possible, but it may also eventually commit the therapist to suspending his interaction—for it is hard to see how he can respond to his patient without cognizance of himself, and once aware of his own values, how he can completely withhold communicating them and continue to interact. This communication is precisely what occurs whenever, for example, a psychotherapist makes the continuation of treatment contingent on the patient's performing or refraining from some behavior. That the value involved for the therapist is a technical rather than a moral one is beside the point. It is *his* value, not the client's, and unless he can communicate it, he cannot function therapeutically.

IMPLICATIONS

If one accepts the notion that psychotherapists are moral agents, and that this agency may be intrinsic to their functions and goals, some important issues take shape.

It becomes apparent, for one thing, that not all the matters dealt with in therapy are mental health matters, even within the broadest meaning of that term. Some of these matters refer to religion, politics, and social and economic behavior of great importance both to individuals and to society. Psychotherapists cannot claim special knowledge or competence in the discussion of such issues, but neither are they apparently free on that basis to disengage themselves from their patients' concerns.

I do not believe that this is an entirely soluble dilemma, but certainly a first step toward its solution would require that therapists become vividly aware of their own personal commitments. Students of therapy have too often been encouraged to regard their clients and themselves exclusively in terms of "dynamics," "relationships," and "perceptions." Insufficient attention has been paid to those aspects of both clients' and therapists' ideologies, philosophies, and moral codes, many of which cannot be interpreted as merely incidental aspects of people's lives.

Secondly, it is apparent that so-called moral neutrality in the psychotherapist is as much a moral position as any more blatant one. It is, from the therapist's side, a libertarian position, regardless of how the client sees it (indeed, in some respects, he may justly see it as insidious). Expressed in a variety of ways, this position is currently in vogue among psychotherapists of quite dissimilar orientations. Some of the concepts that serve to legitimize and popularize moral neutrality are "democracy," "self-realization" or "self-actualization," and "existence." All these concepts are oriented toward people's freedom to do as they please. But even the most democratic general theories, in specifying assumptions and goals, limit their generosity with other terms such as "social responsibility" or "productivity." The latter kind of language seems to suggest that psychotherapists regard themselves as a genuine social force. If so, then to what extent are therapists obligated to represent themselves to the public at large, and to their clients, as a committed social agency? And according to what set of codes? For societies reflect within themselves systems of morality, and a relatively open society, such as that in America, reflects competing and contradictory codes. Is the therapist as moralist obligated, further, to participate publicly in moral arguments as they are reflected in political and economic life—or is he entitled to reserve his participation to his special area of competence?

The question becomes more immediate when it is asked in relation to the individual patient rather than to society at large. At what point, and by what means, is the therapist obligated or entitled to involve himself actively as moralist with his client? Is he entitled, perhaps obligated, to challenge the moral intent of his client when he thinks it inadequate—or immoral? Can he, in good conscience, permit in his patient any kind of behavior that serves to free him permanently of guilt, anxiety, neurosis? If so, will he not thoughtlessly be elevating the goal of personal adjustment to a supreme value—and is this not an inadequate goal for a community of men? And if so, is the therapist free of moral responsibility to that community?

Starting with an altogether technical matter, the sequence of issues that evolve seems inescapable. Either therapists can successfully influence behavior or they cannot, and they have little choice of what to claim. If they wish to say they cannot do so, or may not do so in just those areas where human concern is greatest, and are therefore not at all responsible for the behavior of their clients, one must ask what right they have to be in business. The very validity of the disclaimer destroys their most important function, so the help they can give must then be very narrowly defined.

But if, on the other hand, they affirm some technical expertise and wish to claim a genuine ability to influence people, then they must also assume some responsibility for the nature of that influence. In that event, they must ultimately see themselves as moral agents as they are confronted with moral problems. And the extent to which they are confronted with moral problems depends on the significance of the problems with which they deal, for morals are the ultimate values we assign to our acts.

It is not clear that psychotherapists are suited to assume this role, but it seems certain they cannot escape it. In such a strait, they may best serve themselves and those they hope to aid, by examining this agency to see what it entails.

....

The Cognitive Activity of the Clinician*

PAUL E. MEEHL

SOMEBODY HAS DESCRIBED psychotherapy as "the art of applying a science which does not yet exist." Those of us who try to help people with their troubles by means of that special kind of conversation are uncomfortably aware of the serious truth behind this facetious remark. The clinical psychologist has been able to assuage some of his therapeutic anxiety, and to refurbish his sometimes battered self-image, by keeping one foot planted on what seemed like comparatively solid ground, namely, psychodiagnosis. In recent years, some clinicians have been making a determined effort to assess the validity of our currently fashionable diagnostic instruments, and the findings are not very impressive. The cumulative impact of validation studies is reflected, for example, in Garfield's excellent textbook (1957), where one does not need a highly sensitive third eye to discern a note of caution (or even pessimism?). E. L. Kelly finds that 40% of young clinicians state that they would not go into clinical psychology if they had it to do over again. One suspects that at least part of this professional disillusionment springs either from awareness of the weaknesses in our psychodiagnostic methods or from the chronic intrapsychic (and interprofessional!) strain exacted of those who ward off such a confrontation. Who, for example, would *not* react with discouragement upon reading the recent monograph by Little and Shneidman (1959) where, in an unbiased and well-designed study, we find a very low congruency among interpretation of psychological test data, the test interpreters having been chosen as "experts" on four widely used instruments? Any tendency I felt to rejoice at the slight superiority of the MMPI over the three projective techniques with which it was competing was counteracted by the finding that my favorite test, like the others, does not do at all well when judged in absolute terms.

The cognitive activity of the clinician can be separated into several

* From the *American Psychologist*, 1960, *15*, 19–27.

functions, which I have discussed in a recent paper (Meehl, 1959a). Setting aside for the moment that special kind of cognitive activity which goes on within the therapeutic interview, we can distinguish three classes of functions performed by the psychodiagnostician: *formal diagnosis* (the attachment of a nosological label); *prognosis* (including "spontaneous" recoverability, therapy-stayability, recidivism, response to therapy, indications for differential treatment); and *personality assessment* other than diagnosis or prognosis. This last may be divided, somewhat arbitrarily, into *phenotypic* and *genotypic:* the former being the descriptive or surface features of the patient's behavior, including his social impact; the latter covering personality structure and dynamics, and basic parameters of a constitutional sort.

Quite apart from the validity of current techniques for performing these various cognitive functions, their pragmatic value is open to question. It is commonly believed that an accurate pretreatment personality assessment of his patient is of great value to the psychotherapist. It is not known to what extent, if at all, this is true. However, what do psychotherapists themselves have to say about it? Bernard C. Glueck, Jr. and I have recently collected responses from 168 psychotherapists (both medical and nonmedical, and representing a wide spectrum of orientations: e.g., Freudian, neo-Freudian, Radovian, Sullivanian, Rogerian, eclectic, "mixed") to a questionnaire dealing with 132 aspects of therapeutic technique. One of our items reads: "It greatly speeds therapy if the therapist has prior knowledge of the client's dynamics and content from such devices as the Rorschach and TAT." While the self-styled groups differ significantly in their response to this item (ranging from a unanimous negative among Rogerians to a two-thirds affirmative among George Kelly disciples), all groups except the last tend to respond negatively. The overall percentage who believe that such prior knowledge of the client's personality greatly speeds therapy is only 17%. This low figure, taken together with the fashionable de-emphasis upon nosology and the feebleness of most prognostic studies, at least raises doubts about the practical value of our diagnostic contribution.

Although they do not bear directly upon this question, we have some other interesting results which suggest considerable skepticism among therapists as to the significance of causal understanding itself in the treatment process. For example, 43% state that "Warmth and real sympathy are much more important than an accurate causal understanding of the client's difficulty." Over one-third believe that "Literary, dramatic, aesthetic, or mystical people are likely to be better therapists than people of a primarily scientific, logical, or mathematical bent." Four out of five believe that "The personality of the therapist is more important than the theory of personality he holds." About half believe that "Interpretation as a tool is greatly overrated at present." Two out of five go as far as to say that "Under proper conditions, an incorrect interpretation, not even near to the actual facts, can have a real and long-lasting therapeutic effect." Time does not permit me to read other examples of items which, in the aggregate, suggest minimization of the importance of the therapist's forming a "correct" picture of the client's psyche.

Setting aside the pragmatic question of the therapeutic value of assessment, let us look briefly at the inductive structure of the assessment process. The epistemological rock bottom is a single, concrete, dated slice or interval in the behavior flux, an "episode," identified by certain physical or social properties. Having observed one or more episodes of a given kind, we make an inductive inference as to the strength of low order *dispositions* which these episodes exemplify. Such dispositions are grouped into families, the justification for this grouping being, as Cattell (1946, 1950) has emphasized, some kind of covariation (although not necessarily of Type R) among the members of the disposition-family. It is perhaps possible to formulate the clinician's decision making behavior entirely in terms of such disposition-classes. In such a formulation, clinical inference involves probabilistic transition from episodes to dispositions, followed by the attribution of further dispositions, as yet unobserved. Ideally, such inferences would be based upon an extensive actuarial experience providing objective probability statements. Given a particular configuration of dispositions present in a patient, the statistical frequencies for all other dispositions of practical import would be known within the limits of observational and sampling errors. In practice, of course, this ideal is rarely achieved, the conditional probabilities being subjectively judged from clinical experience without the benefit of an actual tallying and accumulation of observations, and the probabilities being expressed in rough verbal form, such as "frequently" and "likely," rather than as numerical values.

I am still of the opinion (McArthur, Meehl, & Tiedeman, 1956; Meehl, 1954, 1956, 1957) that the practical utility of this approach has been insufficiently explored, and I think that many clinicians are unaware of the extent to which their daily decision making behavior departs from such a model not by being qualitatively different but mainly by being less explicit and, therefore, less exact. However, we must recognize that a purely dispositional approach is not the *only* way of proceeding. An alternative, more exciting (and more congenial to the clinician's self-concept) is to view the clinician's cognitive activity as aiming at the assessment of hypothetical inner states, structures, or events which cannot be reduced to dispositions but which belong to the domain of theoretical entities, crude though the theory may be. Episodes and dispositions are here treated as "signs" or "indicators" of the postulated internal states. These states should not be spoken of as "operationally defined" in terms of the dispositions, because the logical relationship between propositions concerning theoretical entities and those describing dispositions is not one of equivalence, but merely one of degrees of confirmation. The inference *from* dispositions *to* states of theoretical variables is again only probabilistic, partly because statistical concepts occur within the causal model itself (i.e., probability appears, as in the other sciences, in the object-language) and partly because the theoretical network is incomplete and imperfectly confirmed.

A fundamental contribution to the methodology of inference from multiple indicators is the "multitrait-multimethod matrix" of Campbell and Fiske (1959). These authors show that in order to support a claim of construct validity, we must take into account more kinds of correlational data than have been traditionally provided and that it is just as important for some correlations to be low as it is for others to be high. Consider two or more traits (e.g., dominance and sociability), each of which is allegedly measured by two or more methods (e.g., MMPI scores and peer group ratings). Computing all possible intercorrelations, we construct a multitrait-multimethod matrix. The relationships within this matrix may or may not lend support to the claim of construct validity. The monotrait-heteromethod coefficients should be not only statistically significant and respectable in size, but should exceed both the heterotrait-heteromethod and heterotrait-monomethod coefficients. For example, if MMPI dominance and sociability correlate higher than does MMPI dominance with peer group dominance or than MMPI sociability with peer group sociability, we ought to be nervous about the relative contribution of methods factors versus traits under study. Campbell and Fiske point out that the individual differences literature is very weak in this respect, usually failing to provide the necessary data and, when it does, usually showing unimpressive results.

An interesting adaptation of the Campbell-Fiske technique arises if we substitute "persons" for "traits" and deal with Q correlations rather than R correlations. Suppose that a therapist provides us with Q sort descriptions of two patients. From the MMPI profiles these patients are then Q sorted independently by two interpreters. This set-up generates a modified Campbell-Fiske matrix of 15 Q correlations, in which the validity diagonals (i.e., heteromethod-mono*patient* coefficients) represent how similarly the same patient is perceived by the therapist and the two MMPI readers; the monomethod-hetero-patient and heteromethod-heteropatient values reflect the projections, stereotypes, and other idiosyncratic sorting biases of the therapist and of the two interpreters, the extent to which such stereotypes are shared by all three, and the unknown true resemblance of the particular patient pair. Robert Wirt and I have been running a series of such matrices, and thus far our results are as unencouraging as those of the Little and Shneidman study. I have decided to spare you the slides, faintly hoping that the pairs thus far completed will turn out to be atypically bad.

The situation is not much improved by selecting a small subset of "high confidence" items before Q correlating. One disadvantage of Q sort is that it requires the clinician to record a judgment about every trait in the deck. The technique has the advantage that it presents the judge with a standard set of dispositions and constructs and therefore gets judgments which he is able to make but would often fail to make in producing a spontaneous description. But, for this advantage in coverage we have to pay a price. Such a situation is clinically unrealistic: whether we are starting with test data, history, or interview impressions, the particular facets which stand out (whether high or low) will not be the same for different patients. It may be that the meager results of recent validation studies are attributable in part to the calculation of hit frequencies or Q correlations over the entire range of traits, only a minority of which, variable in composition, would willingly be judged by the clinician on any one patient.

I cited earlier the statistic that only one psychotherapist in six believes that he is greatly helped in the treatment process by having advance knowledge of the patient's psychodynamics. One relevant consideration here is the rate at which the psychotherapist's image of

his patient converges to a stable picture. John Drevdahl, Shirley
Mink, Sherman Nelson, Murray Stopol, and I have been looking into
this question. So far, it seems that the therapist's image of his patient crystallizes quite rapidly, so that somewhere between the second
and fourth therapeutic hour it has stabilized approximately to the
degree permitted by the terminal sort-resort reliabilities. Let me show
you a couple of typical results. Figure 1 shows the Q correlations be-

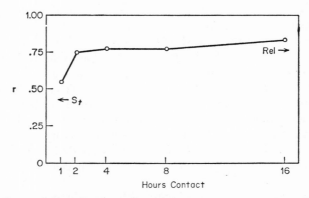

*Fig. 1. Q correlations between therapist's sort at 24 contacts and earlier
sorts. (Phenotypic pool; N = 182 items; Stopol)*

tween Stopol's phenotypic sort after the twenty-fourth hour and his
successive sorts after the first, second, fourth, eighth, and sixteenth
hours. "S_t" indicates correlation of his stereotype with twenty-fourth-
hour sort. "Rel" is sort-resort reliability. (The phenotypic and genotypic ratings are made separately.) Figure 2 shows results for the
genotypic pool. I do not mean to suggest that the therapist's perception at the end of 24 hours is "the criterion," which would involve a
concept of validation that I reject (Cronbach and Meehl, 1955, pp.
284–285, 292–294). But presumably his perception after 24 contacts
is more trustworthy than after only one. Or, if we (a) assume that
some information gained early is subsequently lost by forgetting, erroneous revisions, and the like; (b) take as our standard of comparison the average value of ratings over all six sortings; and (c) treat
this as a kind of "best combined image," the essential character of
the situation remains as shown.

Now this state of affairs presents any psychological test with a
difficult task. If, after two to four hours of therapeutic interviewing,

the therapist tends to arrive at a stable image of the patient which is not very different from the one he will have after 24 contacts, and if that final image is pretty accurate, the test would need to have very high validity before we could justify the expenditure of skilled psychological time in giving, scoring, interpreting, and communicating it.

When we first began this convergence study, our primary interest

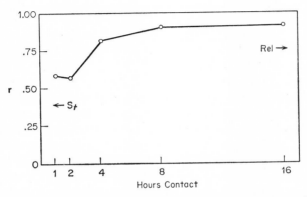

Fig. 2. Q correlations between therapist's sort at 24 contacts and earlier sorts. (Genotypic pool; N = 113 items; Stopol)

was in the pragmatic utility of the MMPI. One way to consider validity (which makes more practical sense than the conventional validation study) is to ask: "How long does it take the psychotherapist to find out what the test would have told him in the first place?" We were interested in plotting the Q correlation between a blind MMPI description of the patient and the successive sorts done by the therapist as he gathered more extensive samples of the latter's behavior during treatment, hoping to find that, as the therapist gets "wised up" by further interviews, he learns what the MMPI would have told him all along. This pleasant fantasy was disturbed by the rapidity with which the therapist's image of the patient converges, even before the Campbell-Fiske correlations were run. It is of some interest to plot the curve of Q correlation between a "good" blind MMPI description of the patient and the successive descriptions by the therapist (Figure 3). These results are surely nothing to write home about!

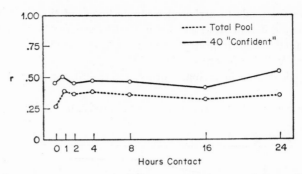

Fig. 3. Q correlations between MMPI reader's sort and successive sorts by therapist. (Phenotypic pool; Meehl and Stopol)

In a recent paper reporting on an empirical study of MMPI sorting behavior (Meehl, 1959b) I listed six factors or circumstances which might be expected theoretically to favor the clinician's brain as a cognizing and decision making instrument in competition with the traditional statistical methods of combining data. Among these six factors is one in which I have a particular interest, I suppose partly because it lends itself more readily to quantitative study than do some of the others. This factor is the presumed ability of the clinician to react on the basis of higher order configural relations (Meehl, 1954, pp. 130–134; Horst, 1954) by virtue of the fact that a system of variables can be graphically represented as a profile; and thereafter, given extensive clinical experience with a particular instrument, the clinician can respond to the visual gestalt. This he could do by *exemplifying* a complex mathematical function which neither he nor anyone else had as yet succeeded in *formulating*. The search for that function could take place in the context of studying the generalization and discrimination of complex visual forms. I recommend to your attention the recent work of Paul J. Hoffman on this subject, some of which has been reported (1958a, 1958b, 1959). Hoffman has undertaken a mathematical analysis of the rating behavior of judges who are presented with multivariable profiles, and the application of his formulas should teach us a great deal about the clinician's cognitive activity.

Comparing the impressionistic judgment of a group of Minnesota clinicians as to the amount of "psychotic tendency" revealed by MMPI profiles with six statistical methods of treating the profiles, I found that the pooled judgment of 21 clinicians was significantly better (against the diagnostic criterion) than the linear discriminant function. In fact, there was a significant tendency (although slight) for even the *individual* clinicians to do a better job than the linear discriminant function. However, the best cross-validative results displayed by any method of sorting these profiles thus far tried utilizes a very complex set of configural rules developed by Grant Dahlstrom and myself (Meehl & Dahlstrom, 1960). Table 1 shows the results of applying these rules to almost a thousand cases from

Table 1. Concurrent validity of Meehl-Dahlstrom rules in eight cross-validation samples

Sample	N	$H\%$	$M\%$	$I\%$	$\dfrac{H}{H+M}$	P
A*	92	55	16	28	.77	<.001
B*	77	45	29	26	.61	<.05
C	103	49	16	35	.75	<.001
D	42	40	21	38	.65	nonsig.
E*	181	45	18	36	.71	<.001
F	166	47	20	33	.70	<.001
G	273	63	12	25	.84	<.001
K*	54	78	5	17	.93	no test
Total	988	53	17	30	.76	.001

* Essentially uncontaminated samples.

eight clinics over the United States. These rules were concocted by a combination of clinical experience with statistical checking; and, while relatively crude and surely failing to extract all of the profile information, they are more efficient at this than a linear combination of scores, the pooled judgments of 29 MMPI readers, or the judgment of the best of 29. Without knowing the form and constants of the mathematical function relating probability of psychosis to the MMPI variables, we cannot answer the question: "How much of the information contained in the profile is extracted by the clinician?" One may plot probability of psychosis as a function of the clinicians' placement of profiles on an 11-step subjective scale of degree (or confidence) of psychoticism. Figure 4 shows probability of psychosis as a function of impressionistic profile placement by the best and worst clinician, and the pooled judgment of a group of 29. Figure 5 shows hit rate (whether neurotic or psychotic) as a function of the amount of consensus among 29 judges.

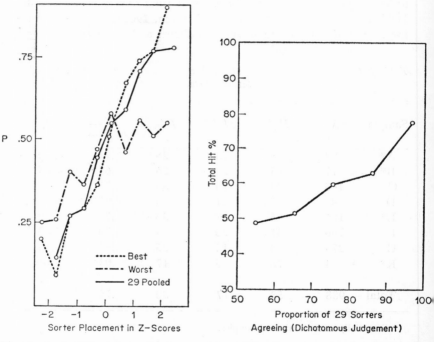

Fig. 4. Probability of psychosis as function of MMPI profile placement by sorters.

Fig. 5. Hit rate as function of MMPI sorter consensus. (neurosis-psychosis)

While our data do indicate that the clinician's judging behavior with respect to the psychoticism variable is significantly configural, the *amount* of departure from a linear, additive model does not appear to be very great. For many years, skeptical statisticians have been pointing out to us clinicians that there is more conversation about nonlinear functions than there is actual demonstration of such and, anyway, that the value of departures from linearity and additivity involved in clinical judgments is likely to be attenuated, if not completely washed out, by the clinician's assignment of nonoptimal weights and the unreliability invariably involved in the impressionistic use of multivariate data.

Lykken, Hoffman, and I plan to utilize some of the MMPI psychoticism data for the kinds of analysis the latter has suggested, but in the meantime I have applied one of Hoffman's formulas to a portion of these data. He suggests that, if we treat the clinician's quantitative sorting as the dependent variable, the multiple R of this variable upon the profile scores should differ from unity only because of the clinician's unreliability, provided his sorting behavior follows a linear model. The multiple R of the 11-step psychoticism ratings for my four best clinicians, when divided by the square root of their reliabilities (Hoffman's "complexity" formula), varies from .871 to .975, with a mean of .942, indicating that the departure of their judging behavior from a linear model is small. It is also interesting that the *inter*sorter reliability (Horst's generalized coefficient) reaches .994 for the four best sorters and .987 for the four worst. Whatever these MMPI readers are doing when asked to judge psychoticism from the profile, they seem to be doing it in very much the same way.

Let me turn next to a brief account of an exploratory study which was a dismal failure and which I am still trying to figure out. All told, there now exist almost 200 different scoring keys for the MMPI item pool, ranging all the way from "dependency" to "baseball talent" and derived by a variety of methods (including factor analysis, face validity, and criterion keying). I thought it might be interesting to treat the patient's MMPI behavior more like the psychoanalyst than like the factor analyst: namely, to overdetermine the psychology of the patient by scoring him on a large number of these scales, in spite of their redundancy. Imagine two patients who produce identical profiles when scored on a very large number of partially overlapping but distinguishable variables. One might hope, except for the intrinsic defects of *coverage* in the MMPI item pool, that such a pair of individuals would be, so to speak, pinpointed in personality space as very close together. In practice it is impossible to find identical (or even nearly identical) profiles as the number of scored dimensions is increased, but perhaps one could get an estimate of this extreme by extrapolating interpatient similarities from lesser degrees of profile resemblance.

Selecting a sample of 20 female outpatients rated by staff psychiatrists or psychologists in connection with a study on the new ataraxic Mellaril (Fleeson, Glueck, Heistad, King, Lykken, Meehl, & Mena, 1958), we calculated the interviewer rating Q correlations for all possible pairs, thus generating an interpatient resemblance matrix of 190 elements. Turning then to the MMPI (by which the clinical raters were, of course, uncontaminated) and eliminating scales of fewer than 10 or more than 80 items, we set up random sets of 10 scales after defining the first set of 10 as the basic profile of clinical scales commonly used. The Cronbach-Gleser distance measure was then computed on the MMPI profiles for the same 190 pairs. Thus we had a matrix of interpatient resemblances as clinically described by skilled interviewers through Q sorts and a corresponding matrix of MMPI profile similarity indices. A *series* of matrices of this latter kind was then generated by progressively extending the profile, adding successive blocks of 10 randomly chosen scales. Thus, the first MMPI matrix was based upon the interpatient distance measures for the usual 10 scores, the second one upon 20 scores (the usual 10 plus 10 randomly chosen), the third one on 30 scores, and so forth up to a profile of 160 variables! The idea, of course, was that through this procedure we would be squeezing all of the blood out of the psychometric turnip and that a second order correlation (apologies to the statisticians) between the corresponding elements of the two matrices would show a steady rise.

It would have been very nice had the asymptote of this intermatrix coefficient, when plotted as a function of the number of MMPI variables entering into the distance measure, approached a very high value. That is, if you measure—however unreliably and redundantly —a huge mass of variables (schizoid trend, recidivism, dominance, defensiveness, baseball talent, dependency, control, ego strength, use of repression, tendency to homesickness, academic potential, etc.), then the psychological resemblance between two patients will be closely related to their profile similarity on this extended list of MMPI scores. It turned out that there was no problem of curve fitting, for the simple reason that the intermatrix resemblances began at zero for the first 10 scales and remained at zero, without the slightest tendency to increase as we included further blocks of scales in computing the distance measures. We know from a good deal of evidence that neither the MMPI nor the clinical Q sorts are quite *that* bad, and I am at a loss to understand these results. My suspicion is that they arise from inadequacies of the distance measure itself, and further analysis of the data is being undertaken with this hypothesis in mind. I still think that it was an interesting idea.

Leaving profile pattern interpretation, I should like to consider one more topic briefly. One of the most important problems in clinical psychology is deciding what kind of language communicates the largest amount of information about a patient. Most clinical practice today is predicated upon the assumption that useful statements about the patient can best be formulated (or at least inferentially mediated) by a theoretical language. The power of theoretical discourse in the other sciences makes this predilection understandable, and the characteristic Allport-Vernon-Lindzey profiles of clinical psychologists reflect strong theoretical interest. However, we learn in undergraduate physics that in order to apply theoretical constructs to the solution of practical problems (specifically, to predict the subsequent course of a particular physical system), one must fulfill two conditions. First, he must possess a reasonably well developed theory. That is, he must know the laws that systems of the given kind obey. Secondly, he must have a technology, a set of measuring instruments, for determining the initial and boundary conditions of the particular system under study. To the extent that either, or both, of these conditions are not fulfilled, predictions arrived at by theoretical inference will be untrustworthy. I do not see how anyone taking an objective view of the enterprise could claim that we fulfill *either,* let alone both, of these conditions in clinical psychology today. For this reason, in spite of my own personal interest in theoretical questions, I remain among that minority who persist in skepticism as to the pragmatic utility of theoretical constructions in daily clinical decision making.

Suppose, however, that some kind of theoretical discourse is to be used; which of the several kinds of theoretical sublanguages is most economical? As a pilot study in connection with a Ford Foundation project now going on at Minnesota, I collected some preliminary data which you may find of interest. Twenty psychotherapists were asked to describe a patient whom they had had in treatment for at least 25 hours, using the 182-item phenotypic pool which generated the curves previously shown. They also described the patient in terms of the 113-item genotypic pool. Although the latter pool was not constructed in any systematic way with respect to theoretical orientation, having been built for a different purpose, one can identify five relatively homogeneous subsets of genotypic items as follows: 25 Murray needs, 14 areas of conflict, 13 mechanisms of defense, 10 value-orientation components, and 7 items referring to dimensions of psychiatric nosology. After calculating the 190 interpatient Q correlations based upon each of these subpools, we may ask how well the pattern of interpatient resemblances in the phenotype is reproduced by the genotypic matrix. Unfortunately, I have not been able to find a statistician who will tell me how to do a significance test on such data, but the coefficients obtained are shown in Table 2. It is remarkable, I think, that the 13 defense mechanisms do about as well in reproducing the 182-item phenotypic matrix as does the entire genotypic pool consisting of almost 10 times as many items. We hope that with a more systematic coverage of the domain the Ford project will give us some definite information about this question.

Table 2. Correlations between interpatient P matrix and G matrices based on various subpools

Variables	r
P (182 items) vs. entire G pool (113 items)	.59
P vs. 13 defense mechanisms	.52
P vs. 25 Murray needs	.22
P vs. 7 nosological components	.22
P vs. 10 value dimensions	.03
P vs. 14 conflict areas	−.03
P vs. all 69 G items in above subpools	.45

Note.—$_{20}C_2$ patients rated; $N = 190$ coefficients.

I have presented some samples of research currently in progress at Minnesota which, while somewhat heterogeneous and difficult to pull together, all treat of what we see as pragmatically important aspects of the clinician's cognitive activity. In order to place any confidence in either the theoretical constructs we employ in discussing patients, or in the instrument-interpreter combinations we use to assess them, studies of convergent and discriminative validity must be carried out. The Campbell-Fiske multitrait-multimethod matrix, or the multiperson-multimethod variant of it, should be useful for this purpose. It seems obvious that even adequate and sophisticated studies of construct validity must be supplemented by data upon the *rate* at which the clinician acquires information from various sources. Since the commonest justification for expenditure of psychometric time is the utility to the therapist of "advance knowledge" (especially of the genotype), the skepticism expressed by our sample of psychotherapists, taken in combination with the convergence curves for the therapist's perception of his patient, put this widely held belief badly in need of experimental support. An important aspect of such data, presumably rather specific to various populations and clinical instruments, is that of differential convergence rates among items. There are probably certain attributes for which a test's validity is insufficient to justify a marked departure from the base rates or mean rating of the given clinical population, and others for which the therapist tends to be in error early in the game and to converge to the truth rather slowly in contrast to the test. I would predict that an example of this is MMPI Scale 6, which is a rather weak scale when used as an exclusion test, but which, when elevated, turns out almost invariably to be right. I have had patients in treatment whose paranoid potential did not manifest itself until 50 or 75 sessions, by which time I had concluded (erroneously) that the MMPI was giving me a false positive.

As has been pointed out by many clinicians, lacking adequate clinical cookbooks (Meehl, 1956) we have in practice to treat our instruments as instrument-interpreter combinations. I believe we can say upon present evidence that no one interpreter succeeds in extracting all of the information contained in a profile and that the development of objective configural methods of profile analysis (of which the Meehl-Dahlstrom rules are a primitive example) is a task of great importance. David Lykken and I are currently engaged in a study comparing more complex functions—such as a second degree polynomial having squares and cross-products—with clinical judgment and the Meehl-Dahlstrom rules. I am betting on the last-named, because—while nonoptimally weighted—they do at least tap configural effects involving interactions up to the sixth order.

Finally, the question of what is the most economical language to employ in describing a patient remains open, although it appears that there are many practitioners who are not sufficiently aware that this problem exists.

I look forward to the next decade of research in clinical psychology with a certain ambivalence. We are asking more sensible questions and being more critical of our procedures; and several research techniques are now available, and in wide use, which should give us some pretty clear answers. The reason for my ambivalence (and I regret that in the role of prophet I have to sound like Jeremiah) is that the evidence already available suggests that the outcomes will look pretty gloomy. My advice to fledgling clinical psychologists is to construct their self-concept mainly around "I am a researcher" or "I am a psychotherapist," because one whose self-concept is mainly "I am a (test oriented) psychodiagnostician" may have to maintain his professional security over the next few years by not reading the research literature, a maneuver which has apparently proved quite successful already for some clinicians. Personally, I find the cultural lag between what the published research shows and what clinicians persist in claiming to do with their favorite devices even more disheartening than the adverse evidence itself.

Psychologists cannot administer shock treatment or pass out tranquilizers, and I do not know of any evidence that we are better psychotherapists than our psychiatric colleagues. If there is anything that justifies our existence—other than the fact that we come cheaper —it is that we think scientifically about human behavior and that we come from a long tradition, going way back to the very origins of experimental psychology in the study of human error, of being critical of ourselves as cognizing organisms and of applying quantitative methods to the outcomes of our cognitive activity. If this methodological commitment is not strong enough to compete with the commitments clinicians have to particular diagnostic instruments, the unique contribution of our discipline will have been lost. I can mobilize some enthusiasm for the next 10 years within the field: while I expect discouraging findings at the level of practice, from the standpoint of the sociology of professions and the history of ideas, the developments should be very interesting to watch.

REFERENCES

CAMPBELL, D. T., & FISKE, D. W. Convergent and discriminant validation by the multitrait-multimethod matrix. *Psychol. Bull.*, 1959, *56*, 81–105.
CATTELL, R. B. *Description and Measurement of Personality.* Yonkers: World Book, 1946.
CATTELL, R. B. *Personality.* New York: McGraw-Hill, 1950.

CRONBACH, L. J., & MEEHL, P. E. Construct validity in psychological tests. *Psychol. Bull.*, 1955, *52*, 281–302.

FLEESON, W., GLUECK, B., HEISTAD, G., KING, J., LYKKEN, D., MEEHL, P., & MENA, A. The ataraxic effect of two phenothiazine drugs on an outpatient population. *Univer. Minn. med. Bull.*, 1958, *29*, 274–286.

GARFIELD, S. *Introductory Clinical Psychology.* New York: Macmillan, 1957.

HOFFMAN, P. J. Criteria of human judgment ability: I. The "clinical" assessment of intelligence and personality. *Amer. Psychologist*, 1958, *13*, 388. (Abstract) (a)

HOFFMAN, P. J. Human judgment as a decision process. *Amer. Psychologist*, 1958, *13*, 368. (Title) (b)

HOFFMAN, P. J. The prediction of clinical prediction. *Amer. Psychologist*, 1959, *14*, 356. (Title)

HORST, P. Pattern analysis and configural scoring. *J. clin. Psychol.*, 1954, *10*, 3–11.

LITTLE, K. B., & SHNEIDMAN, E. S. Congruencies among interpretations of psychological tests and anamnestic data. *Psychol. Monogr.*, 1959, *73*(6, Whole No. 476).

McARTHUR, C. C., MEEHL, P. E., & TIEDEMAN, D. V. Symposium on clinical and statistical prediction. *J. counsel. Psychol.*, 1956, *3*, 163–173.

MEEHL, P. E. *Clinical versus Statistical Prediction.* Minneapolis: Univer. Minnesota Press, 1954.

MEEHL, P. E. Wanted—a good cookbook. *Amer. Psychologist*, 1956, *11*, 263–272.

MEEHL, P. E. When shall we use our heads instead of the formula? *J. counsel. Psychol.*, 1957, *4*, 268–273.

MEEHL, P. E. Some ruminations on the validation of clinical procedures. *Canad. J. Psychol.*, 1959, *13*, 102–128. (a)

MEEHL, P. E. A comparison of clinicians with five statistical methods of identifying psychotic MMPI profiles. *J. counsel. Psychol.*, 1959, *6*, 102–109. (b)

MEEHL, P. E., & DAHLSTROM, W. G. Objective configural rules for discriminating psychotic from neurotic MMPI profiles. *J. consult. Psychol.*, 1960, *24*, 375–387.

SELECTION V

....

Clinical Psychology and Logic*

DAVID BAKAN

THE CONSIDERATIONS IN this essay originate in a prevailing sense of the scientific untenability of clinical psychology among many psychologists. Frequently, clinical psychology is critically envisaged as an art; or if the critic is inclined to be more critical, it may be conceived of as an attempt to obtain knowledge mystically and effect changes magically.

It is the thesis of this essay that a good deal of the difficulty associated with the appropriate scientific delineation and characterization of clinical psychology stems from an inappropriate set of methodological considerations, rather than from any essential defect in the various procedures of this branch of our discipline. This should not be interpreted as a statement to the effect that all is well in the house of clinical psychology. Rather, it is intended simply as a suggestion that many of the *presumptive* ailments, as for example, lack of "experimental" confirmation, are not really what clinical psychology is suffering from.

In this paper we will limit ourselves to one of the major questions associated with clinical psychology: *How is it possible for the clinical psychologist to have any notion at all concerning what is going on in the "mind" of the client?* There are many circumlocutions whereby this question may be asked to avoid the use of the word "mind." But in the interests of simplicity and in the interests of communication—since the experience of the writer has been that there is less trouble in communication with this word than with many others—we will use the word "mind."

We can, however, formulate our question somewhat more generally and perhaps somewhat more complexly: *Is it possible, and in what sense is it possible, for one person to "know" another person's experiences, if experience is, as a certain traditional outlook would have it, utterly and unalterably private?* For purposes of discussion

* From the *American Psychologist*, 1956, *11*, 655–662.

we will refer to that position in the field of psychology which denies the possibility of a psychology of experience, on the grounds of the privacy of experience, as behaviorism.

PREDICTION AND CONTROL

The behaviorist position quickly forces a perplexing antinomy upon our attention, an antinomy which is of very particular significance to clinical psychology. On the one hand, one of the classical arguments associated with the behaviorist position is a form of the pragmatic argument: *That the behaviorist position will lead more quickly and more surely to the satisfaction of the criteria of prediction and control of behavior.* On the other hand, there is an atmosphere which is contemptuous of problems associated with the prediction and control of human behavior that is associated with the behaviorist position. The latter are regarded as impure, applied, etc., kinds of problems, and not quite the proper domain of the "scientist."

This antinomy is not a unique problem of psychologists; there are other sciences which have been able to bear with grandeur the burden of the analogous antinomy for three hundred years or more.

It is indeed strange, and noteworthy, that, among psychologists, where the problem is critically that of predicting and controlling human behavior, the behavioristic orientation seems to have the least cogency; for when we are interested in predicting and controlling the behavior of a human being the most appropriate questions are: "What is he experiencing?" and "What are his wishes and intentions (conscious or unconscious)?" Somehow this is more satisfying, even from the most pragmatic of points of view, than an enumeration and description of his "habits," or "stimulus-response connections," or "behavior tendencies," etc. It is certainly true that in the history of science our ability to predict and control the behavior of *matter* has not profited from such questions. But, evidently, our ability to predict and control the behavior of *human beings* seems to decline as we refrain from attempting to divine the nature of their experiences and motives. The strange thing about this whole situation is that those persons who are most interested in predicting and controlling human behavior, the clinical psychologists, are the very ones who tend to abandon behavioristic modes of thought.

As early as 1934 (*10*) and as late as 1955 (*9*), there have been psychologists who have suggested that if you want to predict and control human behavior, perhaps you had better stop trying to be a "scientist," in the orthodox sense. In 1934 Skaggs wrote:

The writer can see no other conclusion than that scientific psychology is and must be of little *practical value*. At the same time the writer is of the opinion that some of the less scientific psychology is of considerable practical significance. We cannot expect training in scientific experimental psychology to fit one to understand human nature in general. The more scientific the psychologist becomes the more must he retire from the general and complicated problems to more restricted problems and work in isolation from the world at large. There is simply nothing that can be done about the matter. However, the scientific psychologist might be more tolerant of other students of human nature (practical psychologists, novelists, and the like) because much of their knowledge stands the pragmatic test (*10,* p. 576).

A similar kind of conclusion is arrived at by Rogers in his deeply soul-searching article which was recently reprinted in the *American Psychologist* (*9*).

There are other indications in the literature that the logic of the situation presses on to an "impossible" conclusion; that somehow science, as it is conceived, is perhaps more or less incompatible with prediction and control as far as living organisms are concerned. Hebb (*4*), in an article in which he tells how to handle certain kinds of laboratory animals, indicates quite clearly that one is considerably more effective with them if one thinks of their behavior in anthropomorphic terms. And, of course, we must not forget Tolman's classical statement on how to predict the behavior of rats:

But, in any case, I, in my future work, intend to go ahead imagining how, *if I were a rat,* I would behave as a result of such and such an appetite and such and such a degree of differentiation; and so on (*11,* p. 24).

Statements such as these, of course, *a fortiori* indicate a difficulty in the "scientific" approach.

When, as is evident, the press of observations forces us towards a view that there exists a realm of phenomena for which the scientific approach is inappropriate, then we must conclude that the inappropriateness is inherent in that which we conceive science to be.

In other words, the fact that the present conception of science forces honest, astute, and conscientious investigators to look elsewhere for guidance must be interpreted as a shortcoming in the current conceptions of the scientific approach.

THE POSTULATE OF EPISTEMOLOGICAL LONELINESS

In recent history we have become painfully cognizant of the onslaught on the remainder of our knowledge of the results of cultural, historical, psychological, and sociological investigations and modes of thought. We have gotten into the habit of challenging our presumptive bits of knowledge from a culturological point of view. Perhaps we say to ourselves, "that which we believe stems more from our culture, or our need systems, than from what is the case." This kind of doubt has been both devastating and purifying.

We advance the hypothesis that the kind of epistemological scepticism which we inherit from the British empiricists, Locke, Berkeley, Hume and the like, stemmed largely from the state of affairs of their day rather than, say, from the intrinsic necessity of the case. A fundamental characteristic of the thought of the British empiricists is that it conceives of the thinker as essentially alone rather than as a member and participant of a thinking community. Historically, this is indeed both understandable and commendable. These men were pioneers. They were attempting to fashion a world in which they could be free of the traditional prejudices and beliefs. Thus, they were "sceptical" of the knowledge which they obtained from their contemporaries; and they found it necessary to dissociate themselves from their less liberated brethren. Furthermore, they were involved in the development of a new system of ethics and metaphysics in which the single individual was supreme as contrasted with medieval man who was lost in the giant enveloping embrace of the community. In their hunger for a philosophy of individualism they also generated a philosophy in which community had little or no part; a philosophy to which we might refer as a philosophy of *epistemological loneliness.*

It was David Hume, the latest of the great figures of British empiricism, who sensed this characteristic most acutely. In the conclusion of Book I of *A Treatise of Human Nature* (*6,* pp. 263 ff.), Hume gives expression to the relationship between his isolation and the position he advances. His sense of the isolation from the community of men and his reaching out to try to establish communion with the reader are poignant. In the midst of the development of a philosophy in which one of the central distinctions is that between opinion of men and independence of judgment he cries out, ". . . such is my weakness, that I feel all my opinions loosen and fall of themselves, when unsupported by the approbation of others" (6, 264–265).

The world in which he lives his life is one which is different from the world he fashions in his philosophy. He writes:

> I dine, I play a game of back-gammon, I converse, and am merry with my friends; and when after three or four hours' amusement, I would return to these speculations, they appear so cold, and strain'd, and ridiculous, that I cannot find in my heart to enter them any farther (6, p. 269).

What does this have to do with clinical psychology? Our conceptions concerning the privacy of experience as somehow entailed in the logic of science come from such origins. However, insofar as clinical psychology is concerned, a philosophy of loneliness and estrangement does not seem to be the most appropriate foundation. As a matter of fact, it might not be too great a stretch in characterizing many moderns seeking the assistance of clinical psychologists to say that their *disease* is exactly this feeling of loneliness and estrangement; that what they are seeking from the relationship with the clinical psychologist is assistance in overcoming the sense of being, as Thomas Wolfe put it, "forever prison pent."

The recognition that intimacy and community between the therapist and client are critical in effecting a cure for the person seeking help must, of course, be put to the credit of Freud's genius and the whole contemporary psychotherapeutic movement. It is worthwhile in this connection to listen to what Rogers has to say about the way in which he conducts psychotherapy. He writes:

> I launch myself into the therapeutic relationship having a hypothesis, or a faith, that my liking, my confidence, and my understanding of the other person's inner world, will lead to a significant process of becoming. I enter the relationship not as a scientist, not as a physician who can accurately diagnose and cure, but as a person, entering into a personal relationship. Insofar as I see him only as an object, the client will tend to become only an object.
>
> I risk myself, because if, as the relationship deepens, what develops

is a failure, a regression, a repudiation of me and the relationship by the client, then I sense that I will lose myself, or a part of myself. At times this risk is very real, and is very keenly experienced.

I let myself go into the immediacy of the relationship where it is my total organism which takes over and is sensitive to the relationship, not simply my consciousness. I am not consciously responding in a planful or analytic way, but simply in an unreflective way to the other individual, my reaction being based (but not consciously) on my total organismic sensitivity to this other person. I live the relationship on this basis (9, 267–268).

Now Rogers is fully aware that this kind of talk is not very "scientific." However, it is unscientific only when we have a science which is based upon the postulate of epistemological loneliness. The behaviorist who understands only the language of behavior might well confront Rogers with the question: "Dr. Rogers, now just what do you mean when you say that you 'risk' yourself? Can you give me an operational definition of risk?" We are certain that Rogers, in all wisdom, should and probably would, refrain from attempting to answer this question. Although he could probably give a genuinely *operational* definition, he could not give a *behavioristic* one. In the simple dictionary sense we all know what the meaning of the word "risk" is. Our behaviorist is not simply ignorant. But he may be complexly ignorant in that he consciously refuses to refer Rogers' words to his own "risk" of his personality. As a matter of fact, the avoidance of risk in just this sense in many behavioristically-inclined psychologists may be so intense that they cannot deal objectively with the experience of risk.

The behaviorist fashions himself a language which is modeled after the language among strangers. What do we mean? It is characteristic of conversation among strangers that they should talk of the most "public" things. Thus, strangers on a train, say, might talk of the weather, the characteristics of different cities, and the World Series. The language which is used among strangers is generally of the kind which would be accepted by the philosopher of science who calls himself a "physicalist." Thus, the kind of language which is held up to us as an ideal language, i.e., a physicalistic language, is one which, in its essence, is not very good for the kind of intimate coparticipation of the kind suggested by Rogers and other clinical psychologists.

On the basis of this discussion let us then say that we are interested in some kind of view of man which, in addition to having some "face validity," will also seem to be more appropriate to the kind of thing which clinical psychology is. A tempting position, which we must reject, is that somehow, by some unknown mystical process, we are all involved in some single grand communion. This we reject because it fails to satisfy our common sense; and because it is strongly suggestive of a lack of intellectual discipline of which we cannot help but be suspicious.

However, a simpler and more tenable kind of alternative is the assumption that, *after all, we are all pretty much alike.* And insofar as we are alike we might be able to "understand" one another by referring each other's expressions to our own experiences; and by some process which, we will say, is very much like the logical process of inference, we predict and thereby control the behavior of the other person.

It may appear that this postulate is either too novel or too vague. Actually it is not at all novel in the field of psychology. It plays a role in *every general psychological system.* For only if we assume that, after all, we are all pretty much alike, can we have a "general" psychology, a psychology in which the laws, generalizations, abstractions, etc., which are asserted presumably apply to each and every case. And, in the instance of many modern investigations, particularly in the field of learning, the "we" of our postulate is even taken to encompass the white rat. The uniqueness of the individual case is of little concern in a "general" psychology. What matters only are those characteristics in which "after all, we are all pretty much alike." What is novel in our argument is not the postulate itself but that we are carrying it in its implications one step further. Insofar as its vagueness is concerned, it is sufficiently precise to have functioned admirably in even a less sharply delineated fashion in the history of all "general" psychologies.

THE OBSERVED AND THE STUDIED

Before we enter upon the discussion of logic proper, it is essential that another cultural characteristic of modern science be mentioned and perhaps isolated. Centuries of error and their correction lie behind us. Modern man, for whatever reason, experiences deep humiliation when he finds himself in error. There is a great tendency to avoid this humiliation by refraining from making any assertions except those in which one can place only the highest confidence.

The behaviorist guarantees that he will not make errors in attributing experiences to others by *never* attributing any experiences to them—at least not in his role as scientist. In the defense of his position he will tell you that he can *only know what he has observed.* Unfortunately, a critical and basic distinction, that between the "observed" and the "studied," frequently does not bear very much cogency in his thinking. He will assert that since only the behavior of the other person can be observed, only the behavior of the other person can be the object of his study. His parting rejoinder—his last word, so to speak—runs something as follows: "But after all, you can only study the overt behavior of the other one. You cannot study his experiences."

In spite of the compelling quality of such utterances, they are, in the language of the logical positivist, "nonsense." It may be true that one cannot *observe* anything but the manifest behavior of the other person. But this does not prevent one from *studying* many other characteristics of the other person. The fact of the matter is that, except in a limited number of latter-day, die-hard, hyperdisciplined studies, most investigators regard the observations of their studies only as a basis for inference about other things. Our knowledge is almost always the result of *both observation and inference,* and not of observation alone. And if one has to argue that somehow one knows of the other's experiences by *observation and other processes,* the argument is not unique to the field of psychology.

The remainder of this paper becomes somewhat more technical now, and so it might be well to summarize what we have tried to communicate up to this point. We are concerned with the question of how and in what sense one person, particularly a clinical psychologist, might know what is going on in the mind of another, the client. We have strongly suggested that, unless the experience of the other is accepted as a reality, neither clinical success nor theoretical progress along these lines can be made. We have pointed out that there is good reason to believe that the alternative position, i.e., behaviorism, is weakest on a point on which it tends to pride itself the most, the ability to predict and control human behavior. We have dubbed the major postulate of behaviorism the *postulate of epistemological loneliness,* to suggest the social atmosphere, or perhaps the nonsocial atmosphere, which is associated with it; and have attempted to point out that the linguistic behavior which is recommended by the behaviorist as the appropriate form of communication among scientists is modeled along the lines of the social etiquette appropriate among strangers. We have advanced an alternative postulate, that *"after all, we are all pretty much alike."*

THE USE OF LOGIC AS A WAY OF CHARACTERIZING THE INFERENCES OF THE CLINICAL PSYCHOLOGIST

Our major thesis is that the application of certain forms of formal logic to the thought processes which are involved in knowing the other person can result in both increasing our understanding of the clinical process as well as supplying the scientific underpinning which many feel that it needs.

In pointing to logic in connection with the clinical processes it is important that it be recognized that we are not thereby also attempting to connect some of the cultural accretions which are generally associated with logic. Thus, for example, the common expression, "cold logic," we feel is quite inappropriate. Hot logic, lukewarm logic, and cold logic can all be quite logical.

Another point of view, with which we are quite out of sympathy, is that which looks towards logic as a substitute for human thought, and which dreams of the day, perhaps, in which it will replace thought. In the way in which we understand logic it is not and cannot be a substitute for the processes of human thinking. There are probably some people in the field of psychology today who envisage the eventual substitution of some kind of logical or mechanical equipment for the clinician. We sincerely hope that these people will gain no comfort from the reading of this discussion.

The application of logic to the processes of thought has had a thorny history, a history which has generated certain prejudices in us about the possibility of using logic in any direct way for understanding the thought processes. When George Boole wrote his famous *The Laws of Thought* (3), the volume which ushered in the whole train of developments in modern logic, he thought that he was writing what we would call psychology. He thought that the logic as he wrote it was *descriptive* of the processes of thought which man engaged in. When subsequent investigation dramatically showed that in many instances man's thought was not logical, that man often, so to speak, erred, this particular feature of Boole's contribution became quite discredited. The simple alternative to this is that logic is regarded not as *descriptive* but as *prescriptive*. It is to this alternative that most of the work in logic has leaned; and in doing so it has been effectively separated from the discipline of psychology except in some trivial senses.

That which we propose here in the way of using logic in the service of psychology is *neither exactly descriptive nor exactly prescriptive,* although we do not mean to exclude these uses. The alternative which we here propose is to use logic, its terms and its structure, as a heurism whereby we might penetrate more deeply into the nature of the actual processes which are involved. We *consider* the logic as somehow representative of the truth of the situation, but we do not *assert* that it is representative. What we do generally assert, however, is that man engages in processes which are *like* logical processes; and that by the comparison of the actual processes with the corresponding logical processes, our understanding of these processes may be enhanced. An approach of this kind has recently been advanced by Piaget (*8*).

Let us give an example of the kind of thing which we have in mind. I am standing on the street corner and see a car approaching. I engage in some processes which lead me to the conclusion that I can safely cross if I start right now and that I will be on the other side before the car comes near to where I am standing. This whole problem can be completely described in mathematical terms. I can walk so many miles an hour. The distance across the street is such and such of a fraction of a mile. I have the equation that rate times time equals distance. I enter the rate at which I walk, and the distance, and solve the equation for time. Then I estimate the rate at which the car is moving, and the distance it has to go to reach this point, and solve another equation for the time it will take for the car to reach this point. Now, if the time for me to cross turns out to be considerably less than the time for the car to arrive, I conclude that I may cross.

Now actually people generally do not solve problems like this by the solution of equations. They never "think" of equations. But the major point is this: *That they engage in psychological processes which are "like" the mathematical processes.* There must be some —although not necessarily complete or good—isomorphism between the processes which they have engaged in and the mathematical ones.

If we should be interested in gaining an understanding of the nature of this kind of judgment, of what factors make a difference in it, etc., the knowledge of the equations, of the mathematics of the situation, would be basic equipment. For by the comparison of the mathematics with the actual thought processes we can come to understand the thought processes. This would be a use of mathematics in a way in which we assert neither that it is descriptive of, nor prescriptive for, the actual processes.

PROBABILITY AS A BRANCH OF LOGIC

We have talked of logic generally. However, there is a technical problem of choice among different logics. This is not the place to enter into a discussion of the variety of and relations among the various logics which are available. The choice for the purposes for which we intend it must be based upon some apprehension of the fittingness of the important characteristics of the logical system to the important characteristics of the situation to which it is being applied; and upon some sense of the cogency of outcome of such an application. The marriage of a logic with some other enterprise may be either barren or productive of weaklings if the mating is improper.

In our earlier discussion we suggested that knowledge of the other one is somehow to take place by reference to one's own experience. Now, for our present purposes, experiences on the part of the clinical psychologist which are unconscious must be considered as nonexistent. Thus, before we can talk about either logic or the clinical situation in any detail we must presuppose that we have a clinical psychologist in whom a large variety of his experiences are available to him in consciousness. From a psychoanalytic point of view we might speak of an individual in whom many of the repressions have been overcome so that he is able to hold in consciousness, without immediately repressing them, ideas usually revulsive such as, for example, incest-wishes, etc. Thus, for this kind of clinician, the task involved in understanding the other person essentially involves the attribution of one or another of his experiences with a probability value indicative of the likelihood that this is the experience in the client to which the client is referring. It should be evident that whereas our view in general calls for a clinician in whom the appropriate experiences are conscious, it does not necessarily call for the same in the client.

It would seem that the most appropriate logic would be one which is probabilistic in nature. However, it is indeed a very special kind of probability. It cannot be probability in a relative frequency sense since, without stretching a point, there are no samples or populations sufficiently homogeneous from which a sensible ratio may be made; nor does the clinical approach, which is so very much concerned with the particular event, or particular experience under consideration, seem a particularly fitting roost for a frequency theory probability. The probability notion with which we might have some business has more to do with degree of certainty than with objective states of affairs.

It is rather unfortunate for our purposes that probability is too often conceived of as a branch of mathematics rather than logic. The view that probability is primarily a form of logic rather than of mathematics goes back to Leibnitz and finds its current expression in the work of John Maynard Keynes (7).

The Principle of Inverse Probability

The logical problem involved in clinical psychology is this: *The making of inferences about experiences from overt behavior.* The inference may be made, for example, that the individual is experiencing pain from observing him saying "ouch!" Now this may or may not be a valid inference in any given situation. It is indeed possible that a person will say "ouch" even if he is not in pain, as, for example, in the case of malingering. Let us examine the conditions of such an inference. The degree to which we will accept the notion that the person who says "ouch" is in pain is contingent upon a series of other judgments which we make, and therefore we call this a problem in inference.

Let us now introduce the word *probability,* to indicate the degree of tenability to be associated with a proposition. Immediately it becomes evident that the probability that the man is in pain depends upon the probability that he would say "ouch" if he were in pain, and inversely dependent on the probability that he would say "ouch" whether or not he were in pain. It is also evident that the tenability of the proposition that the man is experiencing pain is based on other considerations than whether he does or does not say "ouch." If, for example, we could see his wound we would maintain that it was highly probable that he was experiencing pain.

The essence of our judgment concerning the experience of the other person on the basis of his overt behavior is our estimate of the *contingency of the overt behavior on experience.* The logic of the relations among these judgments seems to be most adequately handled by the principle which is the basic one for nonfrequency theories of probability, the so-called principle of inverse probability, or the Rule of Bayes; and, the greatest portion of our understanding of the contingency of overt behavior on experience comes from self-observation. It is in the combination of inference through the use of inverse probability and self-observation that knowledge concerning the experience of the other person is possible.

In a previous paper the principle of inverse probability was discussed in detail, and the possibility of the use of the principle as a general theory of learning was outlined (*1*). The notion was advanced that one of the critical features involved in learning was a ratio, which was called R. R has many properties in common with what is called a likelihood ratio in contemporary statistical theory.

For the purposes of this paper we will rewrite R as follows:

$$R = \frac{P(B_0/E_0 h)}{P(B_0/\bar{E}_0 h)}$$

to be read as "The probability of behavior B_0 on experience E_0, over the probability of B_0 on not-E_0, all under conditions h." These probabilities can only be ascertained by the individual on the basis of some kind of self-observation; for *behavior and experience together* are available only to a person himself.

According to the logic of inverse probability, the probability of E_0 on B_0 varies directly with R. In other words, the probability of the experience E_0 on the basis of observing behavior B_0 depends directly on $P(B_0/E_0)$ and inversely on $P(B_0/\bar{E}_0)$. If this ratio is large, then the clinician is more inclined to attribute the experience E_0 to the individual.

The critical reader will have observed that we have passed easily from E_0 and B_0 as characteristic of the clinician to having them both characteristic of the client. This technical weakness disappears if it is indeed true that "after all, we are all pretty much alike"; and this technical weakness would make everything we have said complete nonsense if it is false. However, willy-nilly the clinician must be doing something like this. In the last analysis, only the clinician's sense that we are all alike in the more important respects can make tenable either the theory which is being advanced or the kind of therapy talked of by persons like Rogers, the psychoanalysts, etc.

In a paradoxical way the theory not only accounts for correct judgments on the part of the clinical psychologist but also for incorrect ones. It shows how, for example, a clinical psychologist may be "riding a hobby," i.e., explaining wide ranges of behavior on the basis of a limited range of experiences. In a given clinician, the probability of behavior on the basis of a given experience may run very high compared to the probability of that behavior on the basis of other experiences. That is, for a given behavior and a given experience, the R-value is high. This clinician will be inclined to attribute this kind of experience with great certainty, because in himself this R-value is high. It is here that the education of the clinical psychologist is extremely important. What his education should do is to show him the plausibility, within himself, of alternative behaviors on the basis of given experiences, and the multiplicity of experience which may give rise to some specific kind of behavior. If, as has been suggested before, the task of the clinical psychologist is that of finding to which experiences within himself he is to refer the given item of behavior which he observes, it is extremely important that his training shall open up to consciousness the wide ranges of experiences that lie within him. This, of course, is one way of conceiving of the desirability of having psychotherapy for one who is to do psychotherapy.

On Relevance and the Role of Clinical Experience

One of the major problems which faces the clinical psychologist in his daily work is that of relevance. He hears a case history, or listens to his client tell him of many things. Somehow some things which he hears "matter" more than others. As the flow is taking place a vast variety of experiences within the clinician come to be referred to in this complex relationship. Some of the clinician's experiences are brought into focus. Others of them seem to fall out of focus. Then there is the vast amount of experiential material within the clinician which has somehow been untouched by the contact with the client.

What we have said in the above paragraph may be clarified by bringing to bear upon it one of the lessons of probability theory of Keynes. Keynes has an eminently simple definition of relevance which catches the essence of the process to which we are referring. Recasting it into the symbols which we have used, an item of behavior B_0 is relevant to an experience E_0, if the probability of E_0 is modified with the introduction of B_0.

In and of itself this may not appear to be very cogent. However, the use of this formulation can help us in seeing just exactly what the effect of clinical experience may be, and is suggestive of a kind of case-history type of research which may be extremely valuable in opening up previously unseen relevancies. One of the best examples of this kind of research is presented to us in a paper by Josephine Hilgard (5).

She points out that in the study of several cases of rather sudden precipitation of psychoses, the ages of the children of the patients were not considered to be particularly relevant. Then, it became apparent that these patients' children were at an age at which the patients themselves had had rather severe traumatic experiences.

This readily becomes: The probability of becoming psychotic increases as a result of beholding intimately my child who is now as old as I was when (say) my parents died; and by our definition of relevance the age of the child has become relevant. It should be apparent from this that when we say that we are all pretty much alike it does not mean that we must all be psychotic, nor that we must all have children, nor that we must all have had the experience of our parents dying. Not *in point of fact* need we have had these experiences. But rather in the way in which all yearning is the same, and all pain is the same, and all fantasy is the same, etc.—only in this way need we have had these experiences. And the method whereby we may become aware of the relationship between experience and behavior is through the use of systematic self-observation (2).

REFERENCES

1. Bakan, D. Learning and the principle of inverse probability. *Psychol. Rev.*, 1953, *60*, 360–370.

2. Bakan, D. A reconsideration of the problem of introspection. *Psychol. Bull.*, 1954, *51*, 105–118.

3. Boole, G. *The Laws of Thought*. Chicago: Open Court, 1940.

4. Hebb, D. O. Temperament in chimpanzees. I. Methods of analysis. *J. comp. physiol. Psychol.*, 1949, *42*, 192–206.

5. Hilgard, Josephine R. Anniversary reaction in parents precipitated by children. *Psychiatry*, 1953, *16*, 73–80.

6. Hume, D. (Ed. by Selby-Bigge, L. A.) *A Treatise of Human Nature*. Oxford: Clarendon Press, 1951.

7. Keynes, J. M. *A Treatise on Probability*. London: Macmillan, 1948.

8. PIAGET, J. *Logic and Psychology.* Manchester: Manchester Univer. Press, 1953.
9. ROGERS, C. R. Persons or science? A philosophical question. *Amer. Psychologist*, 1955, *10*, 267–278.
10. SKAGGS, E. B. The limitations of scientific psychology as an applied or practical science. *Psychol. Rev.*, 1934, *41*, 572–576.
11. TOLMAN, E. C. The determiners of behavior at a choice point. *Psychol. Rev.*, 1938, *45*, 1–41.

SELECTION VI

....

Clinical Psychology and the Nature of Evidence*

Joseph F. Rychlak

A RATHER STEADY flow of articles dealing with the problems of clinical psychology as science has occupied the pages of this journal since its inception in 1946. This is probably due in part to the postwar self-definition psychologists are attempting, in terms of professionalism, ethics, etc. But the fundamental and pressing question regarding the nature of the clinical endeavor must be recognized. Can a clinician, as an applied member of the field of psychology, call himself a scientist?

Students find themselves caught in this dilemma, generally about the beginning of their second graduate year. They prove an irritating source of questions like: "How can I be a scientist when the obvious fact is that in the clinic I have very little control over all of the variables in operation?" Those of us in the position of educating and training clinicians must face such inquiries with each new group of graduate students after they have learned the facts of life: that clinical psychology is a *science*. What can we answer them? The present paper was undertaken in hopes of clarifying some of the issues present, both historical and philosophical, and also to suggest a form of conceptualization which may help us to understand the source of the dilemma.

RECENT HISTORY

As a point of departure let us take the postwar years, as reflected in the articles and commentaries of the *American Psychologist*. What have they made of clinical as one form of applied psychology? At the very outset, Krech (1946) heralded the "spectre of fission" haunting academic psychology: i.e., the split between experimental

* From the *American Psychologist*, 1959, *14*, 642–648.

and professional psychology. This was really nothing new, having a prewar history as well; but now with the hostilities ended and social needs painfully evident, Krech argued for the study of human beings rather than lower animals, suggesting that the method might prove more difficult but with ingenuity and effort it could be perfected. He proposed a distinction between "pure" experimental and "applied" pure experimental psychology. The former type of psychologist experiments only to shed light on systematic scientific concepts. The latter psychologist experiments to help answer specific questions, whether or not those questions bear on a systematic point of view. Yet both researchers would be "pure" in their experimentation. Crannell (1947) answered Krech with the argument that certain basic laws and principles can better be studied in rats than in men, reaffirming the notion that such a procedure teaches one the basic tools of science.

It was Thorne (1947) who then expressed the belief that:

Although the primary emphasis is on the individual case, the basic methods of clinical science involve the same techniques of description, classification, and explanation as are standard in experimental laboratory science (p. 160).

Here was an issue clearly stated, a suggested parallel between the animal laboratory and the clinical office. But in general over the next few years the issue under presentation was not prominently discussed. Graduate education and VA training programs were of major concern, culminating in the Boulder Conference of August 1949.

The following year Guthrie (1950) discussed the problem in the context of systematic psychology. Drawing a rather heavy analogy between clinical psychology and medicine, Guthrie placed both of these practices out of the realm of science. The reason for this decision was that neither discipline is interested in explanation of what they deal with, disease or behavior as the case may be, except insofar as such explanation facilitates a cure, or presumably a change in behavior. Science, on the other hand, is concerned with explanation per se: "Science aims at generalization and theory. Practitioners aim at cures" (Guthrie, 1950, p. 99). Psychologists need adequate theoretical models, and the psychoanalytical models do not serve for science for they are prescientific. For Guthrie, a scientific model would be one like cybernetics. Summing up, he suggests that the practice of psychology be left to physicians and social workers, whose training will better fit them to the job in the first place, and that psychology take its place as one of the basic sciences.

It would seem, then, that Krech's prediction was taking form, assuming Guthrie's attitude reflected the position of a fair segment of experimentalists. Like Krech, and unlike Thorne who based his argument primarily on the similarity in method, Guthrie suggested that the goal of a discipline defined its nature. However, he added the significant idea that an applied goal was *ipso facto* nonscientific. This is a rather interesting position and can probably be traced in part to Bingham's (1923) well known definition of applied psychology as "psychology in the service of ends other than its own." In any case, as might have been expected, psychologists with an applied interest answered the challenge by stating there were no basic differences between applied and pure research or between the clinician and the systematist (Gabriel, 1950; Newman, 1950).

Rosenzweig (1950) then tapped a truly significant undercurrent of self-definition among clinicians, as reflected in a series of exchanges in the "Comment" department of this journal (Rosenzweig, 1951; Super, 1951). Rosenzweig's general contention was that, as he interpreted several APA committees studying the problems of clinical, the overwhelming emphasis on the training of clinicians was being placed in the area of professional competency. He feared that in our desire to respond to a social responsibility, and define minimal standards of professional competency, we would overlook the fact that at this point in time we cannot state precisely what a clinician should be. Such principles should be based upon firm experimental evidence. He asked that a committee dealing with the coordination of professional and scientific functions of the clinician be formed, lest we face the likelihood that

psychology is destined to become a science foreign to personality—as used to be the case—and a profession foreign to science—as should never be the case (Rosenzweig, 1950, p. 680).

In a series of exchanges that followed, many opinions were voiced and attitudes crystalized; but the upshot of it all was that the clinician refused to accept the inevitability of a schism and was now definitely committed to being scientist as well as practitioner. Fusion replaced fission, and no doubt there were lamentations on both sides.

Hunt (1951) continued in the vein of Thorne and, accepting the affinity of clinical psychology and medicine, took the position that the physician is a scientist using well tested techniques:

Too often we concentrate upon the physician and his bedside manner but overlook the scientific basis of his method (p. 686).

Hunt further underscored the empirical basis of clinical intuition and cited probability theory from Reichenbach. Thus, although he broadened the base somewhat by helping the trend to philosophy of science as a rationale for clinical psychology, Hunt's argument was essentially from the point of view of method rather than goal. Bach (1952) helped develop the latter point by noting that well known practitioners like Freud, Rorschach, and Rogers have stimulated tremendous amounts of significant research. This point of view suggested that a major responsibility and privilege of the clinician is to formulate hypotheses from personal contact with people, such hypotheses to be subsequently evaluated through research. Moreover, the two aspects so delineated were to be viewed as parts of the same process. Rogers (1953) clarified the elements of this argument when he noted that psychologists doing psychotherapy

will develop their hunches, their theories, their concepts, their research projects, not only from knowledge of animals and laboratory subjects, but from intimate contact with the psychological dynamics of individual human beings in a process of change (p. 50).

They would become, then, the "applied" pure psychologists Krech spoke of, but would never participate in ends other than their own.

From this point forward we see attempts on the part of clinicians to bring together—and not merely integrate—the roles of practitioner and scientist. This was and is no easy matter, and not all clinicians took this tack. For example, Tolman (1953) quotes a personal communication of E. L. Kelly, who wrote:

Clinical psychologists must become more and more schizophrenic. When functioning as clinicians, they must behave as intuitively and artistically as do psychiatrists, who as Eysenck points out do not have a satisfactory science to apply as yet. When functioning as scientists . . . they should accept the canons of science and act like scientists. This is not to say that one role is more important or better than another, but they should not be mixed *at the same time* (p. 723).

Here is one man's solution. If followed, clinicians would play dual roles, according to the situation. Presumably the situations would ultimately influence one another, but the important factor E. L. Kelly seems to be stressing is that ground rules in one activity should not dominate or restrict the clinician carrying through in the other activity. Although a feasible program of action, as formulated it seems to have confused some individuals who had difficulty in shifting roles. For example, a student of the period complained about dual roles for experimentally and clinically inclined psychologists (Solomon, 1955). He emphasized, and was supported in this emphasis (Kahn, 1955), that the real difference lay in the opposing interests of individual psychologists, interests which presumably could not be successfully integrated. Fission had now become a highly personal problem, and G. A. Kelly (1955a) as spokesman for the clinical profession noted that the problem was as yet unsolved.

Rogers (1955) next picked up the trend of thought he had helped initiate. His contention was that a clinician can function as *both* scientist and clinical therapist in the *same* situation:

I can abstract myself from the experience and look upon it [i.e., therapy] as an observer, making myself and/or others the objects of that observation. . . . To avoid deceiving myself as observer, to gain a more accurate picture of the order which exists, I make use of all the canons of science. . . . A deeper understanding of therapy . . . may come from living it, or from observing it in accordance with the rules of science, or from the communication within the self between the two types of experience (p. 278).

There are problems in this position, but the approach taken in its support centered about arguments drawn from the philosophy of science, a practice begun earlier but currently of prime importance. Psychologists (Crannell, 1956; Skinner, 1956; Strupp, Castore, Lake, Merrill, & Bellak, 1956) were now asking themselves "what is science?" rather than merely "what is clinical psychology?" Bakan (1956) drew from a discipline usually viewed as a social science, i.e., economics, to justify some of Rogers' contentions. Berenda (1957) reaffirmed some of Oppenheimer's (1956) observations concerning the dangerous practice of patterning our psychological models on an outmoded physical philosophy. Harlow (1957) and Cronbach (1957) gave the applied psychologist a justification for attempting more than one method of studying man, thereby broadening the scope for a science of man. Probably the most highly sophisticated expression of this current school of thought in clinical is that of G. A. Kelly (1955b), who makes every man, psychologically, a scientist in his own right.

Thus, it would appear that in the search for self-definition and justification, clinicians and other psychologists with an applied interest have brought to the fore the question of scientific procedure itself. And the attempt is gradually being made to define science in such a fashion as to include activities carried on in the clinic. "Science" is being defined at least as frequently as is "clinical psychology." In one sense the present article follows this precedent, extending the argument to a consideration of the nature of evidence utilized in the clinic and the nonclinical laboratory situation.

What Is Science?

To say that science does not have an applied goal is inconsistent with the thinking of both Gilbert (Wiener & Noland, 1957, pp. 219–250) and Bacon (Wiener & Noland, 1957, pp. 382–389), people not unimportant in the development of the scientific point of view. Conant (1952) notes what he calls "one of the major significant developments of the last decade" (p. 21) concerning the shift in role of the scientist. And this shift is nothing less than a change from nineteenth century attempts at discovery of natural law to the twentieth century attempt at technological advance. Scientists have become inventors, adding an applied goal to their classical role of explanation for explanation's sake. As to the scientific method: if one tries to pin it down to a circumscribed procedure, it soon becomes apparent that science is situational and varies in method accordingly, at least within certain bounds. Kantor (1953) typifies science as "an enormous accumulation of specific jobs" (p. 4). Conant (1952) is most succinct on this point:

It would be my thesis that those historians of science, and I might add philosophers as well, who emphasize that there is no such thing as *the* scientific method are doing a public service (p. 35).

How then to summarize the scientific point of view for our students? To do so would probably involve a list of authoritative references unnecessary in this context. General principles could probably be underscored in such an array, like those of observation, systematic classification, and experimentation. The attitude of disdain for authority and a healthy suspicion of the easy solutions provided by the intellect would likely be included. Scientists have traditionally viewed themselves as members of a common community, working toward a common goal of knowledge, understanding, and technological advance for mankind. In this connection, psychologists have rightfully patterned themselves after their fellow scientists in physics, etc.; and their psychological theory has followed closely the paradigms of physical science.

Probably the basic and most inclusive characteristic of science relates somehow to the role of evidence. For the scientist qua scientist is never merely and only interested in a thing working (i.e., literally and narrowly, the applied goal); he is interested in *how* and *why* it works.[1] To guide his thinking, to critically evaluate his conclusions he has again and again stressed the role of proof, the nature of truth, and the evidence on which he is to base his beliefs and judgements. It is the contention of this paper that a systematic consideration of the nature of evidence will help to clarify the contradictions in the concept of scientific-clinician. This is so because an inability to shift from one role to another seems contingent upon an inability to appreciate the significance of differing kinds of evidence. A true scientist must appreciate many things, even the significance of his own psychology; and to do this he must learn to make a distinction between the kinds of evidence which motivate his judgement and belief. He must learn something of how and why *he* works.

Two Kinds of Evidence

Evidence refers to the grounds for belief or judgement. Since beliefs and judgements influence action, the issue of evidence is crucial to any consideration of behavior and, in particular, behavioral change. On the basis of evidence we make decisions, state principles of generality, and predict various outcomes. On the basis of evidence we direct our individual behavior. The positivistic scientist refuses to accept a "final word," preferring to deal in probabilities nurtured

---

[1] It should be noted that not all philosophers of science would agree to this statement. Frank, for example, would place questions of "why" in the realm of philosophy, although he suggests that many scientists are also philosophers (1957, p. 23).

on past evidence. The hysteric refuses to accept the findings of the electrocardiograph and insists his heart is stopping. The two situations seem far removed, yet in actuality we can say that both scientist and hysteric are directing their behavior on the basis of the same kind of evidence.

To clarify this similarity it is proposed that a distinction be drawn between validating and procedural forms of evidence.[2] The distinction is rough and arbitrary, and its sole purpose is heuristic in that, if accepted, it facilitates conceptualization and discussion. When we believe a statement or principle on the basis of its observable consequences following a prescribed succession of events designed to test that principle, we do so on the basis of *validating* evidence. The influence of the object of study on the prescribed succession of events is not taken into account and is certainly not a contingency to the acceptance or rejection of the principle being tested. We study an object in a certain way, and its influence on the procedure of study is, or should be, nonexistent. We then act in relation to the principle according to the observed consequences of the succession of prescribed events. We may accept the import of the principle, reject it, or modify it accordingly. This form of evidence includes the familiar notions of experimental or factual evidence and empirical validity.

On the other hand, *procedural* evidence involves the belief in a statement or principle because of its intelligibility, consistency with common sense knowledge, or implicit self-evidence. Although not validated through observing the results of a preconceived succession of events, such a proposition influences behavior on the part of the individual accepting and "believing" its content. Depending upon the level of abstraction one wishes to point to, this form of evidence includes, among others, the notions of philosophical proof, theoretical justification, scientific methodology, construct validity (Cronbach & Meehl, 1955), and (in its most general phrasing) attitudes of common sense.[3]

By common sense is meant the agreed upon or accepted knowledge

---

[2] Philosophical antecedents of this distinction date back to Thomas Aquinas. For the present discussion, the issue of what constitutes truth will be set aside.

[3] Frank (1957) has presented a scholarly analysis of the differences between types of proof he calls I and II which approximates our distinction, except that Type II proof is more technically related to philosophical proof and is not nearly so gross as the procedural distinction made here.

of a group, knowledge which is reflected in its culture and no longer a point of contention among its members. Common sense need not refer only to the sense of the "common man." Different groups have differing senses of common knowledge, and this knowledge can change through innovation so that common sense changes over time. The principles accepted and utilized by a community of psychoanalysts would confuse and possibly embarrass the average layman, if reported to him in a straightforward, simplified fashion. This is because he has not participated in the culture of psychoanalysis and come to accept the significance of its terminology, which embodies its common sense and determines what appears self-evident to its members.

Self-evidence and common sense are concepts many psychologists have felt they successfully dispensed with years ago. The complete rejection of introspectionism carried with it a dismissal of all such "armchair" criteria. In their desire to be scientific, psychologists emphasized the role of validational evidence in the context of laboratory experimentation. Scientific activity has come to mean *nothing but* the utilization of validating evidence. And the fact that procedural evidence also influences behavior has been set aside as an area of study and consideration in psychology, as if it were an unrealistic or at least unscientific problem.

Along with this—since it takes an experimenter working outside of the apparatus to validate an hypothesis—to plan the experiment and assess the significance of the findings, etc., psychologists have succeeded fairly well in taking themselves out of the picture. After all, one studies "that" to validate. And since validation constitutes science, to study oneself is then hardly a scientific endeavor. It is philosophical and semantic. It leads nowhere.

Physicists, on the other hand, have learned over time that their biases must be considered in evaluating their theories, their method, their objects of study, and their empirical findings. And biases hinge upon procedural evidence. One of the most significant and dramatic events in the postwar years was Oppenheimer's (1956) sophisticated exhortation to psychologists to consider their biases, to ask themselves how fruitful it is to use a machine as paradigm, to essentially strike off on their own and trust to their own common sense and knowledge of people. The physical scientists have come to appreciate the importance of procedural evidence—in part, very likely the result of significant advances made when a bold thinker such as

Einstein took a different tack, viewed the universe from a theoretical position outside of and ahead of the common sense of the traditional scientific community, and made significant predictions which are even today being verified for the first time. Feats of this magnificence prompt Conant (1952) to note:

The history of science demonstrates beyond a doubt that really revolutionary and significant advances come not from empiricism but from new theories (p. 53).

Naturally, one cannot contend that theory construction is *only* a question of utilizing procedural evidence. There must be an interplay between hunch and the testing of that hunch. This is an old saw and certainly obvious. The point here under emphasis is that we must push the issue back a notch and realize that how we hypothesize and how we test, not to mention the whos and whys, relate to the biases of the community with which we identify. As already noted, psychologists have tended to identify with the physical sciences. Oppenheimer (1956) is willing to accept psychologists as scientists if they conceptualize people as people rather than electrical machines, refuse to accept the world as completely causal, be unable to define every construct operationally, recognize the importance of individual bias in observation, admit to an inability to predict every event (even in theory), and speak about organic wholes (p. 134). In fact he points out that this is precisely what present day physicists do. Here is an open door for clinical psychology as science. If a physical scientist of this cut were teaching the science courses and laboratory courses our clinical students attend, there might be less conflict for the student in the clinic, because such procedural evidences certainly fit the common sense of the clinician's culture.

Lest the clinical student feel that he is a special case in this cross-cultural conflict, let us hastily note that other areas of study, the best examples of which are hypnotism and extrasensory perception, face the same problem. Murphy, speaking about those psychologists who refuse to accept the validating evidence of extrasensory perception, quotes from Hebb to the extent

that it is not a question of evidence, for the evidence would, in its own right, be adequate. The trouble is that "ESP does not make sense" (Murphy, 1958, p. 69).

Here we have a perfect example of what philosophers and clinicians have noted for a long time: the fact that procedural evidence takes precedence over validating evidence whenever the precepts and/or methods of validation fail to be consistent with the common sense (i.e., procedural evidence) of the individual or group doing the validating.

The other side of the coin is that clinicians have frequently confused the influence of procedural evidence in therapy. If many research psychologists have naively identified scientific activity as exclusively validational in nature, then equally as many clinicians have mistaken procedural evidence as *necessarily* validating a clinical hypothesis.

The Function of Evidence in Therapy

Although the clinician's method may parallel that of the laboratory scientist's in the sense of description, classification, and explanation, we cannot overlook the important difference in the focus of evidence between the two situations. When it comes to psychotherapy, procedural evidence holds sway over validating evidence. But this is the procedural evidence of the client and not of the psychologist. The psychologist, as scientist, must have more to go on than exclusively procedural evidence. If not, he is no different than any of the charlatans who practice in his name.

It is well known that all schools of psychology have certain basic principles in common, such as accepting the client on his own terms, placing the responsibility for most decisions on the client, etc. Our very ethical canons stress the fact that a person must not be coerced into therapy. What is not often made clear is that all such practices emphasize and cultivate the importance of the client's procedural evidence.

The laboratory experimenter does not deliberately encourage his subjects to make shifts in behavior on the basis of their personal procedural evidence. He is not much interested in this question and does not allow their decisions to influence experimental design in any case. He is studying the subject and never the procedure, which he has designed at the outset. The subject has little to say about the procedure, except possibly in the pretesting manipulations, etc. In this fashion the experimenter learns a great deal about a circumscribed hypothesis.

In the clinic, the situation is different. The clinicians must continually take into consideration the client's procedural evidence as an uncontrolled variable. Since it is the client who must come to accept an interpretation, and since he may—like the scientist regarding ESP—exercise his prerogative as a thinking, feeling individual (who can separate the two?), there is every chance that the client will reject perfectly valid evidence. Or, the client may accept 80% of an interpretation, but alter it by 20% to meet with his personal common sense. Frequently this is unverbalized.

Now to the student, who realizes that people can believe many things in the name of common sense, this procedure of therapy seems somehow unscientific. For example, what if we help a paranoid individual reinterpret his past life in terms of witches and goblins, and he improves as a result of this reinterpretation? He believes that now the goblins are gone and therefore people can really like him. Does this mean that clinicians cannot be scientific?

Well, what if an atomic scientist tells us that fallout is going to destroy our children's minds and ultimately the entire race if the atomic tests are not stopped: does this suggestion make him any less a scientist? He may be right, and he may be wrong. Certainly not all scientists agree on this point. But so long as he bases his decision on the validated knowledge of his specialty, who would deny him the right to speak? Further, what we as a nation decide to do about this is up to us. He has fulfilled his professional responsibility.

It is the same with the clinician. He has an ethical responsibility to keep in close contact with, and contribute to when possible, the validated and validatable evidence of his profession (i.e., scientific literature) and to make his therapeutic interpretations in light of these findings. To date, goblins have not stood up too well under validation. If an explicit theory of personality intervenes between research findings and interpretation, so much the better, since you can be certain that an implicit theory will function in its stead—and possibly a naively personal one at that. Scientific knowledge aims at being public knowledge.

In brief, the view here propounded does not consider the clinical office as the appropriate situation for validating certain hypotheses. If one is studying the nature of therapy, then naturally one must validate hunches relating to therapeutic behavioral change in this context. This is what process studies are concerned with. However, though a fruitful source of hypotheses, the clinical relationship should not be considered as the necessary and sufficient criterion for the validation of personality theory. This is so because to date research findings suggest that, no matter what theory the clinician subscribes to and phrases his interpretations in terms of, client changes in behavior and "insights" always serve to validate the theory held by the clinician. This is probably because of other variables functioning in the therapeutic situation than the variables of the clinician's theory of personality (e.g., suggestion), and such extratheoretical variables should be studied in their own right as process studies attempt to do.

Problems result when the clinician takes the client's behavior, made on the basis of the client's personal procedural evidence—an unreliable criterion at best—as *necessarily* validating the clinical interpretation. Personality theories have been developed this way. Many of the constructs so postulated and "clinically validated" have stood up in subsequent experimentation, but many have not. The behavioral change of the client *may* be consistent with a valid principle, but not necessarily so; and we should never rest our case with merely clinical evidence. Clinical practice is a truly fruitful source of hypotheses and may even be viewed as a kind of pretesting; but we should always submit our theories to extraclinical test, particularly since they make reference to life beyond the therapy room. Designing the crucial experiment is a problem in its own right; but we are speaking here of attitude, and in principle we should assume that all relevant experiments can someday be carried out.

By continually accepting therapeutic change as validating theoretical hypotheses we have both learned much and consistently confused issues. This is the reason why clinicians are and must remain scientists, must subject their hypotheses to public trial, and must keep in touch with other points of view (the larger body of scientific knowledge). And the clinical student need not be confused, for he can be a scientist to the extent that he follows such a program. This is nothing more than anyone with an interest in people and a desire to be correct could be expected to do. If he prefers to abstract himself from the larger scientific community, to neglect the research literature, to deride the attempts of his peers to validate some of the notions "he knows" can never be validated, he certainly cannot be considered a scientist. Again, the decision is with him.

REFERENCES

BACH, G. R. Who are the discoverers of psychological knowledge? *Amer. Psychologist*, 1952, *7*, 131–132.

BAKAN, D. Clinical psychology and logic. *Amer. Psychologist*, 1956, *11*, 655–662.

BERENDA, C. W. Is clinical psychology a science? *Amer. Psychologist*, 1957, *12*, 725–729.

BINGHAM, W. V. On the possibility of an applied psychology. *Psychol. Rev.*, 1923, *30*, 289–305.

CONANT, J. B. *Modern Science and Modern Man*. Garden City, New York: Doubleday, 1952.

CRANNELL, C. W. Are rat psychologists responsible for fission? *Amer. Psychologist*, 1947, *2*, 22–23.

CRANNELL, C. W. Fission resolved? *Amer. Psychologist*, 1956, *11*, 636–638.

CRONBACH, L. J. The two disciplines of scientific psychology. *Amer. Psychologist*, 1957, *12*, 671–684.

CRONBACH, L. J., & MEEHL, P. E. Construct validity in psychological tests. *Psychol. Bull.*, 1955, *52*, 281–302.

FRANK, P. *Philosophy of Science*. Englewood Cliffs, New Jersey: Prentice-Hall, 1957.

GABRIEL, E. A clinician answers Guthrie. *Amer. Psychologist*, 1950, *5*, 495.

GUTHRIE, E. R. The status of systematic psychology. *Amer. Psychologist*, 1950, *5*, 97–101.

HARLOW, H. F. Experimental analysis of behavior. *Amer. Psychologist*, 1957, *12*, 485–490.

HUNT, W. A. Clinical psychology: Science or superstition. *Amer. Psychologist*, 1951, *6*, 683–687.

KAHN, T. C. Clinically and statistically oriented psychologists split our profession. *Amer. Psychologist*, 1955, *10*, 171–172.

KANTOR, J. R. *The Logic of Modern Science*. Bloomington, Illinois: Principia Press, 1953.

KELLY, G. A. I itch too. *Amer. Psychologist*, 1955, *10*, 172–173. (a)

KELLY, G. A. *The Psychology of Personal Constructs*. New York: Norton, 1955. 2 vols. (b)

KRECH, D. A note on fission. *Amer. Psychologist*, 1946, *1*, 402–404.

MURPHY, G. Trends in the study of extrasensory perception. *Amer. Psychologist*, 1958, *13*, 69–76.

NEWMAN, S. H. Should psychological theory and practice be divided? *Amer. Psychologist*, 1950, *5*, 495–496.

OPPENHEIMER, R. Analogy in science. *Amer. Psychologist,* 1956, *11,* 127–136.

ROGERS, C. R. The interest in the practice of psychotherapy. *Amer. Psychologist,* 1953, *8,* 48–50.

ROGERS, C. R. Persons or science? A philosophical question. *Amer. Psychologist,* 1955, *10,* 267–278.

ROSENZWEIG, S. Imbalance in clinical psychology. *Amer. Psychologist,* 1950, *5,* 678–680.

ROSENZWEIG, S. (Ed.) Balance in clinical psychology: A symposium in correspondence. *Amer. Psychologist,* 1951, *6,* 208–212.

SKINNER, B. F. A case history in scientific method. *Amer. Psychologist,* 1956, *11,* 221–233.

SOLOMON, L. N. The paradox of the experimental clinician. *Amer. Psychologist,* 1955, *10,* 170–171.

STRUPP, H. H., CASTORE, G. F., LAKE, R. A., MERRILL, R. M., & BELLAK, L. Comments on Rogers' "Persons or science." *Amer. Psychologist,* 1956, *11,* 153–157.

SUPER, D. E. Reply to Rosenzweig. *Amer. Psychologist,* 1951, *6,* 128.

THORNE, F. C. The clinical method in science. *Amer. Psychologist,* 1947, *2,* 159–166.

TOLMAN, RUTH S. Virtue rewarded and vice punished. *Amer. Psychologist,* 1953, *8,* 721–733.

WIENER, P. P., & NOLAND, A. (Eds.) *Roots of Scientific Thought.* New York: Basic Books, 1957.

....

PART TWO

Conceptual Context and Perspective

THE "OBJECTIVITY" OF the scientific endeavor is less an established fact than an elusive ideal. It is quite clear that individual and cultural traits and value systems exert a considerable directive influence at all levels of the scientific process. At any given time such influences are expressed as differences in the nature and focus of the questions posed, in the comprehension of the data generated, and in the application of the knowledge gained. The subject matter of clinical psychology makes this field particularly vulnerable to differences of perspective. Perhaps the easiest thing related to controversial issues in clinical psychology is the finding of them, for differences of opinion are almost ubiquitous. To adapt an old saying, where there are two psychologists there are three points of view.

This state of affairs is not necessarily all to the bad. In our relatively youthful profession diversity of opinion, if accompanied by an openness to persistent and conscientious examination of the conceptual fabric of each position, is to be welcomed as a stimulus to continued growth. Of at least comparable importance is the need for a continuing critical assessment of those basic premises within which we operate that are characterized as much by uniformity of opinion as by diversity. Consensus oftentimes rigidifies inadequate conceptions and practices by blunting both the need to change and the recognition of new patterns of knowledge that make changes necessary and possible. Technical improvements are not enough; if based on questionable conceptual foundations they are apt to hinder rather than advance our purposes in the long run. Agreement as such is, for example, no guarantee that we might not be right for the wrong reasons or that we might be responding merely to trivial or irrelevant aspects of the problems which concern us. Any advance in knowledge is, of course, to be valued in its own right but the greater value lies in the impetus to new discovery. Unless we retain the tolerance to constantly probe the relation between our attitudinal frames of reference and the products of our professional activities we run the risk of merely effecting justification of preconceptions and thereby bringing to our search for understanding a lock rather than a key.

Two pairs of papers have been included in this section as illustrative of the kind of polar positions which are characteristic for many

121

areas of concern within clinical psychology. Other examples of representative controversies could have served as well. However, the Szasz-Ausubel and Eysenck-Strupp papers do present jugular issues which touch closely upon some essential elements of clinical psychology's conceptual framework. Szasz seeks to exorcise the notion of mental illness, to reject the disease model as a way of conceptualizing man's suffering and the limitations of human potential attendant upon the complex problems of living. He submits instead a broader explanatory context encompassing psychosocial, ethical, and legal concepts. In rejoinder, Ausubel defends the use of the term mental illness and submits a rationale for this position which, in certain respects, negates the circle which Szasz has drawn around him by drawing a larger circle to take Szasz in. The differences in orientation remain, however, in sharp focus.

The main substantive issue dealt with in the second set of articles is that of therapeutic outcome, but the differences in attitude and theoretical orientation between Eysenck and Strupp have considerable implication for the whole psychological enterprise as most contemporary clinicians prefer to think of it. Eysenck's interpretation of selected evidence relating to results of psychotherapy leads him to question the very viability of this activity. In contrast, Strupp's critique of the Eysenck position, and his own evaluation of available evidence relating both to treatment process and outcome, permits him to view the psychotherapeutic function not only as viable but as an endeavor which has only barely touched its potential contribution. Such polarity of viewpoint, not uncommon in numerous other contemporary controversies of greater or lesser import, highlights the appropriateness of redirecting impartial scientific effort toward clarifying the context and determinants of our conceptions and misconceptions.

It is particularly of value to turn a questioning mind to areas of traditional thought and practice where dissonance and conflict are not so evident. Dispute at least serves the useful purpose of stimulating effort to defend the particular position espoused or to reject the contrary one, and thus, hopefully, to explore again the specific problems involved. There is less pressure to question that which is generally accepted. This is likely to be especially so if such acceptance is based on what may, by analogy, be conceived as a scientific discipline's "character structure" which serves both defensive and adaptive ends. The paper by Bakan explores the relation of one such "characterological" pattern to some traditionally accepted attitudes and operations which characterize much of contemporary psychological research. In a more general sense, Bakan asks that the quest for knowledge not be isolated from an awareness and comprehension of the psychocultural variables that influence both the mode and the content matter of the quest. Adherence to this injunction promises no easy or reassuring answers. But the willingness to raise difficult questions, to critically reappraise old beliefs regardless of the uncertainty and anxiety it engenders, and to risk new insights does make possible genuine progress toward fulfilling the challenge and responsibility of our profession. The clinical psychologist can do no less.

A.Z.G.

M.A.B.

....

The Myth of Mental Illness*

Thomas S. Szasz

My AIM IN this essay is to raise the question "Is there such a thing as mental illness?" and to argue that there is not. Since the notion of mental illness is extremely widely used nowadays, inquiry into the ways in which this term is employed would seem to be especially indicated. Mental illness, of course, is not literally a "thing"—or physical object—and hence it can "exist" only in the same sort of way in which other theoretical concepts exist. Yet, familiar theories are in the habit of posing, sooner or later—at least to those who come to believe in them—as "objective truths" (or "facts"). During certain historical periods, explanatory conceptions such as deities, witches, and microorganisms appeared not only as theories but as self-evident *causes* of a vast number of events. I submit that today mental illness is widely regarded in a somewhat similar fashion, that is, as the cause of innumerable diverse happenings. As an antidote to the complacent use of the notion of mental illness—whether as a self-evident phenomenon, theory, or cause—let us ask this question: What is meant when it is asserted that someone is mentally ill?

In what follows I shall describe briefly the main uses to which the concept of mental illness has been put. I shall argue that this notion has outlived whatever usefulness it might have had and that it now functions merely as a convenient myth.

MENTAL ILLNESS AS A SIGN OF BRAIN DISEASE

The notion of mental illness derives its main support from such phenomena as syphilis of the brain or delirious conditions—intoxications, for instance—in which persons are known to manifest various peculiarities or disorders of thinking and behavior. Correctly speaking, however, these are diseases of the brain, not of the mind. According to one school of thought, *all* so-called mental illness is of

* From the *American Psychologist*, 1960, *15*, 113–118.

this type. The assumption is made that some neurological defect, perhaps a very subtle one, will ultimately be found for all the disorders of thinking and behavior. Many contemporary psychiatrists, physicians, and other scientists hold this view. This position implies that people *cannot* have troubles—expressed in what are *now called* "mental illnesses"—because of differences in personal needs, opinions, social aspirations, values, and so on. *All problems in living* are attributed to physicochemical processes which in due time will be discovered by medical research.

"Mental illnesses" are thus regarded as basically no different than all other diseases (that is, of the body). The only difference, in this view, between mental and bodily diseases is that the former, affecting the brain, manifest themselves by means of mental symptoms; whereas the latter, affecting other organ systems (for example, the skin, liver, etc.), manifest themselves by means of symptoms referable to those parts of the body. This view rests on and expresses what are, in my opinion, two fundamental errors.

In the first place, what central nervous system symptoms would correspond to a skin eruption or a fracture? It would *not* be some emotion or complex bit of behavior. Rather, it would be blindness or a paralysis of some part of the body. The crux of the matter is that a disease of the brain, analogous to a disease of the skin or bone, is a neurological defect, and not a problem in living. For example, a *defect* in a person's visual field may be satisfactorily explained by correlating it with certain definite lesions in the nervous system. On the other hand, a person's *belief*—whether this be a belief in Christianity, in Communism, or in the idea that his internal organs are "rotting" and that his body is, in fact, already "dead"—cannot be explained by a defect or disease of the nervous system. Explanations of this sort of occurrence—assuming that one is interested in the belief itself and does not regard it simply as a "symptom" or expression of something else that is *more interesting* —must be sought along different lines.

The second error in regarding complex psychosocial behavior, consisting of communications about ourselves and the world about us, as mere symptoms of neurological functioning is *epistemological*. In other words, it is an error pertaining not to any mistakes in observation or reasoning, as such, but rather to the way in which we organize and express our knowledge. In the present case, the error lies in making a symmetrical dualism between mental and physical (or bodily) symptoms, a dualism which is merely a habit of speech and to which no known observations can be found to correspond. Let us see if this is so. In medical practice, when we speak of physical disturbances, we mean either signs (for example, a fever) or symptoms (for example, pain). We speak of mental symptoms, on the other hand, when we refer to a patient's *communications about himself, others, and the world about him.* He might state that he is Napoleon or that he is being persecuted by the Communists. These would be considered mental symptoms *only* if the observer believed that the patient was *not* Napoleon or that he was *not* being persecuted by the Communists. This makes it apparent that the statement that *"X is a mental symptom"* involves rendering a judgment. The judgment entails, moreover, a covert comparison or matching of the patient's ideas, concepts, or beliefs with those of the observer and the society in which they live. The notion of mental symptom is therefore inextricably tied to the *social* (including *ethical*) *context* in which it is made in much the same way as the notion of bodily symptom is tied to an *anatomical* and *genetic context* (Szasz, 1957a, 1957b).

To sum up what has been said thus far: I have tried to show that for those who regard mental symptoms as signs of brain disease, the concept of mental illness is unnecessary and misleading. For what they mean is that people so labeled suffer from diseases of the brain; and, if that is what they mean, it would seem better for the sake of clarity to say that and not something else.

MENTAL ILLNESS AS A NAME FOR PROBLEMS IN LIVING

The term "mental illness" is widely used to describe something which is very different than a disease of the brain. Many people today take it for granted that living is an arduous process. Its hardship for modern man, moreover, derives not so much from a struggle for biological survival as from the stresses and strains inherent in the social intercourse of complex human personalities. In this context, the notion of mental illness is used to identify or describe some feature of an individual's so-called personality. Mental illness—as a deformity of the personality, so to speak—is then regarded as the *cause* of the human disharmony. It is implicit in this view that social intercourse between people is regarded as something *inherently harmonious,* its disturbance being due solely to the presence of "mental illness" in many people. This is obviously fallacious reasoning, for it makes the abstraction "mental illness" into a *cause,* even though this abstraction was created in the first place to serve only as a shorthand expression for certain types of human behavior. It now becomes necessary to ask: "What kinds of behavior are regarded as indicative of mental illness, and by whom?"

The concept of illness, whether bodily or mental, implies *deviation from some clearly defined norm.* In the case of physical illness, the norm is the structural and functional integrity of the human body. Thus, although the desirability of physical health, as such, is an ethical value, what health *is* can be stated in anatomical and physiological terms. What is the norm deviation from which is regarded as mental illness? This question cannot be easily answered. But whatever this norm might be, we can be certain of only one thing: namely, that it is a norm that must be stated in terms of *psychosocial, ethical,* and *legal* concepts. For example, notions such as "excessive repression" or "acting out an unconscious impulse" illustrate the use of psychological concepts for judging (so-called) mental health and illness. The idea that chronic hostility, vengefulness, or divorce are indicative of mental illness would be illustrations of the use of ethical norms (that is, the desirability of love, kindness, and a stable marriage relationship). Finally, the widespread psychiatric opinion that only a mentally ill person would commit homicide illustrates the use of a legal concept as a norm of mental health. The norm from which deviation is measured whenever one speaks of a mental illness is a *psychosocial and ethical one.* Yet, the remedy is sought in terms of *medical* measures which—it is hoped and assumed—are free from wide differences of ethical value. The definition of the disorder and the terms in which its remedy are sought are therefore at serious odds with one another. The practical significance of this covert conflict between the alleged nature of the defect and the remedy can hardly be exaggerated.

Having identified the norms used to measure deviations in cases of mental illness, we will now turn to the question: "Who defines the norms and hence the deviation?" Two basic answers may be offered: (*a*) It may be the person himself (that is, the patient) who decides that he deviates from a norm. For example, an artist may believe that he suffers from a work inhibition; and he may implement this conclusion by seeking help *for* himself from a psychotherapist. (*b*) It may be someone other than the patient who decides that the latter is deviant (for example, relatives, physicians, legal authorities, society generally, etc.). In such a case a psychiatrist may be hired by others to do something *to* the patient in order to correct the deviation.

These considerations underscore the importance of asking the question "Whose agent is the psychiatrist?" and of giving a candid answer to it (Szasz, 1956, 1958). The psychiatrist (psychologist or nonmedical psychotherapist), it now develops, may be the agent of the patient, of the relatives, of the school, of the military services, of a business organization, of a court of law, and so forth. In speaking of the psychiatrist as the agent of these persons or organizations, it is not implied that his values concerning norms, or his ideas and aims concerning the proper nature of remedial action, need to coincide exactly with those of his employer. For example, a patient in individual psychotherapy may believe that his salvation lies in a new marriage; his psychotherapist need not share this hypothesis. As the patient's agent, however, he must abstain from bringing social or legal force to bear on the patient which would prevent him from putting his beliefs into action. If his *contract* is with the patient, the psychiatrist (psychotherapist) may disagree with him or stop his treatment; but he cannot engage others to obstruct the patient's aspirations. Similarly, if a psychiatrist is engaged by a court to determine the sanity of a criminal, he need not fully share the legal authorities' values and intentions in regard to the criminal and the means available for dealing with him. But the psychiatrist is expressly barred from stating, for example, that it is not the criminal who is "insane" but the men who wrote the law on the basis of which the very actions that are being judged are regarded as "criminal." Such an opinion could be voiced, of course, but not in a courtroom, and not by a psychiatrist who makes it his practice to assist the court in performing its daily work.

To recapitulate: In actual contemporary social usage, the finding of a mental illness is made by establishing a deviance in behavior from certain psychosocial, ethical, or legal norms. The judgment may be made, as in medicine, by the patient, the physician (psychiatrist), or others. Remedial action, finally, tends to be sought in a therapeutic—or covertly medical—framework, thus creating a situation in which *psychosocial, ethical,* and/or *legal deviations* are claimed to be correctible by (so-called) *medical action.* Since medical action is designed to correct only medical deviations, it seems logically absurd to expect that it will help solve problems whose very existence had been defined and established on nonmedical grounds. I think that these considerations may be fruitfully applied to the present use of tranquilizers and, more generally, to what might be expected of drugs of whatever type in regard to the amelioration or solution of problems in human living.

THE ROLE OF ETHICS IN PSYCHIATRY

Anything that people *do*—in contrast to things that *happen* to them (Peters, 1958)—takes place in a context of value. In this broad sense, no human activity is devoid of ethical implications. When the values underlying certain activities are widely shared, those who participate in their pursuit may lose sight of them altogether. The discipline of medicine, both as a pure science (for example, research) and as a technology (for example, therapy), contains many ethical considerations and judgments. Unfortunately, these are often denied, minimized, or merely kept out of focus; for the ideal of the medical profession as well as of the people whom it serves seems to be having a system of medicine (allegedly) free of ethical value. This sentimental notion is expressed by such things as the doctor's willingness to treat and help patients irrespective of their religious or political beliefs, whether they are rich or poor, etc. While there may be some grounds for this belief—albeit it is a view that is not impressively true even in these regards—the fact remains that ethical considerations encompass a vast range of human affairs. By making the practice of medicine neutral in regard to some specific issues of value need not, and cannot, mean that it can be kept free from all such values. The practice of medicine is intimately tied to ethics; and the first thing that we must do, it seems to me, is to try to make this clear and explicit. I shall let this matter rest here, for it does not concern us specifically in this essay. Lest there be any vagueness, however, about how or where ethics and medicine meet, let me remind the reader of such issues as birth control, abortion, suicide, and euthanasia as only a few of the major areas of current ethicomedical controversy.

Psychiatry, I submit, is very much more intimately tied to problems of ethics than is medicine. I use the word "psychiatry" here to refer to that contemporary discipline which is concerned with *problems in living* (and not with diseases of the brain, which are problems for neurology). Problems in human relations can be analyzed, interpreted and given meaning only within given social and ethical contexts. Accordingly, it *does* make a difference—arguments to the contrary notwithstanding—what the psychiatrist's socioethical orientations happen to be; for these will influence his ideas on what is wrong with the patient, what deserves comment or interpretation, in what possible directions change might be desirable, and so forth. Even in medicine proper, these factors play a role, as for instance, in the divergent orientations which physicians, depending on their religious affiliations, have toward such things as birth control and therapeutic abortion. Can anyone really believe that a psychotherapist's ideas concerning religious belief, slavery, or other similar issues play no role in his practical work? If they do make a difference, what are we to infer from it? Does it not seem reasonable that we ought to have different psychiatric therapies—each expressly recognized for the ethical positions which they embody—for, say, Catholics and Jews, religious persons and agnostics, democrats and communists, white supremacists and Negroes, and so on? Indeed, if we look at how psychiatry is actually practiced today (especially in the United States), we find that people do seek psychiatric help in accordance with their social status and ethical beliefs (Hollingshead & Redlich, 1958). This should really not surprise us more than being told that practicing Catholics rarely frequent birth control clinics.

The foregoing position which holds that contemporary psychotherapists deal with problems in living, rather than with mental illnesses and their cures, stands in opposition to a currently prevalent claim, according to which mental illness is just as "real" and "objective" as bodily illness. This is a confusing claim since it is never known exactly what is meant by such words as "real" and "objective." I suspect, however, that what is intended by the proponents of this view is to create the idea in the popular mind that mental illness is some sort of disease entity, like an infection or a malignancy. If this were true, one could *catch* or *get* a "mental illness," one might *have* or *harbor* it, one might *transmit* it to others, and finally one could get *rid* of it. In my opinion, there is not a shred of evidence to support this idea. To the contrary, all the evidence is the other way and supports the view that what people now call mental illnesses are for the most part *communications* expressing unacceptable ideas, often framed, moreover, in an unusual idiom.

The scope of this essay allows me to do no more than mention this alternative theoretical approach to this problem (Szasz, 1957c).

This is not the place to consider in detail the similarities and differences between bodily and mental illnesses. It shall suffice for us here to emphasize only one important difference between them: namely, that whereas bodily disease refers to public, physicochemical occurrences, the notion of mental illness is used to codify relatively more private, sociopsychological happenings of which the observer (diagnostician) forms a part. In other words, the psychiatrist does not stand *apart* from what he observes, but is, in Harry Stack Sullivan's apt words, a "participant observer." This means that he is *committed* to some picture of what he considers reality—and to what he thinks society considers reality—and he observes and judges the patient's behavior in the light of these considerations. This touches on our earlier observation that the notion of mental symptom itself implies a comparison between observer and observed, psychiatrist and patient. This is so obvious that I may be charged with belaboring trivialities. Let me therefore say once more that my aim in presenting this argument was expressly to criticize and counter a prevailing contemporary tendency to deny the moral aspects of psychiatry (and psychotherapy) and to substitute for them allegedly value-free medical considerations. Psychotherapy, for example, is being widely practiced as though it entailed nothing other than restoring the patient from a state of mental sickness to one of mental health. While it is generally accepted that mental illness has something to do with man's social (or interpersonal) relations, it is paradoxically maintained that problems of values (that is, of ethics) do not arise in this process.[1] Yet, in one sense, much of psychotherapy may revolve around nothing other than the elucidation and weighing of goals and values—many of which may be mutually contradictory —and the means whereby they might best be harmonized, realized, or relinquished.

[1] Freud went so far as to say that: "I consider ethics to be taken for granted. Actually I have never done a mean thing" (Jones, 1957, p. 247). This surely is a strange thing to say for someone who has studied man as a social being as closely as did Freud. I mention it here to show how the notion of "illness" (in the case of psychoanalysis, "psychopathology," or "mental illness") was used by Freud—and by most of his followers—as a means for classifying certain forms of human behavior as falling within the scope of medicine, and hence (by *fiat*) outside that of ethics!

The diversity of human values and the methods by means of which they may be realized is so vast, and many of them remain so unacknowledged, that they cannot fail but lead to conflicts in human relations. Indeed, to say that human relations at all levels—from mother to child, through husband and wife, to nation and nation—are fraught with stress, strain, and disharmony is, once again, making the obvious explicit. Yet, what may be obvious may be also poorly understood. This I think is the case here. For it seems to me that—at least in our scientific theories of behavior—we have failed to *accept* the simple fact that human relations are inherently fraught with difficulties and that to make them even relatively harmonious requires much patience and hard work. I submit that the idea of mental illness is now being put to work to obscure certain difficulties which at present may be inherent—not that they need be unmodifiable—in the social intercourse of persons. If this is true, the concept functions as a disguise; for instead of calling attention to conflicting human needs, aspirations, and values, the notion of mental illness provides an amoral and impersonal "thing" (an "illness") as an explanation for *problems in living* (Szasz, 1959). We may recall in this connection that not so long ago it was devils and witches who were held responsible for man's problems in social living. The belief in mental illness, as something other than man's trouble in getting along with his fellow man, is the proper heir to the belief in demonology and witchcraft. Mental illness exists or is "real" in exactly the same sense in which witches existed or were "real."

CHOICE, RESPONSIBILITY, AND PSYCHIATRY

While I have argued that mental illnesses do not exist, I obviously did not imply that the social and psychological occurrences to which this label is currently being attached also do not exist. Like the personal and social troubles which people had in the Middle Ages, they are real enough. It is the labels we give them that concerns us and, having labelled them, what we do about them. While I cannot go into the ramified implications of this problem here, it is worth noting that a demonologic conception of problems in living gave rise to therapy along theological lines. Today, a belief in mental illness implies—nay, requires—therapy along medical or psychotherapeutic lines.

What is implied in the line of thought set forth here is something quite different. I do not intend to offer a new conception of "psy-chiatric illness" nor a new form of "therapy." My aim is more modest and yet also more ambitious. It is to suggest that the phenomena now called mental illnesses be looked at afresh and more simply, that they be removed from the category of illnesses, and that they be regarded as the expressions of man's struggle with the problem of *how* he should live. The last mentioned problem is obviously a vast one, its enormity reflecting not only man's inability to cope with his environment, but even more his increasing self-reflectiveness.

By problems in living, then, I refer to that truly explosive chain reaction which began with man's fall from divine grace by partaking of the fruit of the tree of knowledge. Man's awareness of himself and of the world about him seems to be a steadily expanding one, bringing in its wake an ever larger *burden of understanding* (an ex-pression borrowed from Susanne Langer, 1953). *This burden,* then, *is to be expected and must not be misinterpreted.* Our only *rational* means for lightening it is *more understanding,* and appropriate *action* based on such understanding. The main alternative lies in acting as though the burden were not what in fact we perceive it to be and taking refuge in an outmoded theological view of man. In the latter view, man does not fashion his life and much of his world about him, but merely lives out his fate in a world created by superior beings. This may logically lead to pleading nonresponsibility in the face of seemingly unfathomable problems and difficulties. Yet, if man fails to take increasing responsibility for his actions, individually as well as collectively, it seems unlikely that some higher power or being would assume this task and carry this burden for him. More-over, this seems hardly the proper time in human history for obscur-ing the issue of man's responsibility for his actions by hiding it be-hind the skirt of an all-explaining conception of mental illness.

CONCLUSIONS

I have tried to show that the notion of mental illness has outlived whatever usefulness it might have had and that it now functions merely as a convenient myth. As such, it is a true heir to religious myths in general, and to the belief in witchcraft in particular; the role of all these belief-systems was to act as *social tranquilizers,* thus encouraging the hope that mastery of certain specific problems may be achieved by means of substitutive (symbolic-magical) operations.

The notion of mental illness thus serves mainly to obscure the everyday fact that life for most people is a continuous struggle, not for biological survival, but for a "place in the sun," "peace of mind," or some other human value. For man aware of himself and of the world about him, once the needs for preserving the body (and perhaps the race) are more or less satisfied, the problem arises as to what he should do with himself. Sustained adherence to the myth of mental illness allows people to avoid facing this problem, believing that mental health, conceived as the absence of mental illness, automatically insures the making of right and safe choices in one's conduct of life. But the facts are all the other way. It is the making of good choices in life that others regard, retrospectively, as good mental health!

The myth of mental illness encourages us, moreover, to believe in its logical corollary: that social intercourse would be harmonious, satisfying, and the secure basis of a "good life" were it not for the disrupting influences of mental illness or "psychopathology." The potentiality for universal human happiness, in this form at least, seems to me but another example of the I-wish-it-were-true type of fantasy. I do believe that human happiness or well-being on a hitherto unimaginably large scale, and not just for a select few, is possible. This goal could be achieved, however, only at the cost of many men, and not just a few being willing and able to tackle their personal, social, and ethical conflicts. This means having the courage and integrity to forego waging battles on false fronts, finding solutions for substitute problems—for instance, fighting the battle of stomach acid and chronic fatigue instead of facing up to a marital conflict.

Our adversaries are not demons, witches, fate, or mental illness. We have no enemy whom we can fight, exorcise, or dispel by "cure." What we do have are *problems in living*—whether these be biologic, economic, political, or sociopsychological. In this essay I was concerned only with problems belonging in the last mentioned category, and within this group mainly with those pertaining to moral values. The field to which modern psychiatry addresses itself is vast, and I made no effort to encompass it all. My argument was limited to the proposition that mental illness is a myth, whose function it is to disguise and thus render more palatable the bitter pill of moral conflicts in human relations.

REFERENCES

HOLLINGSHEAD, A. B., & REDLICH, F. C. *Social Class and Mental Illness.* New York: Wiley, 1958.

JONES, E. *The Life and Work of Sigmund Freud.* Vol. III. New York: Basic Books, 1957.

LANGER, S. K. *Philosophy in a New Key.* New York: Mentor Books, 1953.

PETERS, R. S. *The Concept of Motivation.* London: Routledge & Kegan Paul, 1958.

SZASZ, T. S. Malingering: "Diagnosis" or social condemnation? *AMA Arch. Neurol. Psychiat.,* 1956, *76,* 432–443.

SZASZ, T. S. *Pain and Pleasure: A Study of Bodily Feelings.* New York: Basic Books, 1957. (a)

SZASZ, T. S. The problem of psychiatric nosology: A contribution to a situational analysis of psychiatric operations. *Amer. J. Psychiat.,* 1957, *114,* 405–413. (b)

SZASZ, T. S. On the theory of psychoanalytic treatment. *Int. J. Psycho-Anal.,* 1957, *38,* 166–182. (c)

SZASZ, T. S. Psychiatry, ethics and the criminal law. *Columbia Law Rev.,* 1958, *58,* 183–198.

SZASZ, T. S. Moral conflict and psychiatry. *Yale Rev.,* 1960, *49,* 555–566.

....

Personality Disorder Is Disease*

DAVID P. AUSUBEL

IN TWO RECENT articles in the *American Psychologist,* Szasz (1960) and Mowrer (1960) have argued the case for discarding the concept of mental illness. The essence of Mowrer's position is that since medical science lacks "demonstrated competence . . . in psychiatry," psychology would be wise to "get out" from "under the penumbra of medicine," and to regard the behavior disorders as manifestations of sin rather than of disease (p. 302). Szasz' position, as we shall see shortly, is somewhat more complex than Mowrer's, but agrees with the latter in emphasizing the moral as opposed to the psychopathological basis of abnormal behavior.

For a long time now, clinical psychology has both repudiated the relevance of moral judgment and accountability for assessing behavioral acts and choices, and has chafed under medical (psychiatric) control and authority in diagnosing and treating the personality disorders. One can readily appreciate, therefore, Mowrer's eagerness to sever the historical and professional ties that bind clinical psychology to medicine, even if this means denying that psychological disturbances constitute a form of illness, and even if psychology's close working relationship with psychiatry must be replaced by a new rapprochement with sin and theology, as "the lesser of two evils" (pp. 302–303). One can also sympathize with Mowrer's and Szasz' dissatisfaction with prevailing amoral and nonjudgmental trends in clinical psychology and with their entirely commendable efforts to restore moral judgment and accountability to a respectable place among the criteria used in evaluating human behavior, both normal and abnormal.

Opposition to these two trends in the handling of the behavior disorders (i.e., to medical control and to nonjudgmental therapeutic attitudes), however, does not necessarily imply abandonment of the concept of mental illness. There is no inconsistency whatsoever in

* From the *American Psychologist,* 1961, *16,* 69–74.

maintaining, on the one hand, that most purposeful human activity has a moral aspect the reality of which psychologists cannot afford to ignore (Ausubel, 1952, p. 462), that man is morally accountable for the majority of his misdeeds (Ausubel, 1952, p. 469), and that psychological rather than medical training and sophistication are basic to competence in the personality disorders (Ausubel, 1956, p. 101), and affirming, on the other hand, that the latter disorders are genuine manifestations of illness. In recent years psychology has been steadily moving away from the formerly fashionable stance of ethical neutrality in the behavioral sciences; and in spite of strident medical claims regarding superior professional qualifications and preclusive legal responsibility for treating psychiatric patients, and notwithstanding the nominally restrictive provisions of medical practice acts, clinical psychologists have been assuming an increasingly more important, independent, and responsible role in treating the mentally ill population of the United States.

It would be instructive at this point to examine the tactics of certain other medically allied professions in freeing themselves from medical control and in acquiring independent, legally recognized professional status. In no instance have they resorted to the devious stratagem of denying that they were treating diseases, in the hope of mollifying medical opposition and legitimizing their own professional activities. They took the position instead that simply because a given condition is defined as a disease, its treatment need not necessarily be turned over to doctors of medicine if other equally competent professional specialists were available. That this position is legally and politically tenable is demonstrated by the fact that an impressively large number of recognized diseases are legally treated today by both medical *and* nonmedical specialists (e.g., diseases of the mouth, face, jaws, teeth, eyes, and feet). And there are few convincing reasons for believing that psychiatrists wield that much more political power than physicians, maxillofacial surgeons, ophthalmologists, and orthopedic surgeons, that they could be successful where these latter specialists have failed, in legally restricting practice in their particular area of competence to holders of the medical degree. Hence, even if psychologists were not currently managing to hold their own vis-à-vis psychiatrists, it would be far less dangerous and much more forthright to press for the necessary ameliorative legislation than to seek cover behind an outmoded and thoroughly discredited conception of the behavior disorders.

THE SZASZ-MOWRER POSITION

Szasz' (1960) contention that the concept of mental illness "now functions merely as a convenient myth" (p. 118) is grounded on four unsubstantiated and logically untenable propositions, which can be fairly summarized as follows:

1. Only symptoms resulting from demonstrable physical lesions qualify as legitimate manifestations of disease. Brain pathology is a type of physical lesion, but its symptoms properly speaking, are neurological rather than psychological in nature. Under no circumstances, therefore, can mental symptoms be considered a form of illness.

2. A basic dichotomy exists between *mental* symptoms, on the one hand, which are subjective in nature, dependent on subjective judgment and personal involvement of the observer, and referable to cultural-ethical norms, and *physical* symptoms, on the other hand, which are allegedly objective in nature, ascertainable without personal involvement of the observer, and independent of cultural norms and ethical standards. Only symptoms possessing the latter set of characteristics are genuinely reflective of illness and amenable to medical treatment.

3. Mental symptoms are merely expressions of problems of living and, hence, cannot be regarded as manifestations of a pathological condition. The concept of mental illness is misleading and demonological because it seeks to explain psychological disturbance in particular and human disharmony in general in terms of a metaphorical but nonexistent disease entity, instead of attributing them to inherent difficulties in coming to grips with elusive problems of choice and responsibility.

4. Personality disorders, therefore, can be most fruitfully conceptualized as products of moral conflict, confusion, and aberration. Mowrer (1960) extends this latter proposition to include the dictum that psychiatric symptoms are primarily reflective of unacknowledged sin, and that individuals manifesting these symptoms are responsible for and deserve their suffering, both because of their original transgressions and because they refuse to avow and expiate their guilt (pp. 301, 304).

Widespread adoption of the Szasz-Mowrer view of the personality disorders would, in my opinion, turn back the psychiatric clock twenty-five hundred years. The most significant and perhaps the only real advance registered by mankind in evolving a rational and humane method of handling behavioral aberrations has been in substituting a concept of disease for the demonological and retributional doctrines regarding their nature and etiology that flourished until comparatively recent times. Conceptualized as illness, the symptoms of personality disorders can be interpreted in the light of underlying stresses and resistances, both genic and environmental, and can be evaluated in relation to *specifiable* quantitative and qualitative norms of appropriately adaptive behavior, both cross-culturally and within a particular cultural context. It would behoove us, therefore, before we abandon the concept of mental illness and return to the medieval doctrine of unexpiated sin or adopt Szasz' ambiguous criterion of difficulty in ethical choice and responsibility, to subject the foregoing propositions to careful and detailed study.

Mental Symptoms and Brain Pathology

Although I agree with Szasz in rejecting the doctrine that ultimately some neuroanatomic or neurophysiologic defect will be discovered in *all* cases of personality disorder, I disagree with his reasons for not accepting this proposition. Notwithstanding Szasz' straw man presentation of their position, the proponents of the extreme somatic view do not really assert that the *particular nature* of a patient's disordered beliefs can be correlated with "certain definite lesions in the nervous system" (Szasz, 1960, p. 113). They hold rather that normal cognitive and behavioral functioning depends on the anatomic and physiologic integrity of certain key areas of the brain, and that impairment of this substrate integrity, therefore, provides a physical basis for disturbed ideation and behavior, but does not explain, except in a very gross way, the particular kinds of symptoms involved. In fact, they are generally inclined to attribute the *specific* character of the patient's symptoms to the nature of his preillness personality structure, the substrate integrity of which is impaired by the lesion or metabolic defect in question.

Nevertheless, even though this type of reasoning plausibly accounts for the psychological symptoms found in general paresis, various toxic deliria, and other comparable conditions, it is an extremely improbable explanation of *all* instances of personality disorder. Unlike the tissues of any other organ, brain tissue possesses the unique property of making possible awareness of and adjustment to the world of sensory, social, and symbolic stimulation. Hence by virtue of this unique relationship of the nervous system to the environment, diseases of behavior and personality may reflect abnormalities in personal and social adjustment, quite apart from any structural or metabolic disturbance in the underlying neural substrate. I would conclude, therefore, that although brain pathology is probably not the most important cause of behavior disorder, it is undoubtedly responsible for the incidence of *some* psychological abnormalities *as well as* for various neurological signs and symptoms.

But even if we completely accepted Szasz' view that brain pathology does not account for any symptoms of personality disorder, it would still be unnecessary to accept his assertion that to qualify as a genuine manifestation of disease a given symptom must be caused by a physical lesion. Adoption of such a criterion would be arbitrary and inconsistent both with medical and lay connotations of the term "disease," which in current usage is generally regarded as including any marked deviation, physical, mental, or behavioral, from normally desirable standards of structural and functional integrity.

Mental versus Physical Symptoms

Szasz contends that since the analogy between physical and mental symptoms is patently fallacious, the postulated parallelism between physical and mental disease is logically untenable. This line of reasoning is based on the assumption that the two categories of symptoms can be sharply dichotomized with respect to such basic dimensions as objectivity-subjectivity, the relevance of cultural norms, and the need for personal involvement of the observer. In my opinion, the existence of such a dichotomy cannot be empirically demonstrated in convincing fashion.

Practically all symptoms of bodily disease involve some elements of subjective judgment—both on the part of the patient and of the physician. Pain is perhaps the most important and commonly used criterion of physical illness. Yet, any evaluation of its reported locus, intensity, character, and duration is dependent upon the patient's subjective appraisal of his own sensations and on the physician's assessment of the latter's pain threshold, intelligence, and personality structure. It is also a medical commonplace that the severity of pain in most instances of bodily illness may be mitigated by the administration of a placebo. Furthermore, in taking a meaningful history the physician must not only serve as a participant observer but also as a skilled interpreter of human behavior. It is the rare patient who does not react psychologically to the signs of physical illness; and hence physicians are constantly called upon to decide, for example, to what extent precordial pain and reported tightness in the chest are manifestations of coronary insufficiency, of fear of cardiac disease and impending death, or of combinations of both conditions. Even such allegedly objective signs as pulse rate, BMR, blood pressure, and blood cholesterol have their subjective and relativistic aspects. Pulse rate and blood pressure are notoriously susceptible to emotional influences, and BMR and blood cholesterol fluctuate widely from one cultural environment to another (Dreyfuss & Czaczkes, 1959). And anyone who believes that ethical norms have no relevance for physical illness has obviously failed to consider the problems confronting Catholic patients and/or physicians when issues of contraception, abortion, and preferential saving of the mother's as against the fetus' life must be faced in the context of various obstetrical emergencies and medical contraindications to pregnancy.

It should now be clear, therefore, that symptoms not only do not need a physical basis to qualify as manifestations of illness, but also that the evaluation of *all* symptoms, physical as well as mental, is dependent in large measure on subjective judgment, emotional factors, cultural-ethical norms, and personal involvement on the part of the observer. These considerations alone render no longer tenable Szasz' contention (1960, p. 114) that there is an inherent contradiction between using cultural and ethical norms as criteria of mental disease, on the one hand, and of employing medical measures of treatment on the other. But even if the postulated dichotomy between mental and physical symptoms were valid, the use of physical measures in treating subjective and relativistic psychological symptoms would still be warranted. Once we accept the proposition that impairment of the neural substrate of personality can result in behavior disorder, it is logically consistent to accept the corollary proposition that other kinds of manipulation of the same neural substrate can conceivably have therapeutic effects, irrespective of whether the underlying cause of the mental symptoms is physical or psychological.

Mental Illness and Problems of Living

"The phenomena now called mental illness," argues Szasz (1960), can be regarded more forthrightly and simply as "expressions of man's struggle with the problem of how he should live" (p. 117). This statement undoubtedly oversimplifies the nature of personality disorders; but even if it were adequately inclusive it would not be inconsistent with the position that these disorders are a manifestation of illness. There is no valid reason why a particular symptom cannot both reflect a problem in living *and* constitute a manifestation of disease. The notion of mental illness, conceived in this way, would not "obscure the everyday fact that life for most people is a continuous struggle . . . for a 'place in the sun,' 'peace of mind,' or some other human value" (p. 118). It is quite true, as Szasz points out, that "human relations are inherently fraught with difficulties" (p. 117), and that most people manage to cope with such difficulties without becoming mentally ill. But conceding this fact hardly precludes the possibility that some individuals, either because of the magnitude of the stress involved, or because of genically or environmentally induced susceptibility to ordinary degrees of stress, respond to the problems of living with behavior that is either seriously distorted or sufficiently unadaptive to prevent normal interpersonal relations and vocational functioning. The latter outcome—gross deviation from a designated range of desirable behavioral variability— conforms to the generally understood meaning of mental illness.

The plausibility of subsuming abnormal behavioral reactions to stress under the general rubric of disease is further enhanced by the fact that these reactions include the same three principal categories of symptoms found in physical illness. Depression and catastrophic impairment of self-esteem, for example, are manifestations of personality disorder which are symptomologically comparable to edema in cardiac failure or to heart murmurs in valvular disease. They are indicative of underlying pathology but are neither adaptive nor adjustive. Symptoms such as hypomanic over-activity and compulsive striving toward unrealistically high achievement goals, on the other hand, are both adaptive and adjustive, and constitute a type of compensatory response to basic feelings of inadequacy, which is not unlike cardiac hypertrophy in hypertensive heart disease or elevated white blood cell count in acute infections. And finally, distortive psychological defenses that have some adjustive value but are generally maladaptive (e.g., phobias, delusions, autistic fantasies) are analogous to the pathological situation found in conditions like pneumonia, in which the excessive outpouring of serum and phagocytes in defensive response to pathogenic bacteria literally causes the patient to drown in his own fluids.

Within the context of this same general proposition, Szasz repudiates the concept of mental illness as demonological in nature, i.e., as the "true heir to religious myths in general and to the belief in witchcraft in particular" (p. 118) because it allegedly employs a reified abstraction ("a deformity of personality") to account in causal terms both for "human disharmony" and for symptoms of behavior disorder (p. 114). But again he appears to be demolishing a straw man. Modern students of personality disorder do not regard mental illness as a cause of human disharmony, but as a co-manifestation with it of inherent difficulties in personal adjustment and interpersonal relations; and in so far as I can accurately interpret the literature, psychopathologists do not conceive of mental illness as a cause of particular behavioral symptoms but as a generic term under which these symptoms can be subsumed.

Mental Illness and Moral Responsibility

Szasz' final reason for regarding mental illness as a myth is really a corollary of his previously considered more general proposition that mental symptoms are essentially reflective of problems of living and hence do not legitimately qualify as manifestations of disease. It focuses on difficulties of ethical choice and responsibility as the particular life problems most likely to be productive of personality disorder. Mowrer (1960) further extends this corollary by asserting that neurotic and psychotic individuals are responsible for their suffering (p. 301), and that unacknowledged and unexpiated sin, in turn, is the basic cause of this suffering (p. 304). As previously suggested, however, one can plausibly accept the proposition that psychiatrists and clinical psychologists have erred in trying to divorce behavioral evaluation from ethical considerations, in conducting psychotherapy in an amoral setting, and in confusing the psychological explanation of unethical behavior with absolution from accountability for same, *without* necessarily endorsing the view that personality disorders are basically a reflection of sin, and that victims of these disorders are less ill than responsible for their symptoms (Ausubel, 1952, pp. 392–397, 465–471).

In the first place, it is possible in most instances (although admittedly difficult in some) to distinguish quite unambiguously between mental illness and ordinary cases of immorality. The vast majority of persons who are guilty of moral lapses knowingly violate their own ethical precepts for expediential reasons—despite being volitionally capable at the time, both of choosing the more moral alternative and of exercising the necessary inhibitory control (Ausubel, 1952, pp. 465–471). Such persons, also, usually do not exhibit any signs of behavior disorder. At crucial choice points in facing the problems of living they simply choose the opportunistic instead of the moral alternative. They are not mentally ill, but they are clearly accountable for their misconduct. Hence, since personality disorder and immorality are neither coextensive nor mutually exclusive conditions, the concept of mental illness need not necessarily obscure the issue of moral accountability.

Second, guilt may be a contributory factor in behavior disorder, but is by no means the only or principal cause thereof. Feelings of guilt may give rise to anxiety and depression; but in the absence of catastrophic impairment of self-esteem induced by *other* factors, these symptoms tend to be transitory and peripheral in nature (Ausubel, 1952, pp. 362–363). Repression of guilt is more a consequence than a cause of anxiety. Guilt is repressed in order to avoid the anxiety producing trauma to self-esteem that would otherwise result if it were acknowledged. Repression per se enters the causal picture in anxiety only secondarily—by obviating "the possibility of punishment, confession, expiation, and other guilt reduction mechanisms" (Ausubel, 1952, p. 456). Furthermore, in most types of personality disorder other than anxiety, depression, and various complications of anxiety such as phobias, obsessions, and compulsion, guilt feelings are either not particularly prominent (schizophrenic reactions), or are conspicuously absent (e.g., classical cases of inadequate or aggressive, antisocial psychopathy).

Third, it is just as unreasonable to hold an individual responsible for symptoms of behavior disorder as to deem him accountable for symptoms of physical illness. He is no more culpable for his inability to cope with sociopsychological stress than he would be for his inability to resist the spread of infectious organisms. In those instances where warranted guilt feelings *do* contribute to personality disorder, the patient is accountable for the misdeeds underlying his guilt, but is hardly responsible for the symptoms brought on by the guilt feelings or for unlawful acts committed during his illness. Acknowledgment of guilt may be therapeutically beneficial under these circumstances, but punishment for the original misconduct should obviously be deferred until after recovery.

Lastly, even if it were true that all personality disorder is a reflection of sin and that people are accountable for their behavioral symptoms, it would still be unnecessary to deny that these symptoms are manifestations of disease. Illness is no less real because the victim happens to be culpable for his illness. A glutton with hypertensive heart disease undoubtedly aggravates his condition by overeating, and is culpable in part for the often fatal symptoms of his disease, but what reasonable person would claim that for this reason he is not really ill?

Conclusions

Four propositions in support of the argument for discarding the concept of mental illness were carefully examined, and the following conclusions were reached:

First, although brain pathology is probably not the major cause of personality disorder, it does account for *some* psychological symptoms by impairing the neural substrate of personality. In any case, however, a symptom need not reflect a physical lesion in order to qualify as a genuine manifestation of disease.

Second, Szasz' postulated dichotomy between mental and physical symptoms is untenable because the assessment of *all* symptoms is dependent to some extent on subjective judgment, emotional factors, cultural-ethical norms, and personal involvement of the observer. Furthermore, the use of medical measures in treating behavior disorders—irrespective of whether the underlying causes are neural or psychological—is defensible on the grounds that if inadvertent impairment of the neural substrate of personality can have distortive effects on behavior, directed manipulation of the same substrate may have therapeutic effects.

Third, there is no inherent contradiction in regarding mental symptoms both as expressions of problems in living *and* as manifestations of illness. The latter situation results when individuals are for various reasons unable to cope with such problems, and react with seriously distorted or maladaptive behavior. The three principal categories of behavioral symptoms—manifestations of impaired functioning, adaptive compensation, and defensive overreaction—are also found in bodily disease. The concept of mental illness has never been advanced as a demonological cause of human disharmony, but only as a co-manifestation with it of certain inescapable difficulties and hazards in personal and social adjustment. The same concept is also generally accepted as a generic term for all behavioral symptoms rather than as a reified cause of these symptoms.

Fourth, the view that personality disorder is less a manifestation of illness than of sin, i.e., of culpable inadequacy in meeting problems of ethical choice and responsibility, and that victims of behavior disorder are therefore morally accountable for their symptoms, is neither logically nor empirically tenable. In most instances immoral behavior and mental illness are clearly distinguishable conditions. Guilt is only a secondary etiological factor in anxiety and depression, and in other personality disorders is either not prominent or conspicuously absent. The issue of culpability for symptoms is largely irrelevant in handling the behavior disorders, and in any case does not detract from the reality of the illness.

In general, it is both unnecessary and potentially dangerous to discard the concept of mental illness on the grounds that only in this way can clinical psychology escape from the professional domination of medicine. Dentists, podiatrists, optometrists, and osteopaths have managed to acquire an independent professional status without rejecting the concept of disease. It is equally unnecessary and dangerous to substitute the doctrine of sin for illness in order to counteract prevailing amoral and nonjudgmental trends in psychotherapy. The hypothesis of repressed guilt does not adequately explain most kinds and instances of personality disorder, and the concept of mental illness does not preclude judgments of moral accountability where warranted. Definition of behavior disorder in terms of sin or of difficulties associated with ethical choice and responsibility would substitute theological disputation and philosophical wrangling about values for specifiable quantitative and qualitative criteria of disease.

REFERENCES

AUSUBEL, D. P. *Ego Development and the Personality Disorders*. New York: Grune & Stratton, 1952.

Ausubel, D. P. Relationships between psychology and psychiatry: The hidden issues. *Amer. Psychologist*, 1956, *11*, 99–105.

Dreyfuss, F., & Czaczkes, J. W. Blood cholesterol and uric acid of healthy medical students under the stress of an examination. *AMA Arch. intern. Med.*, 1959, *103*, 708.

Mowrer, O. H. "Sin," the lesser of two evils. *Amer. Psychologist*, 1960, *15*, 301–304.

Szasz, T. S. The myth of mental illness. *Amer. Psychologist*, 1960, *15*, 113–118.

••

The Effects of Psychotherapy: An Evaluation*

H. J. Eysenck

THE RECOMMENDATION OF the Committee on Training in Clinical Psychology of the American Psychological Association regarding the training of clinical psychologists in the field of psychotherapy has been criticized by the writer in a series of papers (10, 11, 12). Of the arguments presented in favor of the policy advocated by the Committee, the most cogent one is perhaps that which refers to the social need for the skills possessed by the psychotherapist. In view of the importance of the issues involved, it seemed worth while to examine the evidence relating to the actual effects of psychotherapy, in an attempt to seek clarification on a point of fact.

BASE LINE AND UNIT OF MEASUREMENT

In the only previous attempt to carry out such an evaluation, Landis has pointed out that "before any sort of measurement can be made, it is necessary to establish a base line and a common unit of measure. The only unit of measure available is the report made by the physician stating that the patient has recovered, is much improved, is improved or unimproved. This unit is probably as satisfactory as any type of human subjective judgment, partaking of both the good and bad points of such judgments" (26, p. 156). For a unit Landis suggests "that of expressing therapeutic results in terms of the number of patients recovered or improved per 100 cases admitted to the hospital." As an alternative, he suggests "the statement of therapeutic outcome for some given group of patients during some stated interval of time."

Landis realized quite clearly that in order to evaluate the effectiveness of any form of therapy, data from a control group of non-

* From the *Journal of Consulting Psychology*, 1952, *16*, 319–324.

treated patients would be required in order to compare the effects of therapy with the spontaneous remission rate. In the absence of anything better, he used the amelioration rate in state mental hospitals for patients diagnosed under the heading of "neuroses." As he points out:

> There are several objections to the use of the consolidated amelioration rate . . . of the . . . state hospitals . . . as a base rate for spontaneous recovery. The fact that psychoneurotic cases are not usually committed to state hospitals unless in a very bad condition; the relatively small number of voluntary patients in the group; the fact that such patients do get some degree of psychotherapy especially in the reception hospitals; and the probably quite different economic, educational, and social status of the State Hospital group compared to the patients reported from each of the other hospitals—all argue against the acceptance of [this] figure . . . as a truly satisfactory base line, but in the absence of any other better figure this must serve [26, p. 168].

Actually the various figures quoted by Landis agree very well. The percentage of neurotic patients discharged annually as recovered or improved from New York state hospitals is 70 (for the years 1925–1934); for the United States as a whole it is 68 (for the years 1926–1933). The percentage of neurotics discharged as recovered or improved within one year of admission is 66 for the United States (1933) and 68 for New York (1914). The consolidated amelioration rate of New York state hospitals, 1917–1934, is 72 per cent. As this is the figure chosen by Landis, we may accept it in preference to the other very similar ones quoted. By and large, we may thus say that of severe neurotics receiving in the main custodial care, and very little if any psychotherapy, over two-thirds recovered or improved to a considerable extent. "Although this is not, strictly speaking, a basic figure for 'spontaneous' recovery, still any therapeutic method must show an appreciably greater size than this to be seriously considered" (26, p. 160).

Another estimate of the required "base line" is provided by Denker:

> Five hundred consecutive disability claims due to psychoneurosis, treated by general practitioners throughout the country, and not by accredited specialists or sanatoria, were reviewed. All types of neurosis were included, and no attempt made to differentiate the neurasthenic, anxiety,

compulsive, hysteric, or other states, but the greatest care was taken to eliminate the true psychotic or organic lesions which in the early stages of illness so often simulate neurosis. These cases were taken consecutively from the files of the Equitable Life Assurance Society of the United States, were from all parts of the country, and all had been ill of a neurosis for at least three months before claims were submitted. They, therefore, could be fairly called "severe," since they had been totally disabled for at least a three months' period, and rendered unable to carry on with any "occupation for remuneration or profit" for at least that time [9, p. 2164].

These patients were regularly seen and treated by their own physicians with sedatives, tonics, suggestion, and reassurance, but in no case was any attempt made at anything but this most superficial type of "psychotherapy" which has always been the stock-in-trade of the general practitioner. Repeated statements, every three months or so by their physicians, as well as independent investigations by the insurance company, confirmed the fact that these people actually were not engaged in productive work during the period of their illness. During their disablement, these cases received disability benefits. As Denker points out, "It is appreciated that this fact of disability income may have actually prolonged the total period of disability and acted as a barrier to incentive for recovery. One would, therefore, not expect the therapeutic results in such a group of cases to be as favorable as in other groups where the economic factor might act as an important spur in helping the sick patient adjust to his neurotic conflict and illness" (9, p. 2165).

The cases were all followed up for at least a five-year period, and often as long as ten years after the period of disability had begun. The criteria of "recovery" used by Denker were as follows: (a) return to work, and ability to carry on well in economic adjustments for at least a five-year period; (b) complaint of no further or very slight difficulties; (c) making of successful social adjustments. Using these criteria, which are very similar to those usually used by psychiatrists, Denker found that 45 per cent of the patients recovered after one year, another 27 per cent after two years, making 72 per cent in all. Another 10 per cent, 5 per cent, and 4 per cent recovered during the third, fourth, and fifth years, respectively, making a total of 90 per cent recoveries after five years.

This sample contrasts in many ways with that used by Landis.

The cases on which Denker reports were probably not quite as severe as those summarized by Landis; they were all voluntary, non-hospitalized patients, and came from a much higher socioeconomic stratum. The majority of Denker's patients were clerical workers, executives, teachers, and professional men. In spite of these differences, the recovery figures for the two samples are almost identical. The most suitable figure to choose from those given by Denker is probably that for the two-year recovery rate, as follow-up studies seldom go beyond two years and the higher figures for three-, four-, and five-year follow-up would overestimate the efficiency of this "base line" procedure. Using, therefore, the two-year recovery figure of 72 per cent, we find that Denker's figure agrees exactly with that given by Landis. We may, therefore, conclude with some confidence that our estimate of some two-thirds of severe neurotics showing recovery or considerable improvement without the benefit of systematic psychotherapy is not likely to be very far out.

Effects of Psychotherapy

We may now turn to the effects of psychotherapeutic treatment. The results of nineteen studies reported in the literature, covering over seven thousand cases, and dealing with both psychoanalytic and eclectic types of treatment, are quoted in detail in Table 1. An attempt has been made to report results under the four headings: (a) Cured, or much improved; (b) Improved; (c) Slightly improved; (d) Not improved, died, discontinued treatment, etc. It was usually easy to reduce additional categories given by some writers to these basic four; some writers give only two or three categories, and in those cases it was, of course, impossible to subdivide further, and the figures for combined categories are given.[1] A slight degree of subjectivity inevitably enters into this procedure, but it is doubtful if it has caused much distortion. A somewhat greater degree of subjectivity is probably implied in the writer's judgment as to which disorders and diagnoses should be considered to fall under the heading of "neurosis." Schizophrenic, manic-depressive, and paranoid states have been excluded; organ neuroses, psychopathic states, and

---

[1] In one or two cases where patients who improved or improved slightly were combined by the original author, the total figure has been divided equally between the two categories.

character disturbances have been included. The number of cases where there was genuine doubt is probably too small to make much change in the final figures, regardless of how they are allocated.

A number of studies have been excluded because of such factors as excessive inadequacy of follow-up, partial duplication of cases

Table 1. Summary of reports of the results of Psychotherapy.

	N	Cured; much improved	Improved	Slightly improved	Not improved; died; left treatment	% Cured much improved
(A) *Psychoanalytic*						
1. Fenichel [13, pp. 28-40]	484	104	84	99	197	39
2. Kessel & Hyman [24]	34	16	5	4	9	62
3. Jones [22, pp. 12-14]	59	20	8	28	3	47
4. Alexander [1, pp. 30-43]	141	28	42	23	48	50
5. Knight [25]	42	8	20	7	7	67
All cases	760	335		425		44
(B) *Eclectic*						
1. Huddleson [20]	200	19	74	80	27	46
2. Matz [30]	775	10	310	310	145	41
3. Maudsley Hospital Report (1931)	1721	288	900	533		69
4. Maudsley Hospital Report (1935)	1711	371	765	575		64
5. Neustatter [32]	46	9	14	8	15	50
6. Luff & Garrod [27]	500	140	135	26	199	55
7. Luff & Garrod [27]	210	38	84	54	34	68
8. Ross [34]	1089	547	306		236	77
9. Yaskin [40]	100	29	29		42	58
10. Curran [7]	83		51		32	61
11. Masserman & Carmichael [29]	50	7	20	5	18	54
12. Carmichael & Masserman [4]	77	16	25	14	22	53
13. Schilder [35]	35	11	11	6	7	63
14. Hamilton & Wall [16]	100	32	34	17	17	66
15. Hamilton *et al.* [15]	100	48	5	17	32	51
16. Landis [26]	119	40	47		32	73
17. Institute Med. Psychol. (quoted Neustatter)	270	58	132	55	25	70
18. Wilder [39]	54	3	24	16	11	50
19. Miles *et al.* ([31]	53	13	18	13	9	58
All cases	7293	4661		2632		64

with others included in our table, failure to indicate type of treatment used, and other reasons which made the results useless from our point of view. Papers thus rejected are those by Thorley & Craske (*37*), Bennett and Semrad (*2*), H. I. Harris (*19*), Hardcastle (*17*), A. Harris (*18*), Jackson and Wright (*21*), Friess and Nelson (*14*), Comroe (*5*), Wenger (*38*), Orbison (*33*), Coon and Raymond (*6*), Denker (*8*), and Bond and Braceland (*3*). Their inclusion would not have altered our conclusions to any considerable degree, although, as Miles *et al.* point out: "When the various studies are compared in terms of thoroughness, careful planning, strictness of criteria and objectivity, there is often an inverse correlation between these factors and the percentage of successful results reported" (*31*, p. 88).

Certain difficulties have arisen from the inability of some writers to make their column figures agree with their totals, or to calculate percentages accurately. Again, the writer has exercised his judgment as to which figures to accept. In certain cases, writers have given figures of cases where there was a recurrence of the disorder after apparent cure or improvement, without indicating how many patients were affected in these two groups respectively. All recurrences of this kind have been subtracted from the "cured" and "improved" totals, taking half from each. The total number of cases involved in all these adjustments is quite small. Another investigator making all decisions exactly in the opposite direction to the present writer's would hardly alter the final percentage figures by more than 1 or 2 per cent.

We may now turn to the figures as presented. Patients treated by means of psychoanalysis improve to the extent of 44 per cent; patients treated eclectically improve to the extent of 64 per cent; patients treated only custodially or by general practitioners improve to the extent of 72 per cent. There thus appears to be an inverse correlation between recovery and psychotherapy; the more psychotherapy, the smaller the recovery rate. This conclusion requires certain qualifications.

In our tabulation of psychoanalytic results, we have classed those who stopped treatment together with those not improved. This appears to be reasonable; a patient who fails to finish his treatment, and is not improved, is surely a therapeutic failure. The same rule has been followed with the data summarized under "eclectic" treatment, except when the patient who did not finish treatment was definitely classified as "improved" by the therapist. However, in view of the peculiarities of Freudian procedures it may appear to some readers to be more just to class those cases separately, and deal only with the percentage of completed treatments which are successful. Approximately one-third of the psychoanalytic patients listed broke off treatment, so that the percentage of successful treatments of patients who finished their course must be put at approximately 66 per cent. It would appear, then, that when we discount the risk the patient runs of stopping treatment altogether, his chances of improvement under psychoanalysis are approximately equal to his chances of improvement under eclectic treatment, and slightly worse than his chances under a general practitioner or custodial treatment.

Two further points require clarification: (a) Are patients in our "control" groups (Landis and Denker) as seriously ill as those in our "experimental" groups? (b) Are standards of recovery perhaps less stringent in our "control" than in our "experimental" groups? It is difficult to answer these questions definitely, in view of the great divergence of opinion between psychiatrists. From a close scrutiny of the literature it appears that the "control" patients were probably at least as seriously ill as the "experimental" patients, and possibly more so. As regards standards of recovery, those in Denker's study are as stringent as most of those used by psychoanalysts and eclectic psychiatrists, but those used by the State Hospitals whose figures Landis quotes are very probably more lenient. In the absence of agreed standards of severity of illness, or of extent of recovery, it is not possible to go further.

In general, certain conclusions are possible from these data. They fail to prove that psychotherapy, Freudian or otherwise, facilitates the recovery of neurotic patients. They show that roughly two-thirds of a group of neurotic patients will recover or improve to a marked extent within about two years of the onset of their illness, whether they are treated by means of psychotherapy or not. This figure appears to be remarkably stable from one investigation to another, regardless of type of patient treated, standard of recovery employed, or method of therapy used. From the point of view of the neurotic, these figures are encouraging; from the point of view of the psychotherapist, they can hardly be called very favorable to his claims.

The figures quoted do not necessarily disprove the possibility of therapeutic effectiveness. There are obvious shortcomings in any actuarial comparison and these shortcomings are particularly serious when there is so little agreement among psychiatrists relating even to the most fundamental concepts and definitions. Definite proof would require a special investigation, carefully planned and methodologically more adequate than these *ad hoc* comparisons. But even the much more modest conclusions that the figures fail to show any favorable effects of psychotherapy should give pause to those who would wish to give an important part in the training of clinical psychologists to a skill the existence and effectiveness of which is still unsupported by any scientifically acceptable evidence.

These results and conclusions will no doubt contradict the strong feeling of usefulness and therapeutic success which many psychiatrists and clinical psychologists hold. While it is true that subjective feelings of this type have no place in science, they are likely to prevent an easy acceptance of the general argument presented here. This contradiction between objective fact and subjective certainty has been remarked on in other connections by Kelly and Fiske, who found that "One aspect of our findings is most disconcerting to us: the inverse relationship between the confidence of staff members at the time of making a prediction and the measured validity of that prediction. Why is it, for example, that our staff members tended to make their best predictions at a time when they subjectively felt relatively unacquainted with the candidate, when they had constructed no systematic picture of his personality structure? Or conversely, why is it that with increasing confidence in clinical judgment . . . we find decreasing validities of predictions?" (*23*, p. 406).

In the absence of agreement between fact and belief, there is urgent need for a decrease in the strength of belief, and for an increase in the number of facts available. Until such facts as may be discovered in a process of rigorous analysis support the prevalent belief in therapeutic effectiveness of psychological treatment, it seems premature to insist on the inclusion of training in such treatment in the curriculum of the clinical psychologist.

Summary

A survey was made of reports on the improvement of neurotic patients after psychotherapy, and the results compared with the best available estimates of recovery without benefit of such therapy. The figures fail to support the hypothesis that psychotherapy facilitates

156   PERSPECTIVES IN CLINICAL PSYCHOLOGY

recovery from neurotic disorder. In view of the many difficulties
attending such actuarial comparisons, no further conclusions could
be derived from the data whose shortcomings highlight the necessity
of properly planned and executed experimental studies into this important field.

REFERENCES

1. ALEXANDER, F. Five Year Report of the Chicago Institute for Psychoanalysis, 1932–1937.
2. BENNETT, A. E., & SEMRAD, E. V. Common errors in diagnosis and treatment of the psychoneurotic patient—a study of 100 case histories. Nebr. med. J., 1936, 21, 90–92.
3. BOND, E. D., & BRACELAND, F. J. Prognosis in mental disease. Amer. J. Psychiat., 1937, 94, 263–274.
4. CARMICHAEL, H. T., & MASSERMAN, T. H. Results of treatment in a psychiatric outpatients' department. J. Amer. med. Ass., 1939, 113, 2292–2298.
5. COMROE, B. I. Follow-up study of 100 patients diagnosed as "neurosis." J. nerv. ment. Dis., 1936, 83, 679–684.
6. COON, G. P., & RAYMOND, A. A review of the psychoneuroses at Stockbridge. Stockbridge, Mass.: Austen Riggs Foundation, Inc., 1940.
7. CURRAN, D. The problem of assessing psychiatric treatment. Lancet, 1937. II, 1005–1009.
8. DENKER, P. G. Prognosis and life expectancy in the psychoneuroses. Proc. Ass. Life Insur. med. Dir. Amer., 1937, 24, 179.
9. DENKER, R. Results of treatment of psychoneuroses by the general practitioner. A follow-up study of 500 cases. N.Y. State J. Med., 1946, 46, 2164–2166.
10. EYSENCK, H. J. Training in clinical psychology: an English point of view. Amer. Psychologist, 1949, 4, 173–176.
11. EYSENCK, H. J. The relation between medicine and psychology in England. In W. Dennis (Ed.), Current Trends in the Relation of Psychology and Medicine. Pittsburgh: Univer. of Pittsburgh Press, 1950.
12. EYSENCK, H. J. Function and training of the clinical psychologist. J. ment. Sci., 1950, 96, 1–16.
13. FENICHEL, O. Ten Years of the Berlin Psychoanalysis Institute, 1920–1930.
14. FRIESS, C., & NELSON, M. J. Psychoneurotics five years later. Amer. J. ment. Sci., 1942, 203, 539–558.
15. HAMILTON, D. M., VANNEY, I. H., & WALL, T. H. Hospital treatment of patients with psychoneurotic disorder. Amer. J. Psychiat., 1942, 99, 243–247.

16. HAMILTON, D. M., & WALL, T. H. Hospital treatment of patients with psychoneurotic disorder. *Amer. J. Psychiat.*, 1941, *98*, 551–557.

17. HARDCASTLE, D. H. A follow-up study of one hundred cases made for the Department of Psychological Medicine, Guy's Hospital. *J. ment. Sci.*, 1934, *90*, 536–549.

18. HARRIS, A. The prognosis of anxiety states. *Brit. med. J.* 1938, *2*, 649–654.

19. HARRIS, H. I. Efficient psychotherapy for the large out-patient clinic. *New England J. Med.*, 1939, *221*, 1–5.

20. HUDDLESON, J. H. Psychotherapy in 200 cases of psychoneurosis. *Mil. Surgeon*, 1927, *60*, 161–170.

21. JACOBSON, J. R., & WRIGHT, K. W. Review of a year of group psychotherapy. *Psychiat. Quart.*, 1942, *16*, 744–764.

22. JONES, E. *Decennial Report of the London Clinic of Psychoanalysis, 1926–1936.*

23. KELLY, E. L., & FISKE, D. W. The prediction of success in the VA training program in clinical psychology. *Amer. Psychologist*, 1950, *5*, 395–406.

24. KESSEL, L., & HYMAN, H. T. The value of psychoanalysis as a therapeutic procedure. *J. Amer. med. Ass.*, 1933, *101*, 1612–1615.

25. KNIGHT, R. O. Evaluation of the results of psychoanalytic therapy. *Amer. J. Psychiat.*, 1941, *98*, 434–446.

26. LANDIS, C. Statistical evaluation of psychotherapeutic methods. In S. E. Hinsie (Ed.), *Concepts and Problems of Psychotherapy*. London: Heineman, 1938. Pp. 155–165.

27. LUFF, M. C., & GARROD, M. The after-results of psychotherapy in 500 adult cases. *Brit. med. J.*, 1935, *2*, 54–59.

28. MAPOTHER, E. Discussion. *Brit. J. med. Psychol.*, 1927, *7*, 57.

29. MASSERMAN, T. H., & CARMICHAEL, H. T. Diagnosis and prognosis in psychiatry. *J. ment. Sci.*, 1938, *84*, 893–946.

30. MATZ, P. B. Outcome of hospital treatment of ex-service patients with nervous and mental disease in the U.S. Veteran's Bureau. *U.S. Vet. Bur. med. Bull.*, 1929, *5*, 829–842.

31. MILES, H. H. W., BARRABEE, E. L., & FINESINGER, J. E. Evaluation of psychotherapy. *Psychosom. Med.*, 1951, *13*, 83–105.

32. NEUSTATTER, W. L. The results of fifty cases treated by psychotherapy. *Lancet*, 1935, *I*, 796–799.

33. ORBISON, T. J. The psychoneuroses: psychasthenia, neurasthenia and hysteria, with special reference to a certain method of treatment. *Calif. west. Med.*, 1925, *23*, 1132–1136.

34. ROSS, T. A. *An Enquiry into Prognosis in the Neuroses*. London: Cambridge Univer. Press, 1936.

35. SCHILDER, P. Results and problems of group psychotherapy in severe neuroses. *Ment. Hyg., N.Y.*, 1939, *23*, 87–89.

36. SKOTTOWE, I., & LOCKWOOD, M. R. The fate of 150 psychiatric out-patients. *J. ment. Sci.*, 1935, *81*, 502–508.
37. THORLEY, A. S., & CRASKE, N. Comparison and estimate of group and individual method of treatment. *Brit. med. J.*, 1950, *1*, 97–100.
38. WENGER, P. Uber weitere Ergebnisse der Psychotherapie in Rahmen einer Medizinischen Poliklinik. *Wien. med. Wschr.*, 1934, *84*, 320–325.
39. WILDER, J. Facts and figures on psychotherapy, *J. clin. Psychopath.*, 1945, *7*, 311–347.
40. YASKIN, J. C. The psychoneuroses and neuroses. A review of 100 cases with special reference to treatment and results. *Amer. J. Psychiat.*, 1936, *93*, 107–125.

SELECTION X

....

The Outcome Problem in
Psychotherapy Revisited* [1]

HANS H. STRUPP

FOR REASONS WHICH will become more apparent later, the outcome problem in psychotherapy has been receiving relatively scant attention in recent years—not because the problem has lost its importance but rather because of a realization on the part of researchers that a new approach to the issue must be found, and that more pressing matters must be dealt with first before we can address ourselves meaningfully to the question of the effectiveness of psychotherapy. This rationale partly accounts for the great interest in so-called process studies which have swept the scene during the last decade. In this paper I have set myself the task of reexamining the issue in the light of recent research evidence. Furthermore, I shall attempt to redirect attention to the therapeutic situation proper as an important criterion situation; if true, this statement would apply par excellence to the psychoanalytic situation. It appears that in the furor for "easy" quantifications we have largely lost sight of the rich potentialities for research in the transference situation, which unquestionably represents the greatest single methodological discovery for interpersonal research in the twentieth century.

One of the major difficulties in psychotherapy research is that of adequately specifying the independent variable—the psychotherapeutic methods—to which therapeutic changes are being attributed. Knight (1941), for example, cites the following characterizations (among others):

* From *Psychotherapy: Theory, Research and Practice,* 1963, *1,* 1–13.
[1] The writing of this paper was aided by Research Grant No. M-2171 (C3), of the National Institute of Mental Health, Public Health Service.

I am greatly indebted to Dr. Martin Wallach for a critical reading of the manuscript and for a number of valuable suggestions for improvement.

159

(1) With regard to the preponderant attitude taken or influence attempted by the therapist; e.g., suggestion, persuasion, exhortation, intimidation, counseling, interpretation, re-education, re-training, etc.

(2) With regard to the general aim of the therapy; e.g., supportive, suppressive, expressive, cathartic, ventilative, etc.

(3) With regard to the supposed "depth" of the therapy—superficial psychotherapy and deep psychotherapy.

(4) With regard to the duration—brief psychotherapy and prolonged psychotherapy.

(5) With regard to its supposed relationship to Freudian psychoanalysis as, for example, orthodox, standard, classical, or regular psychoanalysis, modified psychoanalysis, "wild" analysis, direct psychoanalysis, psychoanalytic psychotherapy, psychoanalytically oriented psychotherapy, psychodynamic psychotherapy, psychotherapy using the dynamic approach, and psychotherapy based on psychoanalytic principles.

(6) With regard to the ex-Freudian dissident who started a new school of psychotherapy. Thus we have Adler's individual psychology with its Adlerian "analysis," Jung's analytical psychology with its Jungian "analysis," the Rankian "analysis," the Stekelian "analysis," and the Horney modifications (pp. 52–53).

What do these techniques have in common? What are their unique differences? What variance is introduced by the person of the therapist practicing them—his degree of expertness, his personality, and attitudes? These are staggering research problems, and the available research evidence by and large is insufficient. It seems to me that we shall not be satisfied with studies of therapeutic outcomes until we succeed in becoming more explicit about the independent variable. Thus the very extensive research efforts which are beginning to get under way in the area of the therapist's contribution, including his personality and techniques, are crucial as a prerequisite. I shall merely mention in passing that variables in the patient's life situation, social class and other environmental factors, are also increasingly being studied. This work is bound to have a cumulative effect.

Let us stay, however, with the method of treatment and consider further its relation to outcomes. For this purpose let us disregard (what in reality cannot be disregarded) therapist variables and socio-environmental factors. Perhaps it can be agreed that some methods of psychotherapy are more intensive than others—in terms of effort, aim, duration, and the like. If we asked clinicians to rank order different methods of psychotherapy on this continuum, we would undoubtedly find that psychoanalysis, four times a week, for two or more years, would rank at the top and once-a-week supportive therapy in which the patient is seen for a total of 5-10 sessions would be rated somewhere near the bottom. Let us go a step further and predict that therapeutic outcome is (partly at least) commensurate with the effort expended—not an unreasonable assumption in education, training, and child-rearing. It would then follow that, other things being equal, the results achieved by psychoanalysis should be substantially greater than those resulting from minimal treatment methods. We shall for the moment set aside a specification of "greater" but merely suggest that even with crude measuring instruments (which is all we have at present) the demonstration of differences in outcome between the two methods should be a fairly simple matter. The literature, unfortunately, is replete with quasi documentation which has hopelessly befogged the issue.

A brief review of Eysenck's (1952) widely quoted survey, which capitalized upon and added considerably to the existing confusion may be instructive. In order to make any meaningful statements about the effects of psychotherapy, Eysenck reasoned, it is necessary to compare psychotherapy patients with "untreated controls." The effects of psychotherapy, if any, would thus be demonstrated in terms of differences between the two major groups. The "base line" was provided by two studies, one dealing with the percentage of neurotic patients discharged annually as recovered or improved from New York state hospitals, the other a survey of 500 patients who presented disability claims due to psychoneurosis and who were treated by general practitioners with sedatives and the like. The assumption was made in these two studies that the patients did not receive psychotherapy, or, at least not anything resembling "formal" psychotherapy. The amelioration rate in both studies was in the neighborhood of 72 per cent. Typical criteria of recovery were: (a) return to work and ability to carry on well in economic adjustments for at least a five-year period; (b) complaint of no further or very slight difficulties; (c) making of successful social adjustments.

The results of these studies were compared by Eysenck with 19 reports in the literature dealing with the outcomes of both psychoanalytic and eclectic types of psychotherapy. Pooling the results he found that patients treated by means of psychoanalysis improved to the extent of 44 per cent; patients treated eclectically improved to the extent of 64 per cent; patients treated only custodially or by general practitioners improved to the extent of 72 per cent. Thus, paradoxically, it appears that there is an inverse relationship between intensity of psychotherapeutic treatment and rate of recovery. A situation in which clinical experience is completely at variance with statistical data usually calls for a searching analysis to discover possible sources of error. However, Eysenck answered—to his satisfaction—the question that the "control" patients were as seriously ill as the treated patients, and that the standards of recovery were equally stringent for both groups. His paper also shows that contrary to the subsequent popularizations of his findings (by himself) he was well aware of the limitations of the comparison. However, he takes seriously his conclusion that "roughly two-thirds of a group of neurotic patients will recover or improve to a marked extent within about two years of the onset of their illness, whether they are treated by means of psychotherapy or not" (p. 322).

Several writers have taken Eysenck to task for his conclusions, pointing out numerous fallacies in his design. For example, his so-called untreated control groups are almost certainly deficient for the purpose; the criteria for discharge from a state hospital are undoubtedly very different from those of a psychoanalytic treatment center; and the "spontaneous recoveries" may, for all we know, be spurious. If this is true, or even if the "spontaneous recovery" rate is grossly overstated, Eysenck's uncritical acceptance of these figures and his unfortunate conclusion to abandon the training and practice

Table 1 (From Eysenck, 1952). *Summary of reports of the results of psychotherapy*

	N	Cured; much improved	Improved	Slightly improved	Not improved; died; left treatment	% Cure much improve improv
(A) *Psychoanalytic**						
1. Fenichel (1930; pp. 28–40)	484	104	84	99	197	39
2. Kessel & Hyman (1933)	34	16	5	4	9	62
3. Jones (1936; pp. 12–14)	59	20	8	28	3	47
4. Alexander (1937; pp. 30–43)	141	28	42	23	48	50
5. Knight (1941)	42	8	20	7	7	67
All cases	760	335		425		44%

* Part B (Eclectic) omitted.

of psychotherapy forthwith would be rash. Furthermore, if two-thirds of all people who suffer from a "neurosis" "recovered" within two years "after onset," emotional disorder would scarcely be the serious problem which manifestly it is. Finally, one may take issue with Eysenck's assertion that psychotherapists must do significantly better than 72 per cent before they can make any legitimate claim for the efficacy of their procedures.

Even if Eysenck's arguments are ill-founded, it behooves us to take a close look at the results reported by the psychoanalytic treatment centers, because it may be presumed that the most intensive, the most ambitious, and the most thoroughgoing form of psychotherapy is practiced there. Eysenck's data abstracted from published reports are given in Table 1.[2]

Eysenck points out that in this tabulation he classed those who stopped treatment together with those who were rated as not improved. This seemed reasonable to him on the ground that a patient who failed to finish treatment should be considered a therapeutic failure. However, if only those patients are considered who completed therapy—about one-third broke off treatment—the percentage of successful treatments rises to about 66 per cent (Eysenck). Although it may be true that errors in technique may have been responsible for some of the premature terminations, it seems quite unjustified to regard such cases as "therapeutic failures"; by the same token, the efficacy of insulin therapy is hardly adequately represented by including those diabetics for whom it was prescribed but who failed to adhere to the regimen.

Eysenck presented his tabulation of results from therapy under four headings: (a) cured, or much improved; (b) improved; (c)

[2] I have reexamined the original sources quoted in Part A of Eysenck's Table 1 in an attempt to reconcile the two sets of data. I have been utterly unable to do so. To be sure the various reports are not uniform, and it is difficult to bring the figures under common denominators. Nevertheless, on the basis of the published reports the therapeutic results are regularly more favorable to psychoanalysis than is suggested by Eysenck's tabulation—in some instances markedly so. There can be no doubt that Eysenck's zeal has led him to place the worst possible interpretation upon the results. It is also abundantly clear from the reports that exceedingly stringent criteria were employed in classifying outcomes. Thus, the standards employed in these sources were very different from the ones used elsewhere by Eysenck.

It is regrettable that in more recent years psychoanalytic institutes seem to have increasingly desisted from publishing such data, perhaps partly on the grounds that they are easily misinterpreted.

slightly improved; (d) not improved, died, discontinued treatment, etc. This criterion is undoubtedly crude; it may be unreliable; it may reflect an impossibly high standard of perfection; it may be entirely incomparable to the judgments made for the "control" cases or for the studies of "eclectic psychotherapy." But, over-all assessments are often the best we have, and in many areas of psychological measurement they have been shown to have a highly valid core. This would hold true on even stronger grounds where the raters have had ample opportunity to make observations and have intimate knowledge of the person being rated. Where would such conditions be met more perfectly than in psychoanalytic treatment? Irrespective of the validity or meaningfulness of Eysenck's comparisons, the statistics reported by the four[3] psychoanalytic treatment centers may be accepted as reasonable assessments. Still, there is the somewhat disconcerting fact that some 21 per cent of the patients treated were only "slightly improved" and 35 per cent fall into the limbo category "not improved, died, discontinued treatment, etc." However the data are analyzed, we are left with the conclusion that psychoanalysis was only slightly successful or unsuccessful for about 30 per cent of the patients who at one point were accepted for therapy. Since they were accepted for therapy we may presume that at that time, at least, they were considered suitable candidates for this form of psychotherapy. Apart from the fallibility of the criterion measure (which has been considered to be relatively slight), the lack of success may be attributed to the following factors, or a combination of these: (a) errors in judgment about the analysand's suitability; (b) factors in the patient's psychopathology or character structure which emerged as insurmountable obstacles after therapy began; (c) deficiencies in the method of treatment; (d) inadequacies of the therapist's technical skills or shortcomings of his personality; (e) vicissitudes of the particular patient-therapist interaction which resulted in a therapeutic impasse; and (f) variables in the patient's (and/or the therapist's) life situation which produced adverse effects.

Some of these factors may have been predictable at the beginning

[3] The study of Kessel & Hyman (1933) is out of place in Part A of Eysenck's Table 1, which focuses on psychoanalytic institutes and treatment centers. In contrast, the source of Kessel and Hyman's data is obscure, and no information is given about the characteristics of their sample. Most damaging is the fact that the evaluations of treatment outcome were made by unqualified judges (internists), who themselves disavow any competence in psychoanalysis.

of therapy provided more complete information had been available; others may have been completely fortuitous and beyond human control. For example, if we had precise information that patients with a certain character structure fail to benefit markedly from psychoanalysis 80 to 90 per cent of the time, and if we could be sure that Patient X is a member of that class, it would be unwise to recommend psychoanalysis for him. Or, if we had precise information that patients with a certain personality structure in 80–90 per cent of the cases come to grief when entering therapy with a therapist having a particular personality structure, one would advise them accordingly and help them select a more suitable therapist. Fortuitous circumstances (e.g., a fatal illness) need no further illustration. The point to be made is this: Considering the extremely important implications of the decision in advising a patient to enter or not to enter psychoanalysis (or, for that matter, any form of psychotherapy), it would be highly advantageous from the therapist's as well as the patient's point of view to have precise information about the outcome that might reasonably be expected. An increase in the power to predict the outcome of psychotherapy would indeed represent a tremendous advance: not only would it conserve money, energy, and professional manpower, but it would enhance the scientific status of psychotherapy to an unprecedented degree. In order to compete with other forms of treatment, psychotherapy and psychoanalysis need not establish that they are superior to anything else that is available: their claim to existence, survival, and development rests on the establishment of a large number of empirical, highly predictable relationships among key variables which are based on a coherent theory of demonstrable utility, that is, a theory which accounts for highly predictable *and* measurable therapeutic gains.

What is meant by "outcome"? In Eysenck's review and in many of the studies on which it is based, the term is used in extremely loose fashion. Eysenck himself treats neurosis in analogy to a form of physical illness, which allegedly one may contract at one time or another during one's lifetime, which seems to run an almost self-limiting course, and from which the patient somehow recovers through therapy or spontaneously. Anyone having the slightest familiarity with psychopathology and psychodynamics knows how erroneous and misleading such a conception is. I shall not pursue this point at the moment but plan to return to it in a somewhat different context. For the moment, it must be conceded that irrespective of our conception of neurosis or mental disorder there is such a thing as outcome from therapy. But, what kind of criterion is it?

Holt (1958), in an insightful and lucid article, tells us that there is a hidden trick in global predictions because they are not themselves a form of behavior but a judgment made by someone on a great deal of concrete behavior. This is true of grades in college, success in any type of treatment, and the like. "Because it is hidden by the label," Holt says, "there is a temptation to forget that the behavior you should be trying to predict exists and must be studied if it is to be rationally forecast." As long as one relies on global clinical judgments, like outcome, no matter how remarkable clinical judgments may sometimes be, one substitutes something for real information, and where there is no genuine information to begin with, none can be generated.

What needs to be done is "to decide what intervening variables need to be considered if the behavior is to be predicted (and) to deal with the inner constructs that mediate behavior and the determining situational variables as well. . . . The best practice seems to be to give explicit consideration to this step (the formation of clinical judgments), and to supply judgment with as many relevant facts as possible. This means studying known instances, comparing people who showed the behavior in question with others who in the same situation failed to" (p. 2).

To translate Holt's lesson to the therapy situation, it is futile to make judgments and predictions about outcome as long as we have paid insufficient attention to variables in the patient, the therapist, the method of therapy, the patient-therapist interaction, and the surrounding life situation. It is this realization, I believe, which in recent years has caused investigators in the area of psychotherapy to lose interest in "simplistic" (Luborsky's term) outcome studies of the kind we have been discussing and turned them to sustained research upon the psychotherapeutic process itself. Nevertheless, it seems to me, we shall again and again return, armed with more specific data, to the problem of outcome, no matter how arbitrary an end point it may represent.

In the following I shall attempt to deal with two areas having a bearing on the problem of outcome. Both represent important frontiers of research, although clearly they are by no means the only, or even the most important ones. But in both researchers have had more than a modicum of success in mapping it out, in charting it, and in establishing the kinds of empirical connections of which Holt speaks. To be sure, the progress cannot be termed spectacular or a "breakthrough," but it represents the constructive, painstaking, gradual effort which is needed. I am referring to the area of the patient's motivation for therapy, including patient-therapist compatibility; and, secondly, to analyses dealing with the criterion problem. Progress in the former area is more impressive than in the latter, but both unquestionably represent cornerstones on which the scientific edifice of psychotherapy must ultimately rest.

From a fairly large body of converging empirical evidence, which I shall not review here, it is becoming increasingly clear that therapists have fairly specific—and presumably valid—notions about the kinds of attributes which a "good" patient should possess, as well as about those attributes which make a patient unsuitable for the more usual forms of investigative, insight-producing psychotherapy. Patients considered good prognostic risks tend to be young, physically attractive, well-educated, members of the upper middle class, possessing a high degree of ego-strength, some anxiety which impels them to seek help, no seriously disabling neurotic symptoms, relative absence of deep characterological distortions or strong secondary gains, a willingness to talk about their difficulties, an ability to communicate well, some skill in the social-vocational area, a value system relatively congruent with that of the therapist, and a certain psychological-mindedness which makes them see their problems as emotional rather than physical. A number of these attributes appear to be statistically linked to social class. This linkage extends to the patient, the therapist, and the principles of psychotherapy to which he subscribes.[4]

---

[4] This formulation readily lends itself to the misinterpretation that promising candidates for psychotherapy are not really "sick." This inference would be quite unwarranted, and it is in part a reflection upon the primitive status of currently available assessment techniques. By superficial behavioristic standards a person may be described as "mentally healthy" if he meets gross behavioristic criteria of performance, such as functioning in a particular social role, earning a living, absence of gross disturbances in interpersonal situations, absence of gross psychopathology, and the like. Yet, such conformity or seeming adaptation may be achieved at tremendous psychic cost; the individual may feel intensely unhappy, inhibited, conflicted, etc. It appears that, broadly speaking, psychoanalysis pays the closest attention to and evinces the greatest respect for, the individual's intrapsychic organization and its function in the person's *fine* adjustment to himself and others. The latter is completely lost sight of in the

Hence, therapists tend to select those patients whose attributes meet the above criteria. It is hard to say whether therapy is effective because therapists invest their best efforts when these conditions prevail or whether the existence of these conditions in itself presages favorable results. Both statements are probably true to some extent, although variables within the patient and situational variables may play a more important part than the therapist's attitudes and expectations.

Every neurotic patient is unconsciously committed to maintain the status quo, and psychotherapy, particularly if aimed at confronting the patient with his inner conflicts, proceeds against the obstacle of powerful unconscious resistances. Therefore, unless there is a strong conscious desire to be helped and to collaborate with the therapist, the odds against a favorable outcome may be insuperable. Motivation for therapy is a global and a highly complex variable; research has shown that it is made up of combinations of the variables in the patient which have already been mentioned. But, it represents a clinical judgment made by the therapist, which in turn is colored to a significant extent by his own personality and attitudes. Because psychotherapy demands great investments of time and emotional energy from the therapist, it is hardly surprising that his willingness to enter into a therapeutic relationship with a particular patient becomes highly selective. We know that different therapists, depending on their own personality, have highly individual preferences, which it would be important to elucidate. It seems reasonable to hypothesize that therapeutic relationships in which the patient is highly motivated to seek therapeutic help and in which the therapist in turn is highly motivated to put his skills at the patient's disposal have, other things being equal, the greatest chance of success.

For example, Kirtner & Cartwright (1958), studying 42 cases at the University of Chicago Counseling Center, found a significant

---

statistical tabulations dealing with treatment outcomes. Unfortunately, there are no adequate measures of self-respect, a sense of worthwhileness as a person, emotional well-being arising from an ability to be at peace with oneself and others, a sense of relatedness, and identity—values which in this age of materialism largely seem to have lost their meaning. Unless we acknowledge that the integration and full unfolding of the human personality is worth striving for, no matter what the expenditure of therapeutic time and effort may be, and unless it becomes possible to reflect such achievements in tabulations of statistical results, we may be forced to concede that the future lies with tranquilizing drugs rather than with psychological techniques.

association between treatment outcome and the manner in which the client conceptualized and presented his problem in the initial interview. Failure cases tended to intellectualize and discussed external manifestations of internal difficulties. Successfully treated cases, on the other hand, tended to deal with feelings in the therapeutic relationship and were eager to discover how they were contributing to their inner difficulties. No doubt, the second group was considered more suitable by the client-centered therapists. While it cannot be proven, it is entirely possible that those patients who felt they could be helped by client-centered therapy (and by client-centered therapists) continued to work on their problems, whereas those who did not, dropped out. One may also speculate that the therapist's motivation to help the latter group of patients, for a variety of reasons, was less. Thus, the therapist's attitude toward the patient may reinforce corresponding attitudes in the patient, leading to premature termination of therapy. There is no implication that this phenomenon is restricted to one form of therapy or to any one stage of therapy; however, the judgment of therapeutic failure, premature termination, therapeutic impasse, poor motivation for therapy, and the like, wherever it occurs, may signal an unwillingness or inability on the part of the therapist to work with a particular patient as much as it reflects limiting factors within the patient.

Empirical evidence bearing upon this problem has been adduced by our research group in a series of studies dealing with therapists' perceptions of patients, clinical judgments, treatment plans, and therapeutic communications. In some of these studies therapists were presented with a sound film of a therapeutic interview (Strupp, 1958); in others, they based their evaluations on patients seen in diagnostic interviews (Strupp & Williams, 1960); in still others, we presented therapists with written case histories (Wallach & Strupp, 1960). The findings have been remarkably congruent, and are corroborated by similar studies in the literature. Certain systematic differences in therapist responses were traceable to such variables as level of experience, theoretical orientation, and personal analysis. However, in all investigations the therapist's attitude toward the patient as rated by himself showed a highly significant statistical relationship to his clinical judgments and treatment plans, and, where we obtained such data, to the emotional tone of his communications. In recent studies, an item which inquired whether the therapist felt warmly toward the patient proved particularly predictive.

For example: negative attitudes toward the patient were found to be correlated with a more unfavorable diagnosis and prognosis; with recommendations for greater strictness and activity on the part of the therapist; with recommendations for less frequent interviews; with greater unwillingness to treat him, etc. The reverse was also true.

With regard to the therapists' communications, there was a significant relationship between the degree of empathy shown toward the patient and the therapist's self-rated attitude, such that therapists who felt more positively toward the patient also communicated with him more empathically. The variable of personal analysis entered into this statistical relationship in a very interesting way: if the therapist had undergone a personal analysis he was more likely to reveal a high degree of empathy in his communications irrespective of whether he described his attitude toward the patient as positive or negative. This finding was particularly pronounced for the more experienced therapists. Thus it seemed that in the case of experienced therapists their personal attitude toward the patient was less likely to influence the emotional tone of their communications to the patient provided their training had included a personal analysis; if it had not, a negative attitude tended to be associated with lack of empathy.

The implications of these findings relate to the possibility that the therapist's attitude toward the patient, as conveyed by his communications, may bring about a realization of the therapist's conscious as well as unconscious expectations concerning the course and outcome of therapy. For psychotherapy the crux of the matter is not the perceptions and clinical evaluations or even the therapist's conscious attitude toward the patient; rather it is the manner in which these variables influence and structure the therapeutic relationship. This is one of the important problems requiring further exploration.[5]

It is as yet unknown to what extent the patient may fulfill the therapist's unverbalized prophecy. This much, however, is clear: In the absence of a keen and abiding interest and dedication on the part of the therapist, the patient cannot marshal the necessary strength and energy to fight his way to a healthier adaptation, or, to use Dr. Alexander's felicitous term, he cannot undergo a corrective

[5] This discussion and the following paragraphs underscore the interdependence of "process" and "outcome" research and the importance of predictions at the beginning and throughout therapy.

emotional experience. This is particularly true in those situations in which the therapist aims at a thorough reorganization of the patient's personality by inducing him to relive his childhood traumas. Too, the infinite patience which dedicated therapists like Frieda Fromm-Reichmann, Otto Will, Harold Searles, and others have invested in therapy with schizophrenic patients bears eloquent tribute to the proposition that often therapeutic gains are commensurate with the efforts expended by the therapist, provided the patient possesses good basic personality resources.

On the experimental side, numerous studies attest that patients who appear to be motivated for psychotherapy (however the therapist understands this term) tend to be liked by therapists and the prognosis is seen as more favorable (Wallach & Strupp, 1960). Heine & Trosman (1960) have shown that mutuality of expectation is an important factor in the continuation of the therapeutic relationship. In this study, patients who continued in psychotherapy conceptualized their expectations of therapy in a manner more congruent with the therapist's role image, and may therefore have been more gratifying to the therapist. Similarly, Strupp & Williams (1960) found that patients who were judged nondefensive, insightful, likable, and well motivated for therapy were seen by therapists as most likely to improve. In the same vein, Sullivan, Miller, & Smelser (1958) summed up their findings by saying: "those persons who are least equipped to meet life challenges are the ones who stand to gain least from psychotherapy" (p. 7).

Now it may be conceded that a high level of motivation on the part of the patient as well as on the part of the therapist is auspicious for successful psychotherapy, but what about that large group of patients who fail to meet the above high criteria? What shall be done with them? Secondly, nothing has been said about a related question pertaining to the chronicity and severity of the personality disorder which the therapist is attempting to treat. Surely, no matter how highly a patient may be motivated to seek professional help and how eager he may consciously seek to do something about his difficulties, this desire may count for little if his personality structure poses insuperable difficulties to therapy.

To be sure, apart from the patient's motivation for therapy, there are clinical indicators which set limits to the therapist's best efforts. It will be recalled that Freud dealt with these most eloquently and exhaustively in his paper "Analysis Terminable and Interminable" and elsewhere. The therapist cannot perform miracles, and he cannot exceed the limits set by constitutional and hereditary factors; nor can he always undo the crippling conditions brought about by extremely adverse childhood experiences. In this dilemma the therapist has essentially two choices: (a) he can attempt to select patients whom he considers promising candidates for psychotherapy, and with whom he feels he can work productively, rejecting all other applicants; (b) he can recognize the limitations imposed by reality and do his best even if he realizes that in such instances his success may be less than spectacular. What he must not do—and here we return to the experimental findings cited earlier—is to let *irrational* personal attitudes about the treatability or nontreatability of certain patients and clinical conditions influence the best technical efforts he might otherwise put forth. At the present state of knowledge, the dividing lines between clinical indicators and limitations on the one hand, and personal attitudes of the therapist on the other, are unfortunately not as clear as one would like them to be. If they could be disentangled and assessed more objectively, the prediction of therapeutic outcomes would be markedly enhanced, and the percentage of patients who emerge from therapy as "slightly improved" or "unimproved" might dwindle further to approach that ultimate, irremediable hard core contributed by "chance."

Undoubtedly there is no simple relationship between diagnostic indicators and therapeutic outcomes, and much remains to be learned about the problem; in principle there seems to be no reason why it should not be susceptible to conceptual analysis and empirical research—the kind of "job analysis" approach which Holt proposes. Traditionally, the "classical" neurotic conditions, like hysteria, have been considered ideally suited for psychotherapy and psychoanalysis, whereas severe character disorders and the psychoses have been relegated to the opposite end of the treatability continuum of psychotherapy. Partly such judgments are based upon clinical experience; but in part they also reflect subtle value judgments about the kinds of persons with whom psychotherapists prefer to work, as well as an appraisal in socio-cultural terms of the patient's character structure and symptoms. Consequently, a patient meeting the psychotherapist's explicit as well as implicit criteria of a "good" or "promising" patient not only has a better chance of finding a competent therapist, but he may from the beginning elicit greater interest from the therapist, who in turn may become more willing to make an emotional investment in the treatment program and to devote greater energy to the treatment. It is as yet unknown to which extent the patient may fulfill the therapist's unverbalized prophecy. However, it may turn out that a great deal more can be done for certain patients psychotherapeutically once it is possible to approach them and their difficulties in living more objectively.

After many of the variables which need investigation and specification have been sorted out, we may find that only a relatively restricted band of the population meets the criteria for a "good" patient. The available evidence points to a convergent trend, which was aptly summarized by Luborsky (1959): "Those who stay in treatment improve; those who improve are better off to begin with than those who do not; and one can predict response to treatment by how well they are to begin with" (p. 324). It may be noted that the criteria of suitability which have been identified by research coincide remarkably well with those outlined much earlier by Freud. What about the much larger group of people who by these standards are unsuitable for the more common forms of psychotherapy practiced today?

From a practical point of view, the answer seems to lie not in making them more amenable to available methods of psychotherapy —sometimes this can be done, although it is a difficult and time-consuming effort—but in becoming more selective about making the limited facilities and the limited professional manpower available to those who can benefit from it the most. Rather than being "undemocratic," this appears to be a counsel of reality. Research might make an important contribution by refining the selection of particular patients for particular therapists and for particular therapeutic methods. The challenge for the development of alternative techniques and treatment methods for those who cannot readily benefit from customary psychotherapy of course continues and will have to be met. To return once again to the statistical results previously cited, there is a strong possibility that a segment of the failure or near-failure cases can be accounted for in terms of poor selection methods of candidates. In some cases it may be the better part of valor to acknowledge limitations imposed by reality, no matter how painful the consequences may be, rather than to attempt the impossible.

I shall turn next to another major stumbling block in psychotherapy research—the problem of criteria for evaluating results. Before the advent of the "modern era" in psychotherapy research, that is, before sophisticated methodologists and researchers versed in matters of objective investigation and experimental design concerned themselves with these matters, a group of prominent psychoanalysts, including such men as Fenichel, Strachey, Bibring, Bergler, and Nunberg (1937) addressed themselves to the issue. This occurred at the International Congress of Psychoanalysis at Marienbad, in 1936. While this group did not make any formal recommendation for judging outcomes, they dealt with the aims of psychoanalytic therapy and its modus operandi. Knight (1941), in a valuable paper, returned to the problem, listing three major groups of criteria, with several subheadings. Since this compilation has not been substantially improved upon, let me quote it in its entirety:

1. *Disappearance of presenting symptoms*
2. *Real improvement in mental functioning*
   a. The acquisition of insight, intellectual and emotional, into the childhood sources of conflict, the part played by precipitating and other reality factors, and the methods of defense against anxiety which have produced the type of personality and the specific character of the morbid process;
   b. Development of tolerance, without anxiety, of the instinctual drives;
   c. Development of ability to accept one's self objectively, with a good appraisal of elements of strength and weakness;
   d. Attainment of relative freedom from enervating tensions and talent-crippling inhibitions;
   e. Release of the aggressive energies needed for self-preservation, achievement, competition and protection of one's rights.
3. *Improved reality adjustment*
   a. More consistent and loyal interpersonal relationships with well-chosen objects;
   b. Free functioning of abilities in productive work;
   c. Improved sublimation in recreation and avocations;
   d. Full heterosexual functioning with potency and pleasure.

Knight, too, called attention to certain limitations, which may detract from the full effectiveness of the therapeutic method. These will be recognized as the counterparts of the "good patient" variables previously mentioned. Limitations may be due to: (1) the patient's intelligence; (2) native ability and talents; (3) physical factors, such as muscle development, size, personal attractiveness, physical anomalies, sequelae of previous injury or illness, etc.; (4) permanent crippling of the ego in infancy and childhood; (5) life and reality factors which might impose frustrations, privations, etc. against which the patient must do battle, and which might produce relapses; (6) the patient's economic status, whether there is too little or too much money.

It is apparent that Knight's enumeration of criteria goes far beyond a definition of disabling illness and in fact it attempts a definition of positive mental health. It is also clear that the objectives of psychoanalytic therapy have always aspired to this ideal, and the outcome statistics reported by the various psychoanalytic treatment centers leave no doubt on this point. As early as 1930, Fenichel stated in this connection:

We have defined the concept "cured" as rigorously as possible. We have included in this category only cases whose success involves not only symptom removal but which underwent character changes that are rationally and analytically completely understandable and which, where possible, were confirmed through follow-up. In view of this rigor, most of the cases designated as "much improved" are for practical purposes completely coordinate with the "cured" ones. "Improved" cases are those which have remained refractory in one form or another; in this category also belong those cases which for external reasons had to remain partial successes, as well as those which were discharged already in the phase of "transference cure," hence, psychoanalytically speaking they must be considered questionable (p. 19).

By contrast, Eysenck's survey implicitly adopted a much less rigorous standard, oriented around symptom removal. His compilation is a telling example of the confusion which arises when one uncritically mixes studies in which a variety of criteria, frequently unspecified, are adopted. This dilemma, however, cannot be resolved until we succeed in developing more specific empirical indicators of treatment outcomes. Among other things, this requirement entails operational definitions which can be agreed upon by independent observers. For example, there may be reasonable agreement on the meaning of "symptomatic recovery," but a moment's reflection will reveal the difficulties inherent in such judgments as "increased productiveness" or "achievement of sufficient insight to handle ordinary psychological conflicts and reasonable reality stresses."

Knight seems to take it for granted that the evaluations are to be made by the therapist. While it may be conceded that the therapist's knowledge of the patient's psyche is second to none, and that therefore he is in a unique position to perform the evaluative task, it must be remembered that his judgment is vulnerable on a number of grounds, including his personal involvement as well as the necessarily segmental view which he obtains of the patient's life.

In an effort to objectify the therapist's observations many attempts have been made during the last two decades to develop measures of the patient's intratherapy behavior. These have usually taken the form of quantifying aspects of his verbal behavior in therapy. Another large group of studies has followed the phenomenological approach, by asking the patient to evaluate his own status. A third approach has dealt with assessments by means of psychological tests. Zax and Klein (1960), following a review of several hundred investigations, conclude that the most serious failing of these approaches is that the criterion measures have not been systematically related to externally observable behavior in the life space of the patients. Their own proposed solution is to develop:

criteria of sufficient breadth that they are meaningful and representative of a wide range of functioning and yet, at the same time, circumscribed enough to be measured with reliability (p. 445).

They go on to say that the development of such criteria is in its infancy, largely because there is no unifying set of principles (a theory of "normal" behavior) to guide observations. Finally, they express the hope that it might be possible to develop "a relatively limited number of norms reflecting basic interpersonal environments which can be useful." The basic problem here seems to be one of bridging the gap between the person's inner psychic experience and his adaptation to an interpersonal environment.

Clearly, there can be no single criterion of mental health or illness. As Jahoda's (1958) excellent review of current concepts points out, mental health is an individual and personal matter; it varies with the time, place, culture and expectations of the social group; it is one of many human values; and it should differentiate between the person's enduring attributes and particular actions. One value prominent in American culture is that the individual should be able to stand on his own two feet without making undue demands or impositions on others.

From the research point of view, Jahoda discerns six major approaches to the subject:

1. Attitudes of the individual toward himself.
2. Degree to which a person realizes his potentialities through action (growth, development, self-actualization).
3. Unification of function in the individual's personality (integration).
4. Individual's degree of independence of social influences (autonomy).
5. How the individual sees the world around him (perception of reality).
6. Ability to take life as it comes and master it (environmental mastery).

In her searching and incisive discussion of the directions for further research Jahoda clearly indicates that we must develop better empirical indicators of positive mental health in all of the above areas; beyond this it is necessary to specify the conditions under which it is acquired and maintained. The development of outcome criteria in psychotherapy largely overlaps these requirements and must follow a similar course. The patient's behavior in therapy will scarcely suffice as an ultimate criterion, but it will occupy a central position in the cluster of criteria which will undoubtedly emerge. The therapy situation is a unique "test situation" in this respect, whose rich potentialities we have barely begun to exploit. I should like to outline briefly some of the unique advantages as well as some of the limitations.

1. By virtue of its particular structure, the therapeutic situation, and particularly the psychoanalytic situation, removes the conventional restraints in interpersonal communication and makes it possible to observe the patient's "real" feelings and emotional reactions with a minimum of distortions.

2. By inducing regression it uncovers invaluable data about the patient's most enduring patterns of interpersonal relatedness and facilitates the tracing of their genetic development.

3. It provides a penetrating view of the patient's motivational patterns, the manner in which basic strivings are bound intrapsychically, adapted to, and translated into action. Such microscopic observations are carried out over extensive periods of time. Thus it is possible to trace the relationship between an action and its underlying motivation, and to gain considerable information about the

mediating processes. Hence the therapeutic situation avoids a frequent error in psychological research, namely the assumption of an invariant relationship between a behavioral act and the person's underlying motivation.

4. The therapeutic situation simulates an appropriately complex situation and thus meets the objections of oversimplification and artificiality frequently levelled against experimental analogues. (It has been said that the therapeutic situation represents a highly personal situation within a highly impersonal framework.)

5. In the therapeutic situation, the therapist gains important insights into the patient's inner experience, the manner in which he perceives himself, and his self-concept; but he also can assess the patient's social stimulus value—at least in relation to the therapist as a representative of the social environment, and observe discrepancies between inner experience and outward actions. Usually we are restricted in our knowledge of the other person and we can only make inferences from his actions, his verbal communications, and clues we get from his unwitting behavior. In individual therapy, by contrast, the patient himself, through the agency of his observing ego, adds important data about his inner experience to the aforementioned ones. Thus a unique, panoramic view is obtained.[6]

6. The therapeutic situation yields unique data on the manner in which a particular input (clarification, interpretation, etc.) is perceived, experienced, and reacted to on verbal as well as nonverbal levels. Thus, we may gain considerable information about the manner in which an external stimulus is perceived and experienced, and we may note discrepancies between the "objective" aspects of the stimulus (at least as seen by the therapist) and the way in which it is experienced by the patient.

These are some examples to indicate the variety of ways in which the psychotherapeutic situation provides criteria—which in part have their own validity—about human mental functioning. But we demand that intratherapeutic criteria have a counterpart in the external world, that is, a validity beyond the therapeutic situation. It is noteworthy that in the various mental health criteria enumerated by Jahoda the therapeutic situation plays an important part in gathering

---

[6] Although it adds other complexities, group psychotherapy provides more than one representative of the social environment; and it permits the patient to test his motives, actions, inner processes, etc. against the background of the feelings of others.

more precise empirical indicators. It is my thesis, then, that the therapeutic situation itself should be used to a much greater extent than has been heretofore the case to generate and develop criteria of outcome. This conclusion follows from the belief that nowhere else do we have an opportunity to make as penetrating, intensive, systematic, and undistorted observations as in the therapeutic setting.[7] Furthermore, it is in keeping with one of the major working hypotheses of psychoanalysis, that the patient's relationship to the therapist (the transference) is the most faithful replica of the patient's capacity for intimate interpersonal relatedness; as a corollary it states that the patient's adaptation to his human environment outside the therapeutic situation "improves," that is, becomes less conflictual, and more satisfying to the extent that he is able to relate more effectively (in less conflictual ways) to the therapist. The skilled therapist is keenly aware of the shifts in the patient's patterns of relatedness (to him), and he regards them as sensitive indicators of therapeutic change and improvement. What I am advocating, then, is that as researchers we attempt to systematize and objectify these intratherapeutic observations and, wherever possible, relate them to the patient's interpersonal performances outside therapy.

In making this recommendation I am placing major emphasis upon the therapy situation as a miniature life situation, and I am stressing the alignment of psychic forces rather than specific behavioral acts in the outside world. This view is predicted on the (testable) assumption that there is a close association between the quality of the patient's relationship to the therapist and the quality of his relationships with others, including his adaptation to reality. I am also suggesting that the therapist, because he is in possession of incomparably fuller data about the patient's personality, is potentially in a superior position to assess the patient's "mental health." No therapist would maintain that the patient's behavior with close associates or his mastery of life's problems is unimportant, but he is probably correct in insisting that he (in collaboration with

[7] This recommendation is far from original. Already a quarter of a century ago, in the first five-year report of the Chicago Psychoanalytic Institute, Dr. Alexander (1937) concluded that the analyst and the patient are in the best position to judge the actual progress made and the weights to be assigned to analytic insight and the altered life situation in evaluating the therapeutic result. Unfortunately, very little has been done in the interim to design objective research investigations embodying this insight.

the patient) is better equipped to assess the patient's success in living than outsiders irrespective of the degree of their sophistication.

Among the difficulties of using the therapeutic situation as a criterion-generating situation we must note: (1) the problem of conceptualizing, specifying, and quantifying the multidimensional observations made in therapy; (2) the therapist's reliability as an observer (by which is meant more than countertransference); and (3) limitations inherent in the two-person setting, which provide representative, but incomplete, data about the patient's interactions with others. Because of the transference relationship, the therapist tends to get a more or less distorted perspective of the patient's current reality functioning and to some extent he is forced to accept the patient's view of reality, although he will generally be able to make appropriate corrections.

These recommendations, which need to be spelled out in much greater detail before they can be translated into research operations, are in keeping with my conviction that the transference situation, as defined by Freud, is the richest source for observing and studying interpersonal data, and that it has a unique validity of its own. Nowhere else is it possible to study interpersonal processes as systematically, intensively, deeply, and with as much control over extraneous influences. The task for the future is to find ways and means for ordering and quantifying the observations, and to aid the human observer in dealing more systematically and more objectively with the complex data in his auditory-visual field. "Validation" cannot come from experimental analogues and similar devices, and a naive faith in their seeming objectivity may merely serve to deprive us of the potentialities inherent in the transference relationship.

REFERENCES

ALEXANDER, F. *Five Year Report of the Chicago Institute for Psychoanalysis, 1932–1937.*

EYSENCK, H. J. The effects of psychotherapy: an evaluation. *J. consult. Psychol.,* 1952, *16,* 319–324.

FENICHEL, O. Statistischer Bericht über die therapeutische Tätigkeit, 1920–1930. In *Zehn Jahre Berliner Psychoanalytisches Institut.* Vienna: Int. Psychoanalytischer Verlag, 1930. Pp. 13–19.

GLOVER, E., FENICHEL, O., STRACHEY, J., BERGLER, E., NUNBERG, N., & BIBRING, E. Symposium on the theory of the therapeutic results of psychoanalysis. *Int. J. Psychoan.,* 1937, *18,* 125–189.

HEINE, R. W., & TROSMAN, H. Initial expectations of the doctor-patient interaction as a factor in continuance in psychotherapy. *Psychiatry*, 1960, *23*, 275–278.

HOLT, R. R. Clinical *and* statistical prediction: a reformulation and some new data. *J. abn. soc. Psychol.*, 1958, *56*, 1–12.

JAHODA, MARIE. *Current Concepts of Positive Mental Health*. New York: Basic Books, 1958.

JONES, E. *Decennial Report of the London Clinic of Psychoanalysis, 1926–1936*.

KESSEL, L., & HYMAN, H. T. The value of psychoanalysis as a therapeutic procedure. *J. Amer. med. Ass.*, 1933, *101*, 1612–1615.

KIRTNER, W. L., & CARTWRIGHT, D. S. Success and failure in client-centered therapy as a function of initial in-therapy behavior. *J. consult. Psychol.*, 1958, *22*, 329–333.

KNIGHT, R. P. Evaluation of the results of psychoanalytic therapy. *Amer. J. Psychiat.*, 1941, *98*, 434–446.

LUBORSKY, L. Psychotherapy. In P. R. Farnsworth (Ed.), *Annu. Rev. Psychol.*, 1959, vol. 10, 317–344.

STRUPP, H. H. The psychotherapist's contribution to the treatment process. *Behav. Sci.*, 1958, *3*, 34–67.

STRUPP, H. H., & WILLIAMS, JOAN V. Some determinants of clinical evaluations of different psychiatrists. *Arch. gen. Psychiat.*, 1960, *2*, 434–440.

SULLIVAN, P. L., MILLER, CHRISTINE, & SMELSER, W. Factors in length of stay and progress in psychotherapy. *J. consult. Psychol.*, 1958, *22*, 1–9.

WALLACH, M. S., & STRUPP, H. H. Psychotherapists' clinical judgments and attitudes towards patients. *J. consult. Psychol.*, 1960, *24*, 316–323.

ZAX, M., & KLEIN, A. Measurement of personality and behavior changes following psychotherapy. *Psychol. Bull.*, 1960, *57*, 435–448.

....

The Mystery-Mastery Complex
in Contemporary Psychology* [1]

DAVID BAKAN

THE PURPOSE OF this paper is to identify what may be called the mystery-mastery complex in contemporary psychology, and to discuss its significance. I believe that it is this complex which is one of the major forces interfering with our understanding of the nature of human personality, and it is for this reason that it deserves attention. The complex of which I speak consists in the simultaneous pursuit of two objectives: (*a*) to keep the nature of human personality from being understood, to preserve it under a cloak of mystery; and (*b*) to master, or predict and control, the behavior of human beings. Put in this way, it is clear that the two objectives—to keep the nature of the psyche a mystery and master human behavior—are incompatible with each other. What I will try to show in this paper is that a good deal of the methodological juggling which psychologists have engaged in arises out of the attempt to serve these two objectives at the same time. I will also indicate that the mystery-mastery complex which we find in the field of psychology is related to the mystery-mastery complex of the total culture. I will also indicate that there are factors concerning psychology and society which call for the abandonment of the mystery-mastery complex.

The objective of maintaining the psyche in a shroud of mystery can be seen as being rooted both in the nature of the psyche itself, and within certain cultural forces which have tended to reinforce this tendency within the psyche. In the microcosm of the clinical situation this has been identified as repression, where the individual hides his own nature from himself, and resistance, where the indi-

* From the *American Psychologist*, 1965, *20*, 186–191.
[1] This paper, originally entitled "Cultural Inhibitions to a Science of Personality," was presented in a symposium on "Toward a Science of Human Personality," American Psychological Association, Los Angeles, September 1964.

vidual hides his nature from the psychoanalyst. One of the important things which we have learned from the research of the psychoanalysts is that these two forms of mystery keeping are intimately intertwined with each other. The uses of mystery have been amply documented in the psychoanalytic literature, in which mystery has been recognized as a primary defense against insult or injury from within or without.

Perhaps less profound but equally important is the role of mystery, or better, secrecy in all interpersonal relations. In the social spheres one of the major defenses that the individual has, even if it does not entail self-deception as in the case of the individuals involved in the clinical situation, is the keeping of secrets—the secret of his state of affairs, or the secrets of his intentions. We all recognize that in the social, political, economic, and military spheres knowledge of the secrets of others gives one the "advantage," and that discretion, in the sense of revealing only what one wishes to reveal, is valuable both in protecting ourselves from others and in manipulating others. Whereas mystery is the protection against the mastery impulse of others, it is also an objective which must be suspended for thoroughgoing mastery. Because in our total society we would be both masters and yet unmastered, we walk the complicated path of pursuing both the objectives of mystery and mastery.

Certain features of the growth of modern society, in particular the growth of urbanization and industrialization of the nineteenth and twentieth centuries, have worked to encourage the mystery-mastery complex. An outstanding characteristic of these modern developments has been the bringing together into significant interactions persons who were strangers. It is precisely in the interaction among strangers that both mystery and mastery become significant, the former being the *initial condition,* the latter the *issue* among strangers. Ideologically and culturally it was the Protestant ethic, as Max Weber described it (Weber, 1958), which entered as a major support to the mystery-mastery complex. Weber has shown that it was a significant feature in the development of the contemporary world, and David McClelland (1961) has piled up great quantities of data to show its working in the society of today. The Protestant ethic was associated with an intense psychological separation of individual from individual. It had a theology which suggested that the thoughts, feelings, and wishes of each individual were a matter between himself and God alone, and not a matter for another man to concern himself with. It tended to substitute formal and contractual forms of relationship for intimate interpsychic contact. A too great interest in the inner life of another person not only exceeded the bounds of formal relationship, but was also a reminder of the odious Confessional of the Catholic Church. At the same time the Protestant ethic was associated with a vaulting thrust to master the world through industry and through science.[2]

Psychology emerged in the modern world simultaneously with the growth of modern industrialization and urbanization; and this context can help us to understand the developments within our discipline. Thus, for example, this context helps us to understand the emergence on the American scene of its two major psychologies, behaviorism and psychoanalysis. Behaviorism fully deferred to the ideology by dramatically announcing its lack of interest in the psyche, thus insuring that the psyche would remain shrouded in mystery on the assumption that it did not exist, or that it was not subject to scientific investigation. At the same time it committed itself to the mastery objective by announcing that "prediction and control" were its ends. Psychoanalysis, on the other hand, ruthlessly violated the taboo on the mystery of the psyche. Its career in the United States has been very vigorous, but also kind of underworldly. Its major supporters have been the rebels against the alienation associated with modern urban-industrial society, the pockets of resistance among artists, writers, and some intellectuals. Even today, psychoanalysis has not been given much official recognition in the academic institutions. It has received its principal publicity from the popular press and the arts—and the use of psychoanalysis in therapy has been a highly guarded enterprise, and not that widespread. It might be pointed out parenthetically that Rogerian psychotherapy, which has been much more palatable than psychoanalysis in many respects, dealt gingerly with the unveiling of the mystery of the psyche, and has compensated for its small degree of violating the taboo on mystery by simultaneously denouncing the mastery objective, calling itself "nondirective."

It was difficult for psychology, in the simple etymological sense of the term as the study of the psyche, to develop in the larger mystery-mastery context of our society. The great uneasiness, which has been characteristic of psychology, about its status among the

---

[2] Cf. Merton (1936), who shows the intimate relationship between the Protestant ethic and science.

disciplines can be understood as rooted in the awkwardness of fit between its intrinsic objective of understanding the psyche and the mystery-mastery complex. The major point of this paper is that the art of research became to a considerable extent the art of finding a way between the taboo on penetrating the mystery of psychological functioning and the at least symbolic fulfillment of the mastery objective. In order to clarify this let us consider five different but related features which characterize a good deal of the contemporary research enterprise. Each one of these features manages to help the psychologist in living within the mystery-mastery paradox by somehow appearing to serve both of the objectives.

These features are as follows:

1. The scientist-subject distinction
2. The definition of psychology as the study of behavior
3. The choice of lower animals, particularly domesticated animals, as subjects-of-choice in research
4. The specification of the aim of research as the discovery of "laws"
5. The cultural norm that research consists of the testing of pre-conceived hypotheses

I must at this point say that I do not mean to suggest anything so foolish or dogmatic as that these features cannot or have not served to increase our understanding. I in no way wish to disparage the excellent research which has been going on for what is now almost a century. However, I would suggest that a good deal of the understanding which we have won has been through processes which go beyond those suggested by these five features. It is perhaps because psychologists are sensible people in addition to their being possessed of certain methodological tenets that our understanding has been enhanced. It is when psychologists allow themselves to go beyond the scientist-subject distinction, beyond the definition of psychology purely as behavior, beyond lower animals, beyond the presumptive regularities of the laws, and beyond the restriction of research to the testing of hypotheses that discoveries concerning the nature of and functioning of the human psyche have been revealed. If these features in some way constitute the "scientific superego" of psychologists, as I think they often do, then it is in the violation or circumvention of this scientific superego that our total investigatory enterprise has been advanced.

Let me comment briefly on each of these features, and try to point out the way in which they attempt to serve both mystery and mastery:

1. The scientist-subject distinction is often a euphemism for manipulator-manipulated in many research situations. Insofar as the methodological literature on this distinction allows for the existence of the psyche at all, it confounds the issue by presuming at least two different kinds of psyche. It ascribes autonomy, methodicalness, and rationality—which are, by the way, characteristics of Weber's Protestant capitalist—to the one, but rarely to the other. In the methodological literature this is formulated in terms of two "languages," one that the scientist uses in discussing the phenomena, and one which is a "protocol language" used by subjects. If, for example, one might try to understand the nature of the research enterprise by bringing to bear findings concerning the growth of thought, the methodological "sophisticate" cries out "genetic fallacy" as though he were an umpire yelling "foul!" The concept of such two languages characteristically makes the scientist and the subject strangers to each other—a strangeness which, as we have already said, is the underlying condition of the mystery-mastery complex in the first place. In the experimental situation the scientist is the master, the subject the one who is mastered. By the studied ignorance of the meaning of the subject's protocol language the scientist guarantees that he will not enter upon the psyche of the subject. Not that the scientist will not learn something *about* the subject's protocol language; but he will not allow himself to think what the subject's protocol language is really *about*.

2. The definition of psychology as the study of behavior is perhaps the outstanding device whereby the two objectives of mystery of the psyche and mastery are served. It rules out the psyche by *fiat,* and thus guarantees that it is not a fit area for investigation. At the same time it takes as its central concern that which the mastery objective is most critically interested in, the behavior of the other person. For being able to master another person means to master his behavior, to make him act in accordance with the master's wishes.

3. The use of animals as subjects-of-choice in much investigation is particularly interesting from this point of view. The muteness of animals insures that they will not complicate the situation with reports on their thoughts or feelings or wishes. An additional factor

is that psychologists have tended to choose *domestic* animals. Domestic animals are animals which are already given to, selected, and bred for their docility and tractability; i.e., they are easily mastered. The work of the ethologists, of course, represents a significant deviation from this, and should be cited to demonstrate that domesticity of animals is not a prerequisite for their being useful in psychological research.

4. The notion that the aim of psychology is the discovery of laws can be illuminated by an observation which was made by a student of Machiavelli. In a book called *The Statecraft of Machiavelli* Herbert Butterfield (1940) says that the thrust to control other people entails the assumption of an unchanging nature of those who are to be controlled. As has been pointed out by Max Planck (1937), the eminent physicist, and others, such control is also premised on the assumption that those who are being controlled are ignorant of the presumptive regularities that the controller is aware of. This is not the place to enter into a discussion of the various problems associated with the notion of "law." Yet, it should be pointed out that although empirical data have often compromised the notion, it has had a remarkable stubbornness, a stubbornness even greater among psychologists than physicists. The stubbornness of the notion inheres, we believe, in the way in which it appears to serve the two objectives of mystery and mastery. The service of the mastery objective is patent. The mystery is preserved by formulating these laws on the basis of research in which the information concerning the presumptive regularities are concealed from the subjects, and by never allowing a theoretical place for the knowledge of these regularities as factors in human functioning. One of the most ubiquitous fears of investigators is that the human subjects will not be "naive," i.e., that they might be aware of the nature of the phenomenon under investigation. Few things can mess up research as can the subject having read the relevant literature for the study. Put another way we can say that there is a *fact* concerning human functioning that is rarely taken into account: that *human beings make use of their generalizations concerning the nature of human functioning in their functioning*. This is one of the factors involved in the mystery of the psyche which is systematically excluded in the search for laws.

5. I would like to preface what I have to say about the notion of research as the testing of preconceived hypotheses with the observation that there are, in the normal training of the contemporary

psychologist, two important moments in his educational career. The first, which characteristically takes place in his first course in psychology, is when he learns that he should not be interested in mind. Frequently this lesson is learned from a dialogue that the instructor has with the class in the early days of the term. The instructor asks the class what they think psychology is. Before long some student who is proud to be able to show off his primitive knowledge of Greek says that it is the study of the mind. This is the opening that the instructor has been waiting for: "O.K.! What is mind?" The answers which he gets are easily demolished, and then the students are properly prepared. Since we "obviously" do not know what we are talking about when we use the word "mind," why do we not just forget about it, and go on with the study of psychology! The latter consists in large part in bringing the students around to accepting the five features which I have outlined. The second important moment comes early in his graduate career when he learns that research consists in the testing of hypotheses! Curiosity, interest in the phenomena, or even the complex psychodynamics associated with the getting of hypotheses, are brushed aside, or, at best, are regarded as "private processes," about which the least said the better. What the student desperately needs is a *testable hypothesis,* and it is perfectly all right to beg one, borrow one, steal one. What testability in fact consists of is the enumeration of a set of alternatives. The function of the data-collecting process is simply to choose among the alternatives which have been previously conceived of. A good deal of the burden has fallen on "significant" or "not significant," a difference which, as we are painfully becoming aware, is itself not that significant. Again, I must qualify. There is nothing intrinsically wrong with testing hypotheses. It is an important part of the total investigatory enterprise. What I do wish to point out, however, is that by the time the investigatory enterprise has reached the stage of testing hypotheses, most of the important work, if there has been any, has already been done. One is tempted to think that psychologists are often like children playing cowboys. When children play cowboys they emulate them in everything but their main work, which is taking care of cows. The main work of the scientist is thinking and making discoveries of what was not thought of beforehand. Psychologists often attempt to "play scientist" by avoiding the main work.

The elevation of the hypothesis-testing stage to the point where it is conceived of as practically the entire investigatory enterprise is in the service of the mystery-mastery complex. The *pre*conception of the alternatives, and the disciplined limitation of the investigation to them, cuts out the possibility of *surprise,* the learning of something which was not thought of beforehand. (We might point out parenthetically that a good deal of the bickering which has been going on in the literature concerning the use of one-tailed or two-tailed tests hangs precisely on the question as to whether the alternative involving the one-tailed test was *thought of before or after* the time when the data were collected.) The obligation to preconceive the alternatives tends to preserve the mystery of the psyche, by eliminating what is not "proper." To put this in another way, our ideal of research is more in terms of *confirmation* than *discovery.* The mastery objective is served by selection of preconceived alternatives which fulfill it, and elimination of others. This part of the process is hardly acknowledged, hardly evaluated, and hardly the object of critical thought. It is, so to speak, "free"; and insofar as it is free it becomes the likely locus for the operation of the psychological and cultural factors which bind us, and of which we are unaware. For, as we have learned from the various investigations concerning the nature of free responses in projective testing and the like, that which is free is that which is the result of our deepest predilections. To put this yet another way, our deep penchant for "control" of variables in our research enterprise is the facade for our penchant for mastery, not only of the variables in the limited sense in which we use this term, but in the larger sense of the control of the behavior of others. In the interests of control in research, we *select* such sets of alternatives which promise the greatest degree of control of the behavior of those whom we study.

The dynamic associated with the two objectives of mystery and mastery is such that they tend to reinforce each other in spite of the contradiction between them. If the psyche is to be maintained as a mystery, then one is pressed into mastery by default. If one moves to uncover the mystery of the psyche in a condition of interpersonal alienation, then there is an intensification of mystery as a defense. Our clinical experience has made us aware of the way in which an amalgam of mutually reinforcing contradictions can inhibit the psychological growth of the individual. The mystery-mastery complex is the neurotic core of the contemporary psychological research enterprise. This complex of mystery and mastery may not, perhaps, inhibit the multiplication of research papers (although, I am sure that it even does this for some psychologists) as a kind of "repetition compulsion," but it does inhibit the genuine growth of our collective understanding of the nature of human functioning. For understanding necessarily entails the suspension of the taboo on mystery.

But, one may ask, why, if this mystery-mastery complex of which I have been speaking appears to keep at least some of us in motion, should we abandon it? In order to answer this question we need to move to considerations concerning the relationship of psychology to the society at large. I have already indicated that the mystery-mastery complex in psychology is a reflection of the same complex in the larger society, that it is an expression within our science of the same factors which were associated with the development of urbanization and industrialization, i.e., with the making of the modern world.

My answer to this question hinges on the fact that the world is changing, and changing in such a way that psychology has a new and important place in it. Insofar as psychology still maintains the mystery-mastery complex it is participating in the phenomenon of "cultural lag." The mystery-mastery complex has been an important feature in the total development of the society to the present point, but it is rapidly becoming archaic in terms of the changes which are taking place in the larger society itself. The crises of our contemporary society—the cold war, the possibility of nuclear warfare, the problems of educating masses of people, the problems of the interaction of alien cultures, the problems of the underdeveloped nations—all call for an understanding by human beings of each other at a considerably higher level than ever before; and neither mystery nor mastery are sensible objectives anymore.

It may be very bold to attempt to characterize our total society in a few sentences. Yet one can reasonably say that there are two major commitments to which we have come in the last few decades. First, there is the commitment of men to live *with* each other in highly complex interrelationships; and the network of interrelationships continues to enlarge so that before long every person alive on the face of the earth will in someway be related to every other person. Second, there is the commitment of mankind to manage its own affairs. We no longer trust to fate, destiny, "the invisible hand of God" (as Adam Smith put it), unguided natural law, or some single authoritarian "master." It is man in general who is to manage things.

These two commitments tend to make the two objectives of mystery and mastery archaic. We need to understand our own psyches and the psyches of others; we need to stop being strangers to each other. And the mastery of man over man is increasingly intolerable, untolerated, and futile.

For several centuries it has been the physical scientist who has been important in connection with the major social developments. It is from the knowledge gleaned by the physical scientist that great cities and factories were made possible. I believe that what the physical scientists have been to the world in the past, the social scientists will be to the world of the future. As the physical scientists have made it possible to modify the world to increase its habitability, the social scientists will serve the two commitments which I have mentioned.

Yet it would be wrong for the psychologist to enter upon the larger scene in precisely the same social role that the physical scientist has. The knowledge of the physical scientist becomes socially significant as it is mediated, applied, and used in design of processes and equipment. His knowledge of heat, or electricity, or mechanics becomes significant as it is used in making devices of which we avail ourselves without necessarily understanding the nature of heat or electricity or mechanics. The physical scientist was able to turn his knowledge into use *without teaching* us what he knew. But the value of understanding of human functioning *does not inhere in its application in the usual sense, but in its possession.* This is one of the most significant results of the clinical enterprise. In order to help a person who is in psychological difficulties we work to enhance his understanding of himself, and of his relationships to others. If we think in terms of traditional social roles, then the significant place in society of the psychologist will be more that of *teacher* than expert or technician. In order for the psychologist to play a useful social role, it is important that he work to uncover the mystery of the psyche and *teach* people to understand themselves and each other. In this way they can be helped to live with each other, and manage their affairs effectively.

The psychologist is not intrinsically different from other people. All people seek to understand themselves and others in the course of their lives; and all people continually attempt to bring to bear such generalizations in the management of their lives. The special character of the psychologist inheres only in the intensity and systematic nature of his search. The special responsibility that he has is to teach what he learns.

I would like to bring this discussion to a close with an anecdote. Not too long ago a very able graduate student told me that he had decided to leave school, and that he no longer wanted to be a psychologist. I was very much taken aback by this. He was bright, doing well, and was receiving a good stipend. In the course of conversation he made one remark which spoke of his deep feelings about psychology. He told me that he did not want to become a "hollow man," and that he was afraid that if he stayed he would become one. As he spoke I recalled a discussion which we had had about the concept of the "empty organism," and it occurred to me that this may well be a metaphorical projection of the state into which we were trying to discipline our young psychologists. For the mystery-mastery complex forces a conception of hollowness upon both scientist and subject as it tries to keep them apart.

In this discussion, I have presumed one of my conclusions: that the scientist-subject distinction is a reflection of the mystery-mastery complex, and that the mystery-mastery complex needs to be abandoned in favor of understanding. I would like to think that the position that I am advancing is in line with the injunction for psychology to become more *operationistic*. I do not mean this term in the sense in which it is characteristically used by psychologists, but rather in its original sense that we need to be more aware of the factors associated with the knowledge-getting processes. We need to become much more aware of the operation of psychological and cultural factors in our own research operations, for they largely constitute the operations of our investigatory work. What we ordinarily call methodology needs to be expanded to include the culture and psychology of psychologists. By allowing this to happen we can both avoid becoming hollow men and relate more meaningfully to the culture at large.

REFERENCES

BUTTERFIELD, H. *The Statecraft of Machiavelli.* London: B. G. Bell, 1940.

McCLELLAND, D. C. *The Achieving Society.* Princeton, N.J.: Van Nostrand, 1961.

MERTON, R. K. Puritanism, pietism and science. *Sociological Review,* 1936, *28*, 1–30.

PLANCK, M. *The Universe in the Light of Modern Physics.* (Trans. by W. H. Johnston) London: Allen & Unwin, 1937.

WEBER, M. *The Protestant Ethic and the Spirit of Capitalism.* (Trans. by Talcott Parsons) New York: Scribner's, 1958.

PART THREE

Professional Identity and Direction

THE FIRST TWO sections have dealt primarily with issues relating to conceptualizations, procedures, and content areas in clinical psychology. The unifying thread discernible in most of the articles presented has been the recognition of the legitimacy and necessity of including psychologist-related variables and influences in our understanding of psychological phenomena. Whether functioning as diagnostician, therapist, researcher, teacher, or any other role the clinician enters into the pattern of events determining what particular outcome will ensue or be recognized. The editors have referred to the clinician as perhaps the most crucial clinical instrument, in view of his potential for self-awareness and selective variability in the course of the clinical interaction. It is pertinent to consider some of the broader situational influences which have bearing on the effectiveness with which this instrument operates. Perhaps of central importance is the psychologist's self-perception. How adequately he will be able to make use of his capacities in adapting to or more actively shaping the ever changing pattern of cultural needs and attitudes will be largely contingent upon how he defines his own identity and role. At this point in the development of clinical psychology identity and role perceptions are in flux.

The papers included in this final section reflect the complexity and plurality of the problems faced in the struggle for a new self-definition appropriate to the times. Fortunately, there is now a sufficient sense of historical perspective to at least view some of psychology's past successes and failures against a larger background of experience, a background that includes more than parochial intraprofessional concerns. There can be no underestimating the profound impact of the immense technological and social changes of recent years, an impact absorbed throughout the entire fabric of our culture. Perhaps it is the recognition that the identity crisis in clinical psychology is but one facet in a larger flux, and that the trend is toward positive resolution and integration, that permits the generally optimistic tone of the discussion presented. One can discern a sense of excitement and opportunity even where resolution is not yet evident. The view, even where the focus is on current problems of considerable dimension, is toward fulfillment of potential.

Each of the seven discussions presented is in a sense both a personal and public document. Each clearly reflects the deep commitment of the writer and not a little of the anguish which commitment imparts to reflection of this type. While each contributes the benefit of his unique interest and experience, the core problems overlap. Rogers deals primarily with what has usually been perceived as two disparate approaches to comprehension of another person, the scientific and the experiential (what has also been referred to in other contexts as the objective and subjective approaches). He explores the apparent dissonance of these two approaches and offers a resolution which bridges the gap by focusing on the person who can be both scientist and clinician—who can experience and react through diverse yet integrated modes. Wyatt searches for a definition of the clinical identity, for the effective core of the clinical attitude, in the light of some of psychology's developmental vicissitudes and the multiple connotations of the clinical concept. The contributions of Hathaway, Garfield, and Sanford explore some contemporary problems germane to the clinician's present and future identity and role. Each writer presents, in the light of relevant historical data and consistent with his own perspective, his views with respect to various salient problems created or rearoused by recent shifts in cultural attitudes and social needs. Among the questions raised, evaluated, and responded to are: What should be the direction of clinical training? To what form of identity should training be oriented, and to what level of social need? What should be the appropriate relation between professional values and public pressures? This latter issue is dealt with in sharper focus by Messick, in relation to the growing evidence of public concern about psychological assessment procedures on the basis of invasion of privacy. The implications of the psychologist's possible conflict of commitment is this area has obvious repercussions in other areas of psychological activity. With respect to these and other dilemmas it is essential that the clinician be informed, concerned, aware of their implications, and open to considered reflection. These papers cannot bring any answers to the individual clinician. They can only hopefully stimulate him to approach the elements of a possible answer within himself.

A.Z.G.

M.A.B.

Persons or Science?
A Philosophical Question* [1]

Carl R. Rogers

THIS IS A highly personal document, written primarily for myself, to clarify an issue which has become increasingly puzzling. It will be of interest to others only to the extent that the issue exists for them. I shall therefore describe first something of the way in which the paper grew.

As I have acquired experience as a therapist, carrying on the exciting, rewarding experience of psychotherapy, and as I have worked as a scientific investigator to ferret out some of the truth about therapy, I have become increasingly conscious of the gap between these two roles. The better therapist I have become (as I believe I have), the more I have been vaguely aware of my complete subjectivity when I am at my best in this function. And as I have become a better investigator, more "hardheaded" and more scientific (as I believe I have) I have felt an increasing discomfort at the distance between the rigorous objectivity of myself as scientist and the almost mystical subjectivity of myself as therapist. This paper is the result.

What I did first was to let myself go as therapist, and describe, as well as I could do in a brief space, what is the essential nature of psychotherapy as I have lived it with many clients. I would stress the fact that this is a very fluid and personal formulation, and that if it were written by another person, or if it were written by me two years ago, or two years hence, it would be different in some respects. Then I let myself go as scientist—as tough-minded fact-finder in this psychological realm—and endeavored to picture the meaning which science can give to therapy. Following this I carried on the debate which existed in me, raising the questions which each point of view legitimately asks the other.

* From the *American Psychologist*, 1955, *10*, 267–278.
[1] Also published in *Cross Currents: A Quarterly Review*, 1953, *3*, 289–306.

When I had carried my efforts this far I found that I had only sharpened the conflict. The two points of view seemed more than ever irreconcilable. I discussed the material with a seminar of faculty and students, and found their comments very helpful. During the following year I continued to mull over the problem until I began to feel an integration of the two views arising in me. More than a year after the first sections were written I tried to express this tentative and perhaps temporary integration in words.

Thus the reader who cares to follow my struggles in this matter will find that it has quite unconsciously assumed a dramatic form —all of the dramatis personæ being contained within myself; First Protagonist, Second Protagonist, The Conflict, and finally, The Resolution. Without more ado let me introduce the first protagonist, myself as therapist, portraying as well as I can, what the *experience* of therapy seems to be.

THE ESSENCE OF THERAPY IN TERMS OF ITS EXPERIENCE

I launch myself into the therapeutic relationship having a hypothesis, or a faith, that my liking, my confidence, and my understanding of the other person's inner world, will lead to a significant process of becoming. I enter the relationship not as a scientist, not as a physician who can accurately diagnose and cure, but as a person, entering into a personal relationship. Insofar as I see him only as an object, the client will tend to become only an object.

I risk myself, because if, as the relationship deepens, what develops is a failure, a regression, a repudiation of me and the relationship by the client, then I sense that I will lose myself, or a part of myself. At times this risk is very real, and is very keenly experienced.

I let myself go into the immediacy of the relationship where it is my total organism which takes over and is sensitive to the relationship, not simply my consciousness. I am not consciously responding in a planful or analytic way, but simply in an unreflective way to the other individual, my reaction being based (but not consciously) on my total organismic sensitivity to this other person. I live the relationship on this basis.

The essence of some of the deepest parts of therapy seems to be a unity of experiencing. The client is freely able to experience his feeling in its complete intensity, as a "pure culture," without intel-

lectual inhibitions or cautions, without having it bounded by knowledge of contradictory feelings; and I am able with equal freedom to
experience my understanding of this feeling, without any conscious
thought about it, without any apprehension or concern as to where
this will lead, without any type of diagnostic or analytic thinking,
without any cognitive or emotional barriers to a complete "letting
go" in understanding. When there is this complete unity, singleness,
fullness of experiencing in the relationship, then it acquires the "out-
of-this-world" quality which many therapists have remarked upon,
a sort of trance-like feeling in the relationship from which both the
client and I emerge at the end of the hour, as if from a deep well
or tunnel. In these moments there is, to borrow Buber's phrase, a
real "I-Thou" relationship, a timeless living in the experience which
is *between* the client and me. It is at the opposite pole from seeing
the client, or myself, as an object. It is the height of personal subjectivity.

I am often aware of the fact that I do not *know,* cognitively,
where this immediate relationship is leading. It is as though both I
and the client, often fearfully, let ourselves slip into the stream of
becoming, a stream or process which carries us along. It is the fact
that the therapist has let himself float in this stream of experience or
life previously, and found it rewarding, that makes him each time
less fearful of taking the plunge. It is my confidence that makes it
easier for the client to embark also, a little bit at a time. It often
seems as though this stream of experience leads to some goal. Probably the truer statement, however, is that its rewarding character
lies within the process itself, and that its major reward is that it
enables both the client and me, later, independently, to let ourselves
go in the process of becoming.

As to the client, as therapy proceeds, he finds that he is daring to
become himself, in spite of all the dread consequences which he is
sure will befall him if he permits himself to become himself. What
does this becoming one's self mean? It appears to mean less fear of
the organismic, nonreflective reactions which one has, a gradual
growth of trust in and even affection for the complex, varied, rich
assortment of feelings and tendencies which exist in one at the organic or organismic level. Consciousness, instead of being the watch-
man over a dangerous and unpredictable lot of impulses, of which
few can be permitted to see the light of day, becomes the comfortable

inhabitant of a richly varied society of impulses and feelings and thoughts, which prove to be very satisfactorily self-governing when not fearfully or authoritatively guarded.

Involved in this process of becoming himself is a profound experience of personal choice. He realizes that he can choose to continue to hide behind a facade, or that he can take the risks involved in being himself; that he is a free agent who has it within his power to destroy another, or himself, and also the power to enhance himself and others. Faced with this naked reality of decision, he chooses to move in the direction of being himself.

But being himself doesn't "solve problems." It simply opens up a new way of living in which there is more depth and more height in the experience of his feelings, more breadth and more range. He feels more unique and hence more alone, but he is so much more real that his relationships with others lose their artificial quality, become deeper, more satisfying, and draw more of the realness of the other person into the relationship.

Another way of looking at this process, this relationship, is that it is a learning by the client (and by the therapist, to a lesser extent). But it is a strange type of learning. Almost never is the learning notable by its complexity, and at its deepest the learnings never seem to fit well into verbal symbols. Often the learnings take such simple forms as "I *am* different from others"; "I do feel hatred for him"; "I *am* fearful of feeling dependent"; "I do feel sorry for myself"; "I am self-centered"; "I do have tender and loving feelings"; "I could be what I want to be"; etc. But in spite of their seeming simplicity these learnings are vastly significant in some new way which is very difficult to define. We can think of it in various ways. They are self-appropriated learnings, for one thing, based somehow in experience, not in symbols. They are analogous to the learning of the child who knows that "two and two make four" and who one day playing with two objects and two objects, suddenly realizes in *experience* a totally new learning, that "two and two *do* make four."

Another manner of understanding these learnings is that they are a belated attempt to match symbols with meanings in the world of feelings, an undertaking long since achieved in the cognitive realm. Intellectually, we match carefully the symbol we select with the meaning which an experience has for us. Thus I say something happened "gradually," having quickly (and largely unconsciously) reviewed such terms as "slowly," "imperceptibly," "step-by-step," etc., and rejected them as not carrying the precise shade of meaning of the experience. But in the realm of feelings, we have never learned to attach symbols to experience with any accuracy of meaning. This something which I feel welling up in myself, in the safety of an acceptant relationship—what is it? Is it sadness, is it anger, is it regret, is it sorrow for myself, is it anger at lost opportunities—I stumble around trying out a wide range of symbols, until one "fits," "feels right," seems really to match the organismic experience. In doing this type of thing the client discovers that he has to learn the language of feeling and emotion as if he were an infant learning to speak; often, even worse, he finds he must unlearn a false language before learning the true one.

Let us try still one more way of defining this type of learning, this time by describing what it is not. It is a type of learning which cannot be taught. The essence of it is the aspect of self-discovery. With "knowledge" as we are accustomed to think of it, one person can teach it to another, providing each has adequate motivation and ability. But in the significant learning which takes place in therapy, one person *cannot* teach another. The teaching would destroy the learning. Thus I might teach a client that it is safe for him to be himself, that freely to realize his feelings is not dangerous, etc. The more he learned this, the less he would have learned it in the significant, experiential, self-appropriating way. Kierkegaard regards this latter type of learning as true subjectivity, and makes the valid point that there can be no direct communication of it, or even about it. The most that one person can do to further it in another is to create certain conditions which make this type of learning *possible*. It cannot be compelled.

A final way of trying to describe this learning is that the client gradually learns to symbolize a total and unified state, in which the state of the organism, in experience, feeling, and cognition may all be described in one unified way. To make the matter even more vague and unsatisfactory, it seems quite unnecessary that this symbolization should be expressed. It usually does occur, because the client wishes to communicate at least a portion of himself to the therapist, but it is probably not essential. The only necessary aspect is the inward realization of the total, unified, immediate, "at-this-instant," state of the organism which is me. For example, to realize fully that at this moment the oneness in me is simply that "I am deeply frightened at the possibility of becoming something different" is of the essence of therapy. The client who realizes this will be quite certain to recognize and realize this state of his being when it recurs in somewhat similar form. He will also, in all probability, recognize and realize more fully some of the other existential feelings which occur in him. Thus he will be moving toward a state in which he is more truly himself. He will *be,* in more unified fashion, what he organismically *is,* and this seems to be the essence of therapy.

THE ESSENCE OF THERAPY IN TERMS OF SCIENCE

I shall now let the second protagonist, myself as scientist, take over and give his view of this same field.

In approaching the complex phenomena of therapy with the logic and methods of science, the aim is to work toward an *understanding* of the phenomena. In science this means an objective knowledge of events and of functional relationships between events. Science may also give the possibility of increased prediction of and control over these events, but this is not a necessary outcome of scientific endeavor. If the scientific aim were fully achieved in this realm, we would presumably know that, in therapy, certain elements were associated with certain types of outcomes. Knowing this it is likely that we would be able to predict that a particular instance of a therapeutic relationship would have a certain outcome (within certain probability limits) because it involved certain elements. We could then very likely control outcomes of therapy by our manipulation of the elements contained in the therapeutic relationship.

It should be clear that no matter how profound our scientific investigation, we could never by means of it discover any absolute truth, but could only describe relationships which had an increasingly high probability of occurrence. Nor could we discover any underlying reality in regard to persons, interpersonal relationships, or the universe. We could only describe relationships between observable events. If science in this field followed the course of science in other fields, the working models of reality which would emerge (in the course of theory building) would be increasingly removed from the reality perceived by the senses. The scientific description of therapy and therapeutic relationships would become increasingly *unlike* these phenomena as they are experienced.

It is evident at the outset that since therapy is a complex phenomenon, measurement will be difficult. Nevertheless "anything that exists can be measured," and since therapy is judged to be a significant relationship, with implications extending far beyond itself, the difficulties may prove to be worth surmounting in order to discover laws of personality and interpersonal relationships.

Since, in client-centered therapy, there already exists a crude theory (though not a theory in the strictly scientific sense), we have a starting point for the selection of hypotheses. For purposes of this discussion, let us take some of the crude hypotheses which can be drawn from this theory, and see what a scientific approach will do with them. We will, for the time being, omit the translation of the total theory into a formal logic which would be acceptable, and consider only a few of the hypotheses.

Let us first state three of these in their crude form.

1. Acceptance of the client by the therapist leads to an increased acceptance of self by the client.

2. The more the therapist perceives the client as a person rather than as an object, the more the client will come to perceive himself as a person rather than an object.

3. In the course of therapy an experiential and effective type of learning about self takes place in the client.

How would we go about translating each of these[2] into operational terms and how would we test the hypotheses? What would be the general outcomes of such testing?

This paper is not the place for a detailed answer to these questions, but research already carried on supplies the answers in a general way. In the case of the first hypothesis, certain devices for measuring acceptance would be selected or devised. These might be attitude tests, objective or projective, Q technique or the like. Presumably the same instruments, with slightly different instructions or mind set, could be used to measure the therapist's acceptance of the client, and the client's acceptance of self. Operationally then, the degree of therapist acceptance would be equated to a certain score

[2] I believe it is now commonly accepted that the most subjective feelings, apprehensions, tensions, satisfactions, or reactions, may be dealt with scientifically, providing only that they may be given clear-cut operational definition. William Stephenson, among others, presents this point of view forcefully (in his *Postulates of Behaviorism*) and through his Q technique, has contributed importantly to the objectification of such subjective materials for scientific study.

on this instrument. Whether client self-acceptance changed during therapy would be indicated by pre- and post-measurements. The relationship of any change to therapy would be determined by comparison of changes in therapy to changes during a control period or in a control group. We would finally be able to say whether a relationship existed between therapist acceptance and client self-acceptance, as operationally defined, and the correlation between the two.

The second and third hypotheses involve real difficulty in measurement, but there is no reason to suppose that they could not be objectively studied, as our sophistication in psychological measurement increases. Some type of attitude test or Q sort might be the instrument for the second hypothesis, measuring the attitude of therapist toward client, and of client toward self. In this case the continuum would be from objective regard of an external object to a personal and subjective experiencing. The instrumentation for hypothesis three might be physiological, since it seems likely that experiential learning has physiologically measurable concomitants. Another possibility would be to infer experiential learning from its effectiveness, and thus measure the effectiveness of learning in different areas. At the present stage of our methodology hypothesis three might be beyond us, but certainly within the foreseeable future it too could be given operational definition and tested.

The findings from these studies would be of this order. Let us become suppositious, in order to illustrate more concretely. Suppose we find that therapist acceptance leads to client self-acceptance, and that the correlation is in the neighborhood of .70 between the two variables. In hypothesis two we might find the hypothesis unsupported, but find that the more the therapist regarded the client as a person, the more the client's self-acceptance increased. Thus we would have learned that person-centeredness is an element of acceptance, but that it has little to do with the client becoming more of a person to himself. Let us also suppose hypothesis three upheld with experiential learning of certain describable sorts taking place much more in therapy than in the control subjects.

Glossing over all the qualifications and ramifications which would be present in the findings, and omitting reference to the unexpected leads into personality dynamics which would crop up (since these are hard to imagine in advance), the preceding paragraph gives us some notion of what science can offer in this field. It can give us a more exact description of the events of therapy and the changes which take place. It can begin to formulate some tentative laws of the dynamics of human relationships. It can offer public and replicable statements, that if certain operationally definable conditions exist in the therapist or in the relationship, then certain client behaviors may be expected with a known degree of probability. It can presumably do this for the field of therapy and personality change as it is in the process of doing for such fields as perception and learning. Eventually theoretical formulations should draw together these different areas, enunciating the laws which appear to govern alteration in human behavior, whether in the situations we classify as perception, those we classify as learning, or the more global and molar changes which occur in therapy, involving both perception and learning.

Some Issues

Here are two different methods of perceiving the essential aspects of psychotherapy, two different approaches to forging ahead into new territory in this field. As presented here, and as they frequently exist, there seems almost no common meeting ground between the two descriptions. Each represents a vigorous way of seeing therapy. Each seems to be an avenue to the significant truths of therapy. When each of these is held by a different individual or group, it constitutes a basis of sharp disagreement. When each of these approaches seems true to one individual, like myself, then he feels himself conflicted by these two views. Though they may superficially be reconciled, or regarded as complementary to each other, they seem to me to be basically antagonistic in many ways. I should like to raise certain issues which these two viewpoints pose for me.

The Scientist's Questions

First let me pose some of the questions which the scientific viewpoint asks of the experiential (using scientific and experiential simply as loose labels to indicate the two views). The hardheaded scientist listens to the experiential account, and raises several searching questions.

1. First of all he wants to know, "How can you know that this account, or any account given at a previous or later time, is true?

How do you know that it has any relationship to reality? If we are to rely on this inner and subjective experience as being the truth about human relationships or about ways of altering personality, then Yogi, Christian Science, dianetics, and the delusions of a psychotic individual who believes himself to be Jesus Christ, are all true, just as true as this account. Each of them represents the truth as perceived inwardly by some individual or group of individuals. If we are to avoid this morass of multiple and contradictory truths, we must fall back on the only method we know for achieving an ever-closer approximation to reality, the scientific method."

2. "In the second place, this experiential approach shuts one off from improving his therapeutic skill, or discovering the less than satisfactory elements in the relationship. Unless one regards the present description as a perfect one, which is unlikely, or the present level of experience in the therapeutic relationship as being the most effective possible, which is equally unlikely, then there are unknown flaws, imperfections, blind spots, in the account as given. How are these to be discovered and corrected? The experiential approach can offer nothing but a trial-and-error process for achieving this, a process which is slow and which offers no real guarantee of achieving this goal. Even the criticisms or suggestions of others are of little help, since they do not arise from within the experience and hence do not have the vital authority of the relationship itself. But the scientific method, and the procedures of a modern logical positivism, have much to offer here. Any experience which can be described at all can be described in operational terms. Hypotheses can be formulated and put to test, and the sheep of truth can thus be separated from the goats of error. This seems the only sure road to improvement, self-correction, growth in knowledge."

3. The scientist has another comment to make. "Implicit in your description of the therapeutic experience seems to be the notion that there are elements in it which *cannot* be predicted—that there is some type of spontaneity or (excuse the term) free will operative here. You speak as though some of the client's behavior—and perhaps some of the therapist's—is not caused, is not a link in a sequence of cause and effect. Without desiring to become metaphysical, may I raise the question as to whether this is defeatism? Since surely we can discover what causes *much* of behavior—you yourself speak of creating the conditions where certain behavioral results follow—then why give up at any point? Why not at least *aim* toward un-

covering the causes of *all* behavior? This does not mean that the individual must regard himself as an automaton, but in our search for the facts we shall not be hampered by a belief that some doors are closed to us."

4. Finally, the scientist cannot understand why the therapist, the experientialist, should challenge the one tool and method which is responsible for almost all the advances which we value. "In the curing of disease, in the prevention of infant mortality, in the growing of larger crops, in the preservation of food, in the manufacture of all the things that make life comfortable, from books to nylon, in the understanding of the universe, what is the foundation stone? It is the method of science, applied to each of these, and to many other problems. It is true that it has improved methods of warfare, too, serving man's destructive as well as his constructive purposes, but even here the potentiality for social usefulness is very great. So why should we doubt this same approach in the social science field? To be sure advances here have been slow, and no law as fundamental as the law of gravity has as yet been demonstrated, but are we to give up this approach out of impatience? What possible alternative offers equal hope? If we are agreed that the social problems of the world are very pressing indeed, if psychotherapy offers a window into the most crucial and significant dynamics of change in human behavior, then surely the course of action is to apply to psychotherapy the most rigorous canons of scientific method, on as broad a scale as possible, in order that we may most rapidly approach a tentative knowledge of the laws of individual behavior and of attitudinal change."

The Questions of the Experientialist

While the scientist's questions may seem to some to settle the matter, his comments are far from being entirely satisfying to the therapist who has lived the experience of therapy. Such an individual has several points to make in regard to the scientific view.

1. "In the first place," this "experientalist" points out, "science always has to do with the other, the object. Various logicians of science, including Stevens, show that it is a basic element of science that it always has to do with the observable object, the observable other. This is true, even if the scientist is experimenting on himself, for to that degree he treats himself as the observable other. It never

has anything to do with the experiencing me. Now does not this quality of science mean that it must forever be irrelevant to an experience such as therapy, which is intensely personal, highly subjective in its inwardness, and dependent entirely on the relationship of two individuals each of whom is an experiencing me? Science can of course study the events which occur, but always in a way which is irrelevant to what is occurring. An analogy would be to say that science can conduct an autopsy of the dead events of therapy, but by its very nature it can never enter into the living physiology of therapy. It is for this reason that therapists recognize—usually intuitively—that any advance in therapy, any fresh knowledge of it, any significant new hypotheses in regard to it must come from the experience of the therapists and clients, and can never come from science. Again, to use an analogy, certain heavenly bodies were discovered solely from examination of the scientific measurements of the courses of the stars. Then the astronomers searched for these hypothesized bodies and found them. It seems decidedly unlikely that there will ever be a similar outcome in therapy, since science has nothing to say about the internal personal experience which 'I' have in therapy. It can only speak of the events which occur in 'him.' "

2. "Because science has as its field the 'other,' the 'object,' it means that everything it touches is transformed into an object. This has never presented a problem in the physical sciences. In the biological sciences it has caused certain difficulties. A number of medical men feel some concern as to whether the increasing tendency to view the human organism as an object, in spite of its scientific efficacy, may not be unfortunate for the patient. They would prefer to see him again regarded as a person. It is in the social sciences, however, that this becomes a genuinely serious issue. It means that the people studied by the social scientist are always objects. In therapy, both client and therapist become objects for dissection, but not persons with whom one enters a living relationship. At first glance, this may not seem important. We may say that only in his role as scientist does the individual regard others as objects. He can also step out of this role and become a person. But if we look a little further we will see that this is a superficial answer. If we project ourselves into the future, and suppose that we had the answers to most of the questions which psychology investigates today, what then? Then we would find ourselves increasingly impelled to treat

all others, and even ourselves, as objects. The knowledge of all human relationships would be so great that we would know it rather
than live the relationships unreflectively. We see some foretaste of
this in the attitude of sophisticated parents who know that affection
'is good for the child.' This knowledge frequently stands in the way
of their being themselves, freely, unreflectively, affectionate or not.
Thus the development of science in a field like therapy is either irrelevant to the experience, or may actually make it more difficult to
live the relationship as a personal, experiential event."

3. The experientialist has a further concern. "When science trans-
forms people into objects, as mentioned above, it has another effect.
The end result of science is to lead toward manipulation. This is
less true in fields like astronomy, but in the physical and social
sciences, the knowledge of the events and their relationships leads
to manipulation of some of the elements of the equation. This is
unquestionably true in psychology, and would be true in therapy.
If we know all about how learning takes place, we use that knowledge to manipulate persons as objects. This statement places no
value judgment on manipulation. It may be done in highly ethical
fashion. We may even manipulate ourselves as objects, using such
knowledge. Thus, knowing that learning takes place more rapidly
with repeated review rather than long periods of concentration of
one lesson, I may use this knowledge to manipulate my learning of
Spanish. But knowledge is power. As I learn the laws of learning I
use them to manipulate others through advertisements, through prop-
aganda, through prediction of their responses, and the control of
those responses. It is not too strong a statement to say that the
growth of knowledge in the social sciences contains within itself a
powerful tendency toward social control, toward control of the many
by the few. An equally strong tendency is toward the weakening or
destruction of the existential person. When all are regarded as objects, the subjective individual, the inner self, the person in the
process of becoming, the unreflective consciousness of being, the
whole inward side of living life, is weakened, devalued, or destroyed.
Perhaps this is best exemplified by two books. Skinner's *Walden
Two* is a psychologist's picture of paradise. To Skinner it must
have seemed desirable, unless he wrote it as a tremendous satire.
At any rate it is a paradise of manipulation, in which the extent
to which one can be a person is greatly reduced, unless one can be
a member of the ruling council. Huxley's *Brave New World* is

frankly satire, but portrays vividly the loss of personhood which he sees as associated with increasing psychological and biological knowledge. Thus, to put it bluntly, it seems that a developing social science (as now conceived and pursued) leads to social dictatorship and individual loss of personhood. The dangers perceived by Kierkegaard a century ago in this respect seem much more real now, with the increase of knowledge, than they could have then."

4. "Finally," says the experientialist, "doesn't all this point to the fact that ethics is a more basic consideration than science? I am not blind to the value of science as a tool, and am aware that it can be a very valuable tool. But unless it is the tool of ethical *persons,* with all that the term persons implies, may it not become a Juggernaut? We have been a long time recognizing this issue, because in physical science it took centuries for the ethical issue to become crucial, but it has at last become so. In the social sciences the ethical issues arise much more quickly, because persons are involved. But in psychotherapy the issue arises most quickly and most deeply. Here is the maximizing of all that is subjective, inward, personal; here a relationship is lived, not examined, and a person, not an object, emerges; a person who feels, chooses, believes, acts, not as an automaton, but as a person. And here too is the ultimate in science—the objective exploration of the most subjective aspects of life; the reduction to hypotheses, and eventually to theorems, of all that has been regarded as most personal, most completely inward, most thoroughly a private world. And because these two views come so sharply into focus here, we must make a choice—an ethical personal choice of values. We may do it by default, by not raising the question. We may be able to make a choice which will somehow conserve both values—but choose we must. And I am asking that we think long and hard before we give up the values that pertain to being a person, to experiencing, to living a relationship, to becoming, that pertain to one's self as a process, to one's self in the existential moment, to the inward subjective self that lives."

The Dilemma

There you have the contrary views as they occur sometimes explicitly, more often implicitly, in current psychological thinking. There you have the debate as it exists in me. Where do we go?

What direction do we take? Has the problem been correctly described or is it fallacious? What are the errors of perception? Or if it is essentially as described, must we choose one or the other? And if so, which one? Or is there some broader, more inclusive formulation which can happily encompass both of these views without damage to either?

A Changed View of Science

In the year which has elapsed since the foregoing material was written, I have from time to time discussed the issues with students, colleagues, and friends. To some of them I am particularly indebted for ideas which have taken root in me.[3] Gradually I have come to believe that the most basic error in the original formulation was in the description of science. I should like, in this section, to attempt to correct that error, and in the following section to reconcile the revised points of view.

The major shortcoming was, I believe, in viewing science as something "out there," something spelled with a capital S, a "body of knowledge," existing somewhere in space and time. In common with many psychologists I thought of science as a systematized and organized collection of tentatively verified fact, and saw the methodology of science as the socially approved means of accumulating this body of knowledge, and continuing its verification. It has seemed somewhat like a reservoir into which all and sundry may dip their buckets to obtain water—with a guarantee of 99% purity. When viewed in this external and impersonal fashion, it seems not unreasonable to see Science not only as discovering knowledge in lofty fashion, but as involving depersonalization, a tendency to manipulate, a denial of the basic freedom of choice which I have met experientially in therapy. I should like now to view the scientific approach from a different, and I hope, a more accurate perspective.

[3] I would like to mention my special debt to discussions with, and published and unpublished papers by Robert M. Lipgar, Ross L. Mooney, David A. Rodgers, and Eugene Streich. My own thinking has fed so deeply on theirs, and become so intertwined with theirs, that I would be at a loss to acknowledge specific obligations. I only know that in what follows there is much which springs from them, through me. I have also profited from correspondence regarding the paper with Anne Roe and Walter Smet.

Science in Persons

Science exists only in people. Each scientific project has its creative inception, its process, and its tentative conclusion, in a person or persons. Knowledge—even scientific knowledge—is that which is subjectively acceptable. Scientific knowledge can be communicated only to those who are subjectively ready to receive its communication. The utilization of science also occurs only through people who are in pursuit of values which have meaning for them. These statements summarize very briefly something of the change in emphasis which I would like to make in my description of science. Let me follow through the various phases of science from this point of view.

The Creative Phases

Science has its inception in a particular person who is pursuing aims, values, purposes, which have personal and subjective meaning for him. As a part of this pursuit, he, in some area, "wants to find out." Consequently, if he is to be a good scientist, he immerses himself in the relevant experience, whether that be the physics laboratory, the world of plant or animal life, the hospital, the psychological laboratory or clinic, or whatever. This immersion is complete and subjective, similar to the immersion of the therapist in therapy, described previously. He senses the field in which he is interested. He lives it. He does more than "think" about it—he lets his organism take over and react to it, both on a knowing and on an unknowing level. He comes to sense more than he could possibly verbalize about his field, and reacts organismically in terms of relationships which are not present in his awareness.

Out of this complete subjective immersion comes a creative forming, a sense of direction, a vague formulation of relationships hitherto unrecognized. Whittled down, sharpened, formulated in clearer terms, this creative forming becomes a hypothesis—a statement of a tentative, personal, subjective faith. The scientist is saying, drawing upon all his known and unknown experience, that "I have a hunch that such and such a relationship exists, and the existence of this phenomenon has relevance to my personal values."

What I am describing is the inital phase of science, probably its most important phase, but one which American scientists, particularly psychologists, have been prone to minimize or ignore. It is not so much that it has been denied as that it has been quickly brushed off. Kenneth Spence has said that this aspect of science is "simply taken for granted." [4] Like many experiences taken for granted, it also tends to be forgotten. It is indeed in the matrix of immediate personal, subjective experience that all science, and each individual scientific research, has its origin.

Checking with Reality

The scientist has then creatively achieved his hypothesis, his tentative faith. But does it check with reality? Experience has shown each one of us that it is very easy to deceive himself, to believe something which later experience shows is not so. How can I tell whether this tentative belief has some real relationship to observed facts? I can use, not one line of evidence only, but several. I can surround my observation of the facts with various precautions to make sure I am not deceiving myself. I can consult with others who have also been concerned with avoiding self-deception, and learn useful ways of catching myself in unwarranted beliefs, based on misinterpretation of observations. I can, in short, begin to use all the elaborate methodology which science has accumulated. I discover that stating my hypothesis in operational terms will avoid many blind alleys and false conclusions. I learn that control groups can help me to avoid drawing false inferences. I learn that correlations, and t tests and critical ratios and a whole array of statistical procedures can likewise aid me in drawing only reasonable inferences.

Thus scientific methodology is seen for what it truly is—a way of preventing me from deceiving myself in regard to my creatively formed subjective hunches which have developed out of the relationship between me and my material. It is in this context, and perhaps only in this context, that the vast structure of operationism, logical positivism, research design, tests of significance, etc., have their

[4] It may be pertinent to quote the sentences from which this phrase is taken. ". . . the data of all sciences have the same origin—namely, the immediate experience of an observing person, the scientist himself. That is to say, immediate experience, the initial matrix out of which all sciences develop, is no longer considered a matter of concern for the scientist. He simply takes it for granted and then proceeds to the task of describing the events occurring in it and discovering and formulating the nature of the relationships holding among them." Kenneth W. Spence, in *Psychological Theory,* M. H. Marx (Ed.), Macmillan, 1951, p. 173.

place. They exist, not for themselves, but as servants in the attempt to check the subjective feeling or hunch or hypothesis of a person with the objective fact.

And even throughout the use of such rigorous and impersonal methods, the important choices are all made subjectively by the scientist. To which of a number of hypotheses shall I devote time? What kind of control group is most suitable for avoiding self-deception in this particular research? How far shall I carry the statistical analysis? How much credence may I place in the findings? Each of these is necessarily a subjective personal judgment, emphasizing that the splendid structure of science rests basically upon its subjective use by persons. It is the best instrument we have yet been able to devise to check upon our organismic sensing of the universe.

The Findings

If, as scientist, I like the way I have gone about my investigation, if I have been open to all the evidence, if I have selected and used intelligently all the precautions against self-deception which I have been able to assimilate from others or to devise myself, then I will give my tentative belief to the findings which have emerged. I will regard them as a springboard for further investigation and further seeking.

It seems to me that in the best of science, the primary purpose is to provide a more satisfactory and dependable hypothesis, belief, faith, for the investigator himself. To the extent that the scientist is endeavoring to prove something to someone else—an error into which I have fallen more than once—then I believe he is using science to bolster a personal insecurity, and is keeping it from its truly creative role in the service of the person.

In regard to the findings of science, the subjective foundation is well shown in the fact that at times the scientist may refuse to believe his own findings. "The experiment showed thus and so but I believe it is wrong," is a theme which every scientist has experienced at some time or other. Some very fruitful scientific discoveries have grown out of the persistent *disbelief*, by a scientist, in his own findings and those of others. In the last analysis he may place more trust in his total organismic reactions than in the methods of science. There is no doubt that this can result in serious error as well as in scientific discoveries, but it indicates again the leading place of the subjective in the use of science.

Communication of Scientific Findings

Wading along a coral reef in the Caribbean this morning, I saw a blue fish—I think. If you, quite independently, saw it too, then I feel more confidence in my own observation. This is what is known as intersubjective verification, and it plays an important part in our understanding of science. If I take you (whether in conversation or in print or behaviorally) through the steps I have taken in an investigation, and it seems to you too that I have not deceived myself, and that I have indeed come across a new relationship which is relevant to my values, and that I am justified in having a tentative faith in this relationship, then we have the beginnings of Science with a capital S. It is at this point that we are likely to think we have created a body of scientific knowledge. Actually there is no such body of knowledge. There are only tentative beliefs, existing subjectively, in a number of different persons. If these beliefs are not tentative, then what exists is dogma, not science. If on the other hand, no one but the investigator believes the finding, then this finding is either a personal and deviant matter, an instance of psychopathology, or else it is an unusual truth discovered by a genius, which as yet no one is subjectively ready to believe. This leads me to comment on the group which can put tentative faith in any given scientific finding.

Communication to Whom?

It is clear that scientific findings can be communicated only to those who have agreed to the same ground rules of investigation. The Australian bushman will be quite unimpressed with the findings of science regarding bacterial infection. He knows that illness truly is caused by evil spirits. It is only when he too agrees to scientific method as a good means of preventing self-deception, that he will be likely to accept its findings.

But even among those who have adopted the ground rules of science, tentative belief in the findings of a scientific research can only occur where there is a subjective readiness to believe. One could find many examples. Most psychologists are quite ready to believe

evidence showing that the lecture system produces significant incre-
ments of learning, and quite unready to believe that the turn of an
unseen card may be called through an ability labeled extrasensory
perception. Yet the scientific evidence for the latter is considerably
more impeccable than for the former. Likewise when the so-called
"Iowa studies" first came out, indicating that intelligence might be
considerably altered by environmental conditions, there was great
disbelief among psychologists, and many attacks on the imperfect
scientific methods used. The scientific evidence for this finding is
not much better today than it was when the Iowa studies first appeared, but the subjective readiness of psychologists to believe such
a finding has altered greatly. A historian of science has noted that
empiricists, had they existed at the time, would have been the first
to disbelieve the findings of Copernicus.

It appears then that whether I believe the scientific findings of
others, or those of my own studies, depends in part on my readiness
to put a tentative belief in such findings.[5] One reason we are not
particularly aware of this subjective fact is that in the physical
sciences particularly, we have gradually agreed that in a very large
area of experience we are ready to believe any finding which can be
shown to rest upon the rules of the scientific game, properly played.

The Use of Science

But not only is the origin, process, and conclusion of science something which exists only in the subjective experience of persons—so
also is its utilization. "Science" will never depersonalize, or manipulate, or control individuals. It is only persons who can and will do

---

[5] One example from my own experience may suffice. In 1941 a research study
done under my supervision showed that the future adjustment of delinquent
adolescents was best predicted by a measure of their realistic self-understanding
and self-acceptance. The instrument was a crude one, but it was a better pre-
dictor than measures of family environment, hereditary capacities, social milieu,
and the like. At that time I was simply not ready to believe such a finding,
because my own belief, like that of most psychologists, was that such factors
as the emotional climate in the family and the influence of the peer group were
the real determinants of future delinquency and nondelinquency. Only gradually, as my experience with psychotherapy continued and deepened, was it
possible for me to give my tentative belief to the findings of this study and
of a later one (1944) which confirmed it. (For a report of these two studies
see "The role of self understanding in the prediction of behavior" by C. R.
Rogers, B. L. Kell, and H. McNeil, *J. consult. Psychol.*, 1948, *12*, 174–186.)

that. This is surely a most obvious and trite observation, yet a deep realization of it has had much meaning for me. It means that the use which will be made of scientific findings in the field of personality is and will be a matter of subjective personal choice—the same type of choice as a person makes in therapy. To the extent that he has defensively closed off areas of his experience from awareness, the person is more likely to make choices which are socially destructive. To the extent that he is open to all phases of his experience we may be sure that this person will be more likely to use the findings and methods of science (or any other tool or capacity) in a manner which is personally and socially constructive.[6] There is, in actuality then, no threatening entity of "Science" which can in any way affect our destiny. There are only people. While many of them are indeed threatening and dangerous in their defensiveness, and modern scientific knowledge multiplies the social threat and danger, this is not the whole picture. There are two other significant facets. (a) There are many other persons who are relatively open to their experience and hence likely to be socially constructive. (b) Both the subjective experience of psychotherapy and the scientific findings regarding it indicate that individuals are motivated to change, and may be helped to change, in the direction of greater openness to experience, and hence in the direction of behavior which is enhancing of self and society, rather than destructive.

To put it briefly, Science can never threaten us. Only persons can do that. And while individuals can be vastly destructive with the tools placed in their hands by scientific knowledge, this is only one side of the picture. We already have subjective and objective knowledge of the basic principles by which individuals may achieve the more constructive social behavior which is natural to their organismic process of becoming.

A New Integration

What this line of thought has achieved for me is a fresh integration in which the conflict between the "experientialist" and the "scientific" tends to disappear. This particular integration may not be acceptable to others, but it does have meaning to me. Its major tenets have been

[6] I have spelled out much more fully the rationale for this view in two recent papers: "The concept of the fully functioning person" (unpublished manuscript), and "Toward a theory of creativity," *ETC*, 1954, *11*, 249–260.

largely implicit in the preceding section, but I will try to state them here in a way which takes cognizance of the arguments between the opposing points of view.

Science, as well as therapy, as well as all other aspects of living, is rooted in and based upon the immediate, subjective experience of a person. It springs from the inner, total, organismic experiencing which is only partially and imperfectly communicable. It is one phase of subjective living.

It is because I find value and reward in human relationships that I enter into a relationship known as therapeutic, where feelings and cognition merge into one unitary experience which is lived rather than examined, in which awareness is nonreflective, and where I am participant rather than observer. But because I am curious about the exquisite orderliness which appears to exist in the universe and in this relationship I can abstract myself from the experience and look upon it as an observer, making myself and/or others the objects of that observation. As observer I use all of the hunches which grow out of the living experience. To avoid deceiving myself as observer, to gain a more accurate picture of the order which exists, I make use of all the canons of science. Science is not an impersonal something, but simply a person living subjectively another phase of himself. A deeper understanding of therapy (or of any other problem) may come from living it, or from observing it in accordance with the rules of science, or from the communication within the self between the two types of experience. As to the subjective experience of choice, it is not only primary in therapy, but it is also primary in the use of scientific method by a person. I have even come to see that freedom of choice is not necessarily antithetical to the determinism which is a part of our framework for thinking scientifically. Since I have recently tried to spell out this relationship elsewhere,[7] I will not take the space to do so here.

What I will do with the knowledge gained through scientific method—whether I will use it to understand, enhance, enrich, or use it to control, manipulate, and destroy—is a matter of subjective choice dependent upon the values which have personal meaning for me. If, out of fright and defensiveness, I block out from my awareness large areas of experience—if I can see only those facts which support my present beliefs, and am blind to all others—if I can see only the objective aspects of life, and cannot perceive the subjective

---

[7] In my paper on "The concept of the fully functioning person."

—if in any way I cut off my perception from the full range of its actual sensitivity—then I am likely to be socially destructive, whether I use as tool the knowledge and instruments of science, or the power and emotional strength of a subjective relationship. And on the other hand if I am open to my experience, and can permit all of the sensings of my intricate organism to be available to my awareness, then I am likely to use myself, my subjective experience, *and* my scientific knowledge, in ways which are realistically constructive.

This, then, is the degree of integration I have currently been able to achieve between two approaches first experienced as conflicting. It does not completely resolve all the issues posed in the earlier section, but it seems to point toward a resolution. It rewrites the problem or reperceives the issue, by putting the subjective, existential person, with the values which he holds, at the foundation and the root of the therapeutic relationship and of the scientific relationship. For science too, at its inception, is an "I-Thou" relationship with the world of perceived objects, just as therapy at its deepest is an "I-Thou" relationship with a person or persons. And only as a subjective person can I enter either of these relationships.

....

What Is Clinical Psychology?[*][1,2]

FREDERICK WYATT

ANY ATTEMPT AT defining clinical psychology at this point in the history of psychology would have to begin with a sampling of meanings. It would have to use the benefits of linguistic philosophy and literally examine the *ordinary language* both of official psychology and of common psychological usage. Furthermore, any designation of clinical psychology will have to explain the difference between *normative* and *casual* practice. *Normative* refers to official designations. These, as we shall see, have been so widely drawn that with the burden of so much comprehensiveness and caution they cannot explain why their subject should be so controversial. *Casual* refers to what clinical psychologists are actually doing. A great variety of things, it turns out: sometimes different ones under the same name, sometimes similar operations under very different names. This may explain why neither a definition by subject matter (e.g., psychopathology) nor by aim (e.g., rehabilitation, helping people) will do the matter justice.

Psychology, for better or worse, is a profession of strong convictions. It has a subject so encompassing that it extends to all aspects of human existence. Yet there is no unity of approach in psychology. There is only a common subject, and that in the most perfunctory sense. Psychologists may agree that they are concerned with behavior. But that may mean almost anything in human experience, or only a very small portion of its scope. In other words, the subject of psychology implies another normative designation, a command,

[*] Prepared for this volume.

[1] This paper is dedicated to the memory of Frederick Lyman Wells, 1884–1964.

[2] This paper developed from a quasi-minority statement contributed to the Report of the Ad Hoc Committee (Watson, 1964). An earlier version of the paper itself was read at the Congress of the International Association of Applied Psychology in Ljubljana, Yugoslavia, 1964. I am indebted to Joseph Adelson, Frithjoff Bergmann, Donald Hall, John Higham, James Meisel, Ingo Seidler, and Eric Wolf for their helpful criticism.

as it were, to attend to some things and ignore others. Several of the most consequential schools in psychology have actually defined the subject of their investigation by the method they wanted to stress and by certain basic assumptions the method was supposed to realize. Behaviorism (Koch, 1964) is a good example. One can easily see that psychologists' notorious divisions come straight from the immense scope and the overwhelming plurality of their subject. For what they have undertaken to study, man's experience and his conduct, is not only encompassing but is also in a state of becoming, forever in transition, and at all times determined by interaction and context. The characteristic disagreements of psychology derive from a problem of corresponding size: namely, how to grasp all this, and by what rationale. Clinical psychology has been the pawn of partisanship practically since its beginning. It is not merely an area of psychology but the shibboleth of psychological sentiments. It is an area whose intellectual understanding is assessed according to the fixed ideas of the observer. The present controversy as to what clinical psychology really is and does would be described more accurately as an argument about what clinical psychology *ought* to do. This, too, has to be kept in mind when an attempt is made to define clinical psychology.

Intellectual enterprises, like people, are determined by a broad spectrum of social conditions. The conduct of a person is never entirely functional, even in his most rational moments. Just as he never serves exclusively the aims by which he claims to be directed, so is no scientific enterprise as completely functional as its partisans like to have it. At no time is the shape of scientific endeavor determined by utility alone. Mixed into the task—sometimes indiscernibly, sometimes starkly obvious—is always a certain amount of tradition, of conviction long before observation, and, of course, also of fashion. The last point is often the most important one. Its principle, "Now we do things this way!" is true for all times even if the ways change quite rapidly from one fashion to the next. It takes courage and stubbornness to follow a course of which the collective righteousness of the scientific establishment disapproves. To do so invites, next to many obvious external risks, the internal one of making a theory of oppositionism rather than of reasoned observation. The argument for the best, the truly scientific, approach to behavior is also vitiated by a common sequence in the history of ideas. People identify with each other by kinship of disposition and form schools of thought, but in order to define themselves and to protect the group from disruption they must project their ambivalence on the deviants and nonconformists. Ideas quickly harden into ideologies as this process continues, and an increasing vigorousness of partisanship often signifies that the reasons and the original points of departure for a theory have been obscured beyond recognition. In short, the experimental psychologist, bent on rigorous method, apparently finds it as hard to admit the non-functional aspects of his conviction as does his clinical colleague, eager to understand what makes people tick. In order to appreciate the plural and controversial nature of clinical psychology, a schematic survey of ideas bearing upon its history is indicated.

Clinical psychology began when the general theories of psychology were first applied to normal and subnormal people. In this sense Binet's test belongs to the origins of clinical psychology; by attempting to screen children from the point of view of intelligence, Binet implicitly used his method also for the *understanding* of subnormal or deviant children. The term "clinical" itself seems to have been established in this context when Leitmer Wittmer founded the first department of clinical psychology at the Pennsylvania Hospital in Philadelphia. The next developments especially need to be understood in terms of available technology and of its widely publicized use. The idea of testing intelligence and some of the techniques for it had already been developed when, at the occasion of the First World War, Bingham, Yerkes, and their associates applied such techniques on a large scale to the selection of manpower. Slowly the scope of clinical psychology widened. The study of psychological impairment had gone alongside the expansion of measuring general intelligence and specific abilities, such as memory, and had concerned itself largely with the differentiation of classes and types of disorder. Clinical psychologists looked for patterns in the variation of abilities and for the relation of differential impairment to pathological traits.

This account is not only brief and schematic but also one-sided. But the aim here is to stress the convergence of some ideas which, in my opinion, decisively affected the present appearance of clinical psychology and its controversial scope. No attempt is made to do justice to all the major ideas and to the personalities representative of them; nor to the social circumstances so obviously affecting the development of clinical psychology. A fuller account of influences prior to Freud and in addition to Freudian psychoanalysis would have had to include Janet, G. Stanley Hall and William James (perhaps the two most important beneficent ancestral spirits), Mc-Dougall, Otto Rank and Jessie Taft and their influence on the counseling movement, Jung's influence on H. A. Murray and others, and John Dewey and the advent of applied pragmatism and the Progressive Education movement. Such an account would have had to deal with a change of attitude far beyond that pointedly expressed in the surge of interest in psychoanalysis and psychotherapy which became manifest in many disciplines. While the growth of this new attitude was greatly accelerated by the sudden and immense social dislocation caused by the Second World War which put psychological rehabilitation into social prominence, its appearance as a major event of social change had been in the making for much longer. Among the social conditions bearing upon the expansion of clinical psychology those of the war and post-war period would have to be mentioned as specific, unique conditions. The large-scale immigration of European intellectual and professional workers in the years immediately preceding the war also belongs in this category. Yet all these events may have only been catalysts for the slow ground-swell of social change implied in the increasing urbanization and industrialization and the consequent transformation of family structure and sex roles. Some aspects of the profound revision of elementary beliefs about the individual's nature and possibilities which accompanied this change will be discussed later in this essay.

To return to some specific intellectual currents affecting the development of clinical psychology: a decisive new impulse came with the ascendance of psychoanalysis and the emergence of projective methods. The history of these developments, too, has been described previously (Kelly, 1966; Watson, 1953; Wyatt, 1948) and needs to be touched upon here only briefly. During the first official tenure of clinical psychology no ideology was at hand that would have accounted comprehensively for the etiology of psychological disorders and for the motives of conduct in general.[3] Clinical psycholo-

---

[3] The term *conduct* is used here and throughout to characterize persistent patterns of behavior, modes and fixed forms of adjustment. I am aware that *conduct* connotes the moral aspects of behavior, but there is no reason to object to the moral innuendo of this concept as it is appropriate to the purpose at hand. No observer can help responding to what impresses him as the "good" or "bad" in the comprehensive pattern of an individual's behavior, even though afterwards he may for the sake of objectivity detach the "moral aspect" from his impressions (as he should) or deny it (as he should not).

gists based their work on theories such as Wundtian associationism, none of which were capable of providing a general theory of behavior broad enough to explain maladjustment. They were primarily concerned with abilities (what later came to be called cognition) by which they could meaningfully relate their observations to current psychiatric theories and, even more so, to classifications of maladjustment, such as that proposed by Kraepelin. Other psychologists had begun to rely increasingly on the measurement of traits and dispositions by means of tests. Their view was that, as E. L. Thorndike put it, whatever exists must exist in some quantity and can therefore be measured. Thus, if properly measured, everything should fall into place and the results themselves should point to the principles by which specific traits are lawfully related to each other. Thus the hope was that measurement, if only carried out long enough, would ultimately lead to a valid theory. This hope did not materialize. No other system of psychology was then available to deal with behavior in real-life situations, including behavior in which pathological forms of adjustment were manifest (Koch, 1964). The absence of any comprehensive theory of motivation applicable to the conduct of people and to their quandaries provided an impetus for the ascendance of psychoanalysis, apart from its own indigenous contributions.

The innovations brought about by psychoanalysis must be understood therefore in several ways. Above all, psychoanalysis provided a universal theory capable of explaining discrete symptoms and relating them systematically to a general theory of motivation and development. Until then psychopathology had mostly been a bizarre spectacle, leaving the baffled observer with the impression that the victim either had been stricken by an awful predicament or that

---

These elementary acts of judgment are inevitably affected by subjective needs and beliefs—here lies, for instance, the manifest origin of transference. This does not detract, however, from the potentially objective relevance of such impressions as long as the observer is able to recognize his involvement and keep it apart. There is, at least in English terminology, no word to refer to on-going behavior in real-life situations. The term *behavior* which, perhaps in competition with "mentalistic" concepts, has lately become more accommodating and inclusive, will not do even though we shall be forced by the paucity of language to continue its use. But we should be aware that the term does not afford us enough distinction between what behavior is like when it is first sampled and what is left of it after it has been scientifically processed. Perhaps *conduct* can be used to fill this gap, at least in a conspectus such as this one.

he was perpetrating a shameful hoax. The first contribution of psychoanalysis to clinical psychology was to make psychological disruption meaningful by putting it into a coherent and comprehensive frame of reference. Psychologists had been accustomed to view mental disorder as the jagged profile of cognitive deficit or, if they followed the psychiatrists, as deviations occurring in some regularity, but a regularity all the more tantalizing because it made no sense as such. Now psychopathology began to be viewed as an expression of the individual's elementary concerns—a disguised and frantic set of messages. These messages, moreover, became astonishingly meaningful once they were properly interpreted in terms of individual history and its universal sequences and crises of development. Furthermore, psychoanalysis insisted on behavior as a dynamic and transactional process; according to this conception personality is continuously striving, driven by appetites, primarily concerned with release and fulfillment and with the avoidance of anguish and bodily pain. Thirdly, the psychoanalytic distinction between conscious and unconscious motivation gave fantasy a new significance; it could now be recognized as the characteristic mode of resolving need tensions and as the repetition of unsettled conflicts in the implied hope of mastering them.

From the psychoanalytic concept of fantasy issued a new approach to the study of personality—projective tests. The interpretation of dreams and parapraxes in psychoanalysis supplied the model for the development of tests designed to induce self-revealing fantasies independent of sleep and the anarchy of dreams. The Rorschach Test, still the paragon of projective tests, however, rests as much or more on the organizatory and expressive facilities of personality as on its appetitive ones. While clearly influenced by psychoanalytic theory, this test has a certain margin of theoretical and operative autonomy. It anticipated the subsequent shift of focus to a psychoanalytic psychology of the ego and helped prepare clinical psychologists for it.

The possession of new instruments and of a new theory of personality profoundly changed the status of clinical psychologists. Suddenly they found themselves possessed of tests which promised to achieve in a relatively short time what before had to be accomplished by observation so extended that it sometimes missed its purpose. Psychologists now felt that they had gained access to the carefully guarded aspirations and anxieties of the individual, including those motives of which the individual was not clearly conscious; gained access also to the structural qualities of his thinking, his subjective modes of apprehending reality and his ways of coping with it. The time had come, in short, when psychiatric residents might hesitate to state a diagnosis until the psychologist had presented the results of *his* psychodiagnostic studies.

The ascent of the psychologist to the role of star-diagnostician was based on the convergence of several factors. The increasingly wide use of psychoanalytic propositions for explaining the genesis and structure of psychopathological phenomena provided a common conceptual language for diagnostician and therapist. Of particular significance, these propositions offered an immensely effective frame of reference when applied to the individual case. Psychologists were quick to realize them in their diagnostic formulations and their researches, making use of a proliferating variety of projective devices designed (or readapted) to comprehend and demonstrate the workings of these psychoanalytic principles. Psychoanalysis made possible for the first time specific psychological hypotheses about conduct and provided models for its deviations and breaks. If this statement seems exaggerated, consider that disorders of conduct had heretofore been relegated, although never very conclusively, to histogenic and metabolic pathology. Psychoanalysis provided a framework for the first time in which the incidents of disruption could be related to the entire psychophysical scope of the individual, both to his own history and to his interaction with the social ambience. Consider also that psychoanalysis implied a complete reorganization of the meanings of *normal* and *abnormal* and their significance in the growth of personality which, to this date, has not been fully explored.

At the end of the last world war mental health facilities began to expand on an unprecedented scale. By then, the social and ideological appearance of the clinical psychologist had changed in the following ways: (1) his theoretical scope had been greatly expanded by the inclusion of psychoanalytic concepts; (2) the range of his clinical activities had been significantly enlarged by the inclusion of psychotherapy; (3) the development of new projective tools, in conjunction with the changes in theoretical orientation, had extended the psychologist's stock of diagnostic instruments and had prepared him for a bigger and more incisive task; (4) the clinical psychologist had progressed from earlier linear measures—fragmentary because of the neglect of dynamic and affective conditions—to a conception of deviation in terms of genesis and structure. He had come to recognize psychopathology as a variant of ordinary psychological growth, a special form of adjustment resulting largely from the arrests and breaks of regular development; (5) the clinical psychologist, in addition to attaining more status in an increasingly more coordinated effort which came to be known as the mental health team, also made a spectacular advance as a specialist in research on psychopathology and on mental health in general.

A fuller understanding of the latter point again necessitates a return to historical and sociological considerations. Psychologists had done research in clinics and mental hospitals for a long time, and from their somewhat isolated and anonymous departments had published some very good work. This research rarely brought them deserved attention, partly because what they investigated had no great appeal at that time and partly because they themselves did not have sufficient prestige in their essentially heterogeneous community. Only during the years following the war, as the issue of mental health became more of a public concern, did the competence of psychologists for research emerge into public and institutional awareness. At the same time it also became clear how little we knew of the conditions underlying mental health now that we had, at long last, become aware of its impact. Research in mental health developed apace with the expansion of mental health services and the spread of popular interest in the new science of adjustment. When it came to the prerequisites of systematic inquiry, psychologists, by dint of training and preparation, were obviously best equipped to plan and conduct research.

In retrospect, however, it appears that psychologists had been conceded leadership in research not only because they were the ones best equipped for it, but because in this way they could also be kept out of the highly privileged and socially visible role of the healer and psychotherapist reserved for the medical practitioner. As a rule, psychiatrists found it easier to acknowledge psychologists as research specialists than as psychotherapists. To yield the former role to psychologists might keep them from being identified publicly as practicing therapists, a prospect more vexing than the somewhat abstract and peripheral status of the research expert. On the other hand, many psychologists, who had been studiously trained to avoid consideration of actual, global, in-life behavior because of its refractoriness to rigorous methodology, found clinical encounters little to their taste. They often insisted that research was the true function for the psychologist, and enjoined other psychologists to this view. Without intending to do so, they supported the psychiatrists' argument that psychologists, for one reason or another, should not do therapy (Tryon, 1963).

During the war the acute needs for selection and rehabilitation simply had to be met as they came. In the period of that new awareness of adjustment and mental health that followed, the new psychological approaches of diagnostic testing and psychotherapy had come to the fore. Yet they remained outside the ken of official or laboratory psychology. Considering with what rigor traditional psychology had defined its task, it is small wonder that these approaches were held to rest on doubtful premises which were unacceptable in practically all respects. The ambiguity of clinical propositions seemed excessive, and the explanation of such ambiguity in terms of the psychological level to which these propositions referred was considered as nothing short of an outrage. The frankly mentalistic quality of clinical concepts appeared to many to be a regression into ancient errors (Skinner, 1956; 1964). They felt the inferential and intuitive reasoning of clinical interpretation, the essential operation of the new approach (Erikson, 1958), to be so peculiar and arbitrary as to render it unscientific if not specious. Despite the work of the Gestalt school, the clinician's insistence on context, configuration, interaction, and meaning struck traditional psychologists as an obfuscation. Its only purpose could be to dodge or embarrass the methodological designs made mandatory by the deutero-physicalism of psychology. The complexities of conduct which psychoanalytically oriented clinical psychologists proposed to examine, and the recession of established principles such an orientation imposed, were at least as intolerable to the traditional psychologist as was the do-good pragmatism of clinical service. For what should scientists make of aims such as that of assisting people in psychological distress? After the first enthusiasm for these innovations had spent itself, the traditional ideology of psychology asserted itself again. By then, however, clinical psychology had become a conspicuous and populous segment of psychology as a whole. To stress the clinical psychologist's research function seemed the best way to bring him back into the fold. It will be seen, in the light of these comments, that the emergence of the clinical psychologist as the research specialist of the mental health area must be understood as a result of several converging yet highly disparate trends.

Let us now return to the ascendance of a new attitude toward mental health and individual adjustment. The rise of mental health into public consciousness after the war represents a profound change in man's expectations of what life can give him—the collective image of his destiny. It is, as I have argued elsewhere (Wyatt, 1956), a profound change in man's image of himself and of his destiny —what he must accept as his unalterable lot, such as illness and death, and what he can hope to modify and improve, such as the course and frequency of illness. Up to the advent of modern theories of personality, and especially of psychoanalysis, there was little differentiation between what is unchanging in the self, such as character, and what can be modified, such as traits, attitudes, or sentiments. Popular psychology, that perennial conglomerate of collective notions about the nature of man to which the explication of his self and his conduct had been left, oscillated between two extremes. According to one common-sense principle nothing much can be done once a person is formed. According to the other the individual is admonished to "know thyself" and to improve or modify his conduct according to his insights. He was, for instance, instructed to "conquer" himself in moral quandaries. Although external pressure was not to sway him from his purpose in some situations, he was at the same time expected to curb his desires by the conscious use of will and reason. Then there were the exceptions. Character might change under special circumstances, under great duress or by special dispensation. In short, the absence of any universal theory of adjustment made it impossible to distinguish conflict-generated from conflict-free behavior. What we would now regard as neurotic character traits or as explicit neurotic symptoms were, in the still-recent past, regarded as idiosyncratic, admirably eccentric, or strangely disturbing. Victorian biographies in particular are full of such examples. Only when symptoms became too bizarre or too compulsive were they attributed, according to the predilection of the age, either to demoniacal possession, to degeneracy, or to subtle organic changes.

The new orientation to mental health implies a far-reaching transformation of some of the basic assumptions of our culture. Man suddenly found himself in the possession of more freedom over his destiny than he could have dreamed of a generation earlier. *Character* had been equated with *destiny* before; but if character was in important respects the result of the circumstances in which it developed, and especially if its more troublesome aspects rested on the perpetuation of childish misapprehensions, then it also might be modified later on. Shyness and diffidence or consuming obsessions were no longer integral parts of the self with which an individual simply had to live, but were the results of a somewhat devious development which under favorable circumstances could be recovered and corrected. The idea of therapeutic modification had profoundly changed the image of man, even though it would take still more time until the implications of this change were fully realized. Yet as the range of man's self-determination expanded, his vulnerability expanded too. The grave importance assigned to the developmental process made evident the need to protect it from disturbance and thereby to prevent later maladjustment. Man's view of himself, in conjunction with his new lease on self-determination, had also become more emphatically historical than ever before. His current liabilities and assets now seemed largely products of his own past development, which introduced a peculiarly retrospective cast even in the informal psychological assessment of everyday life.

Man's changed perception of himself was reflected in the emergence of social institutions designed to protect him from maladjustment and to assist him in his rehabilitation. The mental health professions were now on the way to becoming an institution parallel to but increasingly differentiated from that of Medicine, and perhaps destined to a larger role. Healing had undergone incisive modifications ranging from revisions of etiology and treatment (as in psychosomatic disorders) to the planful guidance of individual interaction and group behavior, quasi-therapeutic endeavors for which the traditional connotation of therapy is obviously no longer appropriate. A new vocabulary will have to be designed to define more adequately what *de facto* are new forms of social control no more analogous to individual therapy than to economic planning. The phase now unfolding is that of Community Mental Health. The role of the clinical psychologist in it seems to be expanding from the more succinct and limited one of therapist, diagnostician, and research specialist to that of a broadly gauged psychological consultant to the community.

Fortified by a purview of its history, we should have no difficulty recognizing why the definitions of clinical psychology are so unavoidably controversial. Official definitions such as those sanctioned by the American Psychological Association must, inasmuch as they represent the norms of the profession, emphasize pluralism in an attempt to keep divergent dispositions under one professional roof (Raimy, 1950; Shakow, 1945). Sociologically speaking, this is simply a necessity.[4] But we must also be attentive to the consequences. Once a definition has been institutionalized it will, by feedback, itself define training and employment opportunities and eventually mold the expectations of individuals. *Casual* definitions of clinical psychology are implied and abstracted in the *normative* (official) statements. By their very nature they cannot be made explicit because they refer both to what the individual manifestly does in the practice of clinical psychology and to his aims and attitudes, the cognitive and effective motives of his pursuit.

Clinical psychology is a summary concept; it refers to everything and everybody, to activities and aims and jobs, to training and tasks, to techniques and attitudes. Like most inclusive concepts of this kind it implies that all these endeavors have something in common and that they hang meaningfully together. Of course they do, but less neatly than the concept would lead us to believe. What is common to the endeavors of clinical psychology is the psychological viewpoint, not more, and sometimes rather less. For the psychological viewpoint, a broad and elementary orientation, is itself highly inclusive and full of differences. We shall be well advised, therefore, to take clinical psychology for what it really is—a social aggregate organized around a number of discrete foci.

As a summary concept clinical psychology cannot be easily encompassed by a unitary definition. Clinical psychology is defined by *subject matter,* i.e., the problems of disordered, discordant, or socially deviant behavior subsumed under the concept of psychopathology; but it is also defined by *operation.* The operations may be transactional, as in diagnosis and especially in psychotherapy when the therapist's modification of the behavior of his client modifies, in turn, the subsequent operations of the therapist. Or, these opera-

---

[4] Holt (1962) and Kelly (1966), from a somewhat different point of view, have warned us against any dogmatic insistence that clinical psychology should be exactly this or exclusively that. One cannot but agree; a growing yet inchoate specialty or profession cannot be bound by a definition which is itself the product of transition. The plurality of interests and ideologies in clinical psychology is as much a fact of life as is the plurality of functions. This does not mean, however, that we should not seek to define more accurately what mental sets and attitudes are involved in this pursuit.

tions may be non-transactional and non-mutual when the behavior of the investigator is in essence prescribed by both his ends and his method, and will be affected in only a limited way by the behavior of his subject. This definition makes the characteristic goals of clinical psychology, such as relief of discomfort, treatment of psychological disorders, or rehabilitation, an aspect of the operation. As there is a relatively clear-cut difference between transactional and non-transactional operations, a definition of clinical psychology by *aim* either has to be inclusive and accept different and possibly contrary aims or it has to emphasize one aim at the expense of the other, which is often the case. The cleavage and controversy within clinical psychology between research and service seems related to these alternatives.

When we speak of clinical psychology we may mean any combination of subject and operation. We may have in mind criteria of training, of a job title, or of an agency. Such criteria are obviously important for the place clinical psychologists have in the complicated texture of a bureaucratic mass-society. However, it must also be obvious that we will not fully comprehend what *being* a clinical psychologist means to the one who has chosen this role for himself and identified with it if we leave its definition on a purely descriptive level. Kelly (1966) and Watson (1953) point out correctly that hardly any of the engagements used to characterize the clinical psychologist are really exclusive to him. There must be something else in an emergent social role: a quality by which it is experienced, the convictions implicit in it, and a specific set of attitudes, no less effective if they are not fully conscious. Considering the intense affects underlying such attitudes, the current argument about clinical psychology much more likely has its roots in the assertion of such an identity (the fusion of self and role) and in the reaction of others to it than in training schedules and job descriptions. *Identity* suggests more than doing a task regularly and with some functional efficiency. It implies an integration between intellectual conviction and affective consent; it affirms that the role into which task and operations are organized makes sense and is relevant at this time and in this place (Erikson, 1956). It "makes sense" because it helps the individual who has adopted it to integrate a plethora of complex, subtle, and deeply personal dispositions into a meaningful idea and into meaningful action.

Of course there is nothing in the idea of identity that prescribes what convictions and engagements it should comprise. The vocational identity of an experimental psychologist, too, would be vested in his attitude toward his science. His principal approach would be the same whether he is concerned with normal or abnormal people. But we can empirically observe what kind of attitudes are commonly found among clinical psychologists, and may then infer which of them seem most germane to the task at hand and most essential to the identity of those performing it. Undeniably, some judgment is involved in such an assessment which cannot claim to be entirely objective. But for the point at hand it is sufficient to stress the relevance and the logical utility[5] of the position presented. The term *clinical* will be more useful if it refers to essence rather than to circumstances. A definition of clinical psychology would certainly become both more succinct and more relevant if it seized upon something constant and essential in the engagements of the clinical psychologist. The definition we shall now consider appears to be inherent in any transactional engagement.

The essence of the clinical attitude, I submit, is its concern with actual behavior and with the actual urges, interests, and apprehensions of people in on-going life. The emphasis is on the importance of the stream of experience, in its affective as well as cognitive aspects; an emphasis which includes the plurality of experience (several things going on simultaneously), the changes in self-awareness, the metaphorical and symbolic quality of thought and, especially, the important consequences of the mind's capacity for creating meaning. The term *clinical*, furthermore, suggests the psychologist's willingness to study the behavior of people through direct observation, frequently in transactional settings involving varying degrees of participation and interaction. Finally, implied in the concept *clinical* is a clear transition and distinction, but no absolutist separation, between observing, understanding, and acting in the service of readaptive goals. The idea of "doing something about it" is indigenous to clinical psychology; it denotes a more inclusive and diffuse concept than that of research, which is indeed more exclusive, specific, and self-limiting. I should like to illustrate this point from the experience of psychoanalytic psychotherapy and its effect on the

[5] I am under no illusion that the argument for logical utility could not be also used for an entirely different point of view. The significance of the attitudes described is a matter of opinion; their presence and frequency, however, is a massive matter of fact demonstrated by an enormous body of writing. For two widely differing examples see Erikson (1958) and Watson (1964).

conceptual organization of the therapist. The therapist is likely to recognize that observation in psychotherapy, comprising a combination of acts of observation and intervention based on tentative organization of available data, gives access to dimensions of behavior and experience not grasped by pre-clinical psychological categories. The vistas opened by psychotherapy do not only pertain to content, such as the vicissitudes of drives and conflicts, but also to the flexibility of focus, the plurality of context, and the convergence of many layers of experience in the expression of the moment. The therapist will also learn quickly that the logic of the events of which he is the observer, partner, and moderator simply does not fit the physicalist conception and methodology which is so prevalent in present-day psychology. In this sense psychotherapy is not only a source of data but a paradigm. One can spurn or ignore either, or one can acknowledge the paradigm and accept what it implies as an approach essential to the scope of psychology and complementary to other approaches.

To the normative definitions of clinical psychology should be added the statement that a psychological approach is *clinical* to the extent that it attempts to understand people in their natural complexity and in their continuous adaptive transformations. The clinical approach will, therefore, be concerned with the inner awareness of experience—its "feel"—as much as with its outward appearance. It will stress the *meaning* of behavior, such as its conscious and unconscious intent, its multiple aims, and its changing objects.[6] Such a conception of behavior will be configurational by axiom, historical in perspective, and oriented toward development as an irreversible process.

Because of its reliance on observation in transactional settings (such as that of psychotherapy) and, consequently, on empathy and intuition, this approach to the study of behavior has often been

---

[6] This does not mean that on the strength of such a definition we can now exclude from clinical psychology all psychologists not in accord with this view. If nothing else, the embarrassing spectacle of classifying out of science all those who do not acknowledge physicalist methodology as its sole criterion should warn us against any such attempt. I do believe that it would be useful if the part played in clinical work by the attitudes described in this paper could be made more explicit. I also believe that in its present usage the term *clinical* generally implies just what these attitudes denote. However, the emphasis here is on explicitness and differentiation, and not on preempting a term so that it can be used to conceal the uneasiness of dogmatism.

debarred from science and, with unmistakable condescension, likened to "art." But there is no reason to believe that science and art are antithetic; as complex psychological sets they seem to overlap as much as they diverge. Clinical psychology does, in fact, by mode of comprehension and even by aim, have some affinity with the arts. This is especially so with literature, which (if we may for the moment bracket its aesthetic aims and means) does often look like informal clinical psychology. In spite of this affinity, however, the clinical approach as defined here is entirely capable of retaining the epistemic quality of science, the commitment to systematic explanation and the search for underlying principles. Hence its concern with a universal theory of motivation relating normal to abnormal behavior, one of the primary criteria for a scientific clinical psychology.

Such a psychology will continually try to test heterogeneous psychological theories for its own uses. Its place is in the front line of psychological exploration whence it can report its own formulations of the qualitative substance of human experience to the laboratory for a more detailed investigation and confirmation. Conversely, it is in a good position to try out the results of laboratory research in the intensive observation of conduct. The historical significance of abnormal behavior is obvious, and the clinic is still an indispensable training ground for clinical psychologists. There is no reason, however, why either subject matter or professional location should determine the scope of clinical psychology.

REFERENCES

ERIKSON, E. H. The problem of ego identity. *Psychol. Issues,* 1959, *1,* 101–168.

ERIKSON, E. H. The nature of clinical evidence. *Daedalus,* 1958, *87,* 65–87.

HOLT, R. R. What is a clinical psychologist? *Newsletter of the Division of Clinical Psychology,* Amer. Psychol. Assoc., 1962, *15* (No. 2), 4–5.

KELLY, E. L. Clinical psychology: The postwar decade. In I. N. Mensh (Ed.), *Clinical Psychology: Science and Profession.* New York: Macmillan, 1966. Pp. 104–121.

KOCH, S. Psychology and emerging conceptions of knowledge as unitary. In T. W. Wann (Ed.), *Behaviorism and Phenomenology: Contrasting Bases for Modern Psychology.* Chicago: University of Chicago Press, 1964. Pp. 1–41.

RAIMY, V. C. (Ed.). *Training in Clinical Psychology.* New York: Prentice-Hall, 1950.

SHAKOW, D. Sub-committee report on graduate internship training in psychology. *J. consult. Psychol.*, 1945, *9*, 243–266.

SKINNER, B. F. Behaviorism at fifty. In T. W. Wann (Ed.), *Behaviorism and Phenomenology: Contrasting Bases for Modern Psychology.* Chicago: University of Chicago Press, 1964. Pp. 79–97.

SKINNER, B. F. Critique of Psychoanalytic Concepts and Theories. In H. Feigl & M. Scriven (Eds.), *The Foundations of Science and the Concepts of Psychology and Psychoanalysis.* Minneapolis: University of Minnesota Press, 1956. Pp. 72–87.

TRYON, R. C. Psychology in flux: The academic-professional bipolarity. *Amer. Psychologist*, 1963, *18*, 134–143.

WATSON, R. I. A brief history of clinical psychology. *Psychol. Bull.*, 1953, *50*, 321–346.

WATSON, R. I. Toward definitions of clinical psychology. Report of the Ad Hoc Committee on the Definition and Description of Clinical Psychology of the Division of Clinical Psychology of the American Psychological Association. Washington, D.C., 1964.

WYATT, F. Climate of Opinion and Methods of Readjustment. *Amer. Psychologist*, 1956, *11*, 537–542.

WYATT, F. Clinical psychology and orthopsychiatry. In *Orthopsychiatry 1923–1948: Retrospect and Prospect.* American Orthopsychiatric Association, New York: 1948. Pp. 217–236.

....

A Study of Human Behavior: The Clinical Psychologist* [1]

Starke R. Hathaway

I set for myself the task of describing the clinical psychologist[2] in a way similar to what we do in evaluating clients and patients. That is, if we are to understand and predict human behavior of any kind, we should dispassionately identify cultural values and pressures that motivate behavior. Presumably, insofar as the human organism is rational, the interactional outcomes of cultural pressures and the organism's special characteristics produce behavior which, classified over a period of time, provides predictive genotypic statements characteristic of future behavior. More in keeping with my role of clinical psychologist, I shall discuss personal elements that relate to the question whether psychologists—clinical psychologists—will be scientific or professional: whether we will become researchers and teachers of a basic science to service personnel or continue as an aggressive profession while accepting requirements of competition and service devotion characteristic of a service profession. In discussing this topic—cast as a series of alternatives—I shall review some of the complex interactions of clinical psychologists and our culture which is shifting in its demands and its rewards.

The Advent of the Clinical Psychologist

I do not know when clinical psychologists first appear in history because I cannot be certain, even today, of the accurate identification of the species. I am, in any case, quite sure that the Greeks must have provided some examples. And, of course, Wundt was an origin

* From the *American Psychologist,* 1958, *13,* 255–265.
[1] Address given to the Minnesota Psychological Association, April 5, 1957.
[2] The reader should understand that the "clinical" of this article is referent to the more medical connotation. The clinical psychologists are predominantly those in recognized clinics.

for things psychological, and McDougall and James were clinical, much more clinical than were their behaviorist successors who so strongly characterized the psychology of the earlier decades of this century.

At the time I came into the field of psychology, there was no widely accepted definition of a clinical psychologist. The forebearers were mental testers; the psychologists in institutions for exceptional children, then crudely called feebleminded; and the psychologists in child guidance clinics. In the 1920's many psychologists, influenced by the empirical stimulus of Watsonian behaviorism, turned to physiological psychology. Franz and Lashley were pioneers. Then came Jacobsen, Lindsley, Klüver, Halstead, Darrow, and others who were often initially oriented to physics and engineering before shifting to the nervous system. Usually this shift was impelled by the open field for those who could build electronic amplifiers or recording galvanometers. To many younger psychologists it may seem strange that these powerful new research instruments were not then available in kits; but, if one wanted an audio amplifier or a polygraph or a galvanic skin response apparatus, he had to design and build it himself. These early psychologists began also to take courses in anatomy and physiology, particularly those at Chicago and Minnesota. I believe Calvin Stone was one of the first of the long line of Minnesota psychologists who studied neuroanatomy with the medical students. These physiological psychologists were not very numerous over the country, but they were conspicuous and their contacts and experiments helped to lay a foundation for a later acceptance of the psychologist in closer working contact with medicine.

There was, at that time, no wide public acceptance of the psychologist as a clinician except as a mental tester. Psychologists like Lightner, Witmer, and E. B. Twitmyer were independent and solidly respected pioneers, but they were not typical of the specialty. On the one hand, the mental tester was professionally tolerated as were all psychologists who worked with behavior problems in children. But most mental testers had an ancillary role in work with physicians, and they ultimately lost out in the evolution of the clinical field. The passive role and low prestige of the mental testers, as viewed by established professions like law and medicine, frustrated some; and such frustration constituted an early pressure in the evolution of the modern clinical psychologist. For example, while some states gave recognition to mental tests in laws relating to legal guardianship and feeblemindedness, the physician with no mental test training was usually given major responsibility in such situations. In my interpretation, the role of mental tester generated so much avoidance behavior that many psychologists still recall predictable negative reactions to the word "psychometrist" and to the phrase "just mental testing." On the other hand, Terman, Thorndike, Wallin, Pintner, Porteus, Bronner, Paterson, Pressey, and others were able to give some status to testing but largely through research emphasis—a significant development in the evolutionary process.

Abnormal psychologists were also forerunners of the modern clinical psychologist. Ultimately they also became professionally extinct and contributed a mildly negative motive in the total process. With great expertness, they taught an abstract subject matter in psychopathology—abstract because they taught what had been handed on to them by Kraepelin and other early medical workers with the insane. Our heritage from them includes beautifully discrete classes of mental illness which some modern clinical psychologists still look for in vain. When our APA Division of Clinical Psychology was first organized, it was called the Division of Clinical and Abnormal Psychology. There was a real distinction in interests of these two types of members. And at first the abnormal psychologists were strong in the division, but the clinicians were more vigorous, although less scholarly and much less well organized in subject matter. Later the growing and overpowering strength of the clinicians came from the service needs of the Armed Services and of the Veterans Administration programs.

But engineering and physiological knowledge was at that early date the easier gate leading to the fascinating field of clinical work with human beings. This is the more pronounced path of development, although some animal and experimental psychologists and clinical persons like Landis, Wechsler, Wells, Rogers, and Shakow also provided stock for evolution.

As everyone knows, when the recent two wars got under way, the demand for psychologists of any kind was very great. Selection and placement of military manpower created an urgent need for accuracy and speed, and the tests of the psychologists were at hand. The First World War gave impetus to intelligence testing, and the Second World War created a comparable impetus for personality testing.

Psychologists were given great freedom and responsibility and discovered that their psychological tools were surprisingly prestigeful in the eyes of the public. And all of a sudden there was a mass exodus from the laboratories out into the world of applied psychology. There was an evolutionary upsurge toward modern clinical psychology. Almost overnight there appeared a number of psychologists gestated in the safety of the university ivory towers. They emerged as ready to do psychotherapy and personality diagnosis of mental illness and all sorts of practical things with which they had had no real clinical experience and for which their professional techniques were not established as valid.

A BADGE OF OFFICE

Scientific and professional support for this upsurge came from mental testing. The Terman-Binet, the Wechsler-Bellevue, and the Strong and the Kuder interest tests, among others, had won public acceptance for expansion into varied applications. These psychometric successes suggested that similar success could be achieved with personality evaluation thereby decreasing the number of psychological failures in combat, for example. What the public did not know was that these objective tests were valid enough in measuring aptitudes, abilities, and interests, but the objective measurement of personality had seemed to be signally unsuccessful. Tests yielding number scores in the critical field of personality measurement were routinely considered to be useless by psychologists. Responding to the public need with this uneven background, the early clinical psychologists gave themselves a promissory note that they would later develop valid measures of personality (2, p. 27). Since they had to do something at once, they used, in addition to the Wechsler-Bellevue and the Stanford-Binet tests, projective tests which "seemed" valid and in any case could not be proved invalid in any simple way. To go with these securities on the note, they espoused a complicated neo-Adlerian dynamic jargon and began to collect badges indicating credit-ability—they subjected themselves to analysis.

Those psychologists who had thought of themselves as physiological, medical, or clinical (medical) psychologists suddenly found themselves part of a horde of these psychologists, claiming close generic relationship, who set about creating the bureaucratic structure and the training programs that have influenced the recent development of clinical psychology. Some psychologists we had known as animal psychologists or experimental psychologists or academic counselors or general psychology teachers soon dominated national circles as authorities on what the new clinical training should be for preparation to work in medical settings and in other professional positions. Only here and there had one of these psychologists been closely and professionally supervised in a clinical setting or had practiced professionally responsible psychotherapy with child or adult patients. For instance, hardly one in four of the psychologists at the important Boulder Conference was a trained and experienced clinician as ABEPP would now define it.

Let me assert that I do not detract from the significant contribution that we "grandfather" clinicians have made. Clinical psychology would not have its present position if we had not used the help at hand in the early days of development. Indeed the evolutionary impulse would have died for lack of offspring without these "adopted" clinicians. For example, our forebearer psychologists feelingly crystallized the pressure that the new clinical training programs should be directed toward the doctorate degree.

But, like many other humans, these psychologists had striven to feel significant in the world and to gain cultural and financial security, and the physician was the most obvious and desirable example for imitation by an educated person who wanted to work with people as was required in the Armed Services and the Veterans Administration clinical settings. Other professions were secure and respected for direct public service, but the new clinical psychologist inherited a will to be a scientist from his behaviorist progenitors, and they also gave him the wish to be scientific in applied psychological work. The intellectual path to power and achievement was clearly established for use. From the culture, the physician not only carried the prestigeful power of life and death but also was reputed to have great psychological wisdom in what used to be called the philosophy of living. People sought the physician for information about sex; and, if anyone was troubled in ways that appeared not obviously criminal or that appeared a bit deviant from ordinary behavior, then the physician (actually any physician, not just the psychiatrist) was the accepted advisor. He had to keep things in confidence, and he had studied and dissected human bodies; he was the only person, except family, before whom the opposite sex could appear undressed with propriety and to whom one would bring psychological and physical excreta. Naturally, our clinical progenitors were attracted by the applied psychological aspects of so secure a position.

The Ph.D. was not a professional degree, of course, except rather loosely for the profession of college teaching; but one *was* called a doctor, and it was difficult for the lay person to differentiate the various kinds of doctors—some clients readily attributed some of the features of the physician to anyone called a doctor. The ivory tower psychologists who had suddenly been born into clinical psychology were sensitive to these cultural conditions. They had accumulated a considerable amount of frustration from their identification with the science of human behavior, implying that they knew why people behave as they do; yet they observed that the psychiatrist and even the general physician were accepted public authorities about human behavior, especially the interesting clinical aspects of it. Moreover, in many clinical variations of human behavior, the physicians had the power to turn the psychologist on and off, to use him where they wished, to say which of the things he said were valid and which were not. As I say, the newly born clinical psychologists were suffering from professional frustration, and this frustration made it likely that a descendent service profession of clinical psychology would emphasize the Ph.D., whether it was appropriate to the service practice of psychology or not.

A case in point is the forgotten proposal made at the Boulder Conference to prohibit the teaching of mental testing to any student not already committed to a clinical Ph.D. program. Under this proposal, the use of psychological tests might be the "defining" professional power, as was the use and prescription of drugs one of the distinctive powers of the physician (2, p. 59). This evolutionary trend, if pursued, might have been fairly successful in establishing status. A few state laws use tests in this way, but the spectre of the old mental tester was frightening; and, anyway, educators and personnel workers have to use tests too. And no one knew how to convert objective test data into dynamically useful statements. Thus the search for a technique which would "define" the new clinician turned elsewhere, to the Ph.D.

This Ph.D. upgrading of clinical psychologists, including the officially extinct mental tester, produced a new frustration. Some of us protested even at that early time that, recognizing the virtue of higher education and the halo value of the title "doctor," the great mass of things that had to be done in a psychology service would not be done better because of the training that went into the current Ph.D. (2, pp. 34 ff.). Also, the public could ill afford Ph.D.s to do mental testing; and, if we were not experts in psychometry, what did we offer that was new? My own clinical experience, like that of the few others who had been active for several years in clinical psychology, had seemed to indicate that most of the training required for the Ph.D. was unneeded in daily clinical practice, even in psychotherapy.

Turning to another characteristic, the clinical psychologist who is suitable Ph.D. material is often the victim of mixed self concepts. He sees himself as a "doctor," but he does not identify readily with socal workers, nurses, medical technicians, and the like; moreover, he cannot completely accept himself as comparable to a physician. He does not want to be "on call" or forced to be responsible for the minutiae of medical "care" for sick and dependent patients. He is not a "doctor" of much of anything according to modern lay context. He is not a doctor of physic, not a doctor of dentistry; he is, rather, a doctor of philosophy, and in that family he becomes a doctor of psychology which is a very, very broad field and not easily comparable to "real doctors." It is small wonder that he sometimes emphasizes that the "doctor" title is historically more proper for the Ph.D. than for the M.D., a latecomer.

THE PROMISED LAND OF RESEARCH

The clinical psychologists who emerged from the ivory tower solved some of the problem of their unrelated training by a major emphasis on research. In shifting to this point, predictable for them, they made a masterful move in that they laid the foundation for a prestige and security that is still fairly unique among the service professions. This research strategy, however, produced frustration for many of the new clinical trainees, not really interested in research but in clinical psychology as a service profession—in helping people in trouble. Some of these young psychologists are now further frustrated: being able to help people is glamorous mainly as private practitioners or as psychoanalysts, but the same help given under other circumstances is without the communicable tradition of a profession. And so the young, service minded (and therefore more fundamentally professional) psychologist is like the psychiatrist, forced to base his security on training in science and research which no one can closely relate to or use in routine diagnostic and psychotherapeutic work.

But, for many, the promised land of research has been a fairly successful refuge, although there is often an undercurrent of unrest. In the first place, if the clinical psychologist wants to emerge from the ivory tower part of the time to do practical clinical research in a prestigeful setting, he feels that he should be working with psychologically maladjusted persons willing publicly to admit that they need help. That is, he is not satisfied to work with his friends, students, or the friends of students as clients or counselees. But in most instances and under the present organization of clinics and with the present attitudes of public agencies, the clients with whom the clinical research psychologist would like to work are rarely under his control. When the psychiatrist does not control the subjects, the social worker does; and the social worker has been understandably jealous in protecting himself, partly by using the shadow of the psychiatrist, even when he is working in clinics independent of psychiatric supervision. Clearly established professions like psychiatry and social work can point to their recognized responsibility for patients, and they must reserve the right to veto any procedure that might adversely affect the patient. The clinical psychologist who wishes to use patients as subjects has to maneuver around such a block in order to pursue his research interests. We can understand much of his behavior if we will keep this point in mind.

A transitional adjustment in the evolution of clinical psychology is found in the psychology department clinic. Clinicians in these luxury devices can use psychiatrists and social workers as consultants and are thus free of heavy responsibilities by operating with financial deficits and by the fact that any patient who decides he is really sick can go to a "real" clinic. In department clinics the psychologist is king, and therefore research and intellectuality reign. But these clinics are not appropriate to the activities of academic departments and usually cause some schism within the department faculty. They are thus only partial solutions to the problems.

Unfortunately, the achievement of freedom to work with patients frequently also traps the psychologist into the position of having professional responsibility for those patients. That is, when he is treating them or is otherwise responsible, he faces heavy demands on his time which may sabotage his research efforts. When he is working with animals, the psychologist does not have to be much concerned about their personal affairs and does not have a heavy cultural responsibility to be professionally available to them during night and day. One simply does not use a group of human subjects for an experiment and then sacrifice the lot to buy or breed new subjects when they are needed.

But even when he can achieve free access to subjects and general freedom to do clinical research, the criterion problems for clinical work in psychology are found to be far more difficult than in medicine generally and even in some other branches of psychology. The results of experiments in education and of variations in personnel policies are more likely to show identifiable changes in behavior and to provide relevant criteria than are experiments with psychotherapy or studies of insane or delinquent persons. These problems of research design have driven many a promising clinical psychologist back to student-subject research with verbal behavior or even to the animal laboratories. One may sometimes observe a tendency toward inbreeding and even a reappearance of the recessive strain of abnormal psychologists among teachers and researchers in psychodynamics or psychophysiology whose only contact with "real" patients came from personal therapy, their training apprenticeship, or from patients herded into their research quarters by orders to the responsible clinician that specify quantity and kind of subjects needed for a project.

Moreover, the clinical psychologist is under pressure because he knows that his psychometric tools are objectively weak, although they are his mainstay as a scientist. Following his cultural heritage, he basks in the expectation among his professional peers and the public that predictions made, either statistically or clinically, with the application of tests will be more accurate about what is therapeutically best, about the outcomes of psychotherapy, and about the causes of maladjustment than is presently possible with our knowledge (2, p. 26).

SCIENCE AND PRACTICE

But the applied clinical psychologist's ambivalences include others. His genealogy has led to rigorous training in critical thinking and in research. He is taught to have particular reverence for objective data, reproducible data, and he is not permitted the easy unawareness of the problem of validity that is a negative asset to the other helping professions. This rigorous training, part of the heritage of the ivory tower, comes into direct conflict with the forced routine of daily clinical decisions from inadequate evidence. The "good" psychologist should withhold decisions and actions unless he has reasonable probability that he is doing better than chance; but almost everything in the practicing psychologist's work demands decisions even when evidence is inadequate.

The worst part of this conflict is that the most satisfying rewards and personal recognition for a service oriented psychologist often come from the most obviously unscientific items of his behavior. That is, a good part of the time he is rewarded for defying his training in scientific thought and action. For example, he contributes to decisions about which therapy to use, when to discharge the patient, even when to operate on patients. He sometimes does psychotherapy with friends and patients. For these tasks he knows that his decisions are based upon no better evidence than those of his less scientifically oriented peers; but the patients who get better express admiration and indebtedness. Then, too, professional peers, frustrated in the face of our general clinical impotence, are rewardingly thankful if we will, under some scientific guise, make decisions for them. Such expressions of appreciation come in our professional field as a natural consequence of our culture that uncritically identifies us with science and professional competence.

On attempting to adjust to the many aspects of this problem, it is not surprising that the clinical psychologist should do as the psychiatrist did before him and thus preserve some of the trappings of science to soften the painful contact with established objectivity. Projective methods and dynamics are examples of such an adaptive trend. If one takes a projective test and interprets it dynamically or, in general, if one talks in dynamic terms, one is in apparent line with "good," modern science. I am not deprecating the values of these procedures for research or for theory, but I am examining their values in the relief of the clinician's anxiety. One assures one's self and eagerly assures others that the Rorschach is a measuring instrument and properly respectable for scientific study and that psychoanalysis is a new and powerful scientific method. It is possible to pick up a figure drawing or a set of TAT stories or even an MMPI profile and to talk about unconscious mechanisms without the threat of an objective accusation that the test was administered and interpreted incorrectly.

This is a very important source of assurance. The mental testers did not have this source of freedom. That is, a Binet test produced an IQ that might be challenged definitively. Similarly, for the psychiatrist, if he goes wrong in inferring latent schizophrenia, nothing but a more authoritative voice can contradict him; contrastingly, if he overlooks a tumor, his shame is inevitable. One thing that has made such an adjustment unsatisfactory for the clinical psychologist is the very fact that what relieves him of tiresome drill and study may open the path to psychologists in other specialties and to other professional clinical workers who can also suggest mechanisms from figure drawings and inkblots and thus compete in the spinning of dynamic statements.

Another field of frustration for the modern clinical psychologist who wants to practice is that he has, in part, been attracted to the specialty by false ideas about his ultimate role. He, for example, may see himself as a wise person to whom people come for help with their problems. It is prestigeful to be thought of in this way. Every young psychologist is adapted to the fact that when he goes to parties or is in any contact with persons not in psychology, he receives a certain amount of "free" adulation. It is a pretty strong young psychologist who can wholly resist pleasure in the role of the mind reader or a person intimate with the more juicy secrets of daily living.

This tends to give a prestigeful character to practicing psychotherapy, and among clinical psychologists one of the most jealously sought after roles is that of the psychotherapist. Unfortunately, the professional psychotherapeutic work is not so satisfying as the culture makes it seem. Most of the people who need psychotherapy are not college-type people, not verbally bright; many of them are somewhat uncouth and with uninteresting problems and uncomplicated personalities. The psychologist, who usually does not want to be in private practice and thus who is not well paid for working with these people, soon finds that a routine of psychotherapy with complaining patients he cannot refuse is often a pretty undesirable way to live. Also, he finds he must work harder than the psychiatrist because he cannot collect fees from shock, drugs, and other medical prerogatives. Consequently, he sometimes attempts to achieve a position where he can get the cream of patients; that is, where he can work with the attractive young person, the easy situational problem, or whatever constitutes an interesting and rewarding case.

Many of the theoretical formulations about psychotherapy are built upon practice with such patients, "cream of the crop," who are more often like the therapist himself: bright, verbal, good at producing intriguing associations and fascinating dreams. Of course, this psychotherapeutic cream is usually skimmed off by the supervisory staff. The young clinical psychologist will accept the leavings while in training, but he finds it difficult to go on with the same skimmed remnant after he has graduated, even at the expense of risking his professional position.

Under the guise of training, the fledgling psychologist is sometimes maneuvered into doing the diagnostic testing and summary report writing that express the scientific "ticket" for the practice of clinical psychology as the chiefs of service would like it. Not only are these tests weak in useful validity, but also the related duties do not increase self-respect because they do not require intellect and knowledge comparable to his "high" Miller score and, indeed, his test based, diagnostic statements rarely produce a dramatic effect in therapy. Finally, the procedures on which they are drilled in training are not really respected by the teaching faculty who themselves often do not use the same psychometric devices and other more scientifically respectable procedures in their own practice. That is, both clinical psychologists and psychiatrists have fallen into the habit of teaching one thing and privately doing another.

Another cultural trap for the young clinical trainee is that his training faculty in psychology tends to be oriented toward theory and academic things in general, and so the students who are selected for training also develop (or profess to have) a wish to be identified with these ideals. The father-figure is a professor or research chief who does a little research or psychotherapy with interesting subjects or friends and peers—who is able to play all roles with the advantages of each.

Thus it is that there is now a mixed reward offered the young clinical psychologist. He can work with clinical cases and enjoy satisfactions that are provided in feeling that he is intimate with people and has directly helped them in the best tradition of the origins of the medical, nursing, and social work professions. Or he can work for the satisfactions of contributing to knowledge, of becoming scientifically known, of becoming a great teacher, and other characteristic rewards of a scholar. Such is the dilemma of the professional man or scientist.

Clinical psychology is now established among psychologists and to a large extent in the public culture. Indeed, in the recent series of *Life* magazine, termed "psychology," the discussion included psychiatry. Out of this heritage and with these ambivalences, the clinical psychologist of today has gained some prestige. Where he has gained a foothold, he has prestige over the social worker and nurse with his research competence and his doctorate. He has succeeded in transposing from the psychiatrist a considerable standing in the eyes of the public; partly this is due to his success in publicizing his field, and partly there has been a breakdown in the overly high confidence that the public had in psychiatry with some consequent drift toward the psychologist. Finally, the psychologist has derived some benefit by the mixture of being a doctor but not being identified with the mentally ill person. Here psychiatry's efforts to keep the psychologist out of psychotherapy have somewhat backfired in that, if he is not in psychotherapy, he is not working with ill persons; and "high-K" people who feel they need psychological help find it easier to go to a psychologist than to a psychiatrist because of the magic escape from considering themselves psychologically ill. Some psychologists themselves achieve the same type of escape by taking psychotherapy from a psychiatrist (!) and calling their therapeutic sessions "training sessions."

TODAY AND TOMORROW

I have reviewed some of the cultural forces operating today on clinical psychologists. I have not described their resultant behavior in the detail you would like. By this review of the personal and cultural forces, I have sought to establish the variety of emphases current in clinical psychology. Nearly every adjustment pattern observed among clinicians has occurred as a resultant of training and experience in some university, school, or clinic. As yet, no completely satisfying or dominant component of needs has been discovered for the training and role of the clinical psychologist. Local specialties like dust bowl empiricism, extinction of conditioning, nondirection, and other expedient items are partly compensatory emphases that have had some adjustive value.

But it is a backward step to discard special curricular requirements for clinical psychologists, as has been done by several large universities and as is implicitly signified in the denial of a differentiation of counselors and clinical psychologists. Social psychologists, experimental psychologists, counselors, and other psychological specialists should contribute to our service programs; but, if these variously trained psychologists are not marked as different from specially trained clinical psychologists, I believe no psychologists can be given direct professional responsibility for patients.

True clinical emphasis is on "patients," not "clients" or "counselees," even though a continuum of behavior is involved. Laws and the culture itself do not leave much doubt that patients are different from counselees. To these patients and their problems, the clinical psychologist should come with a prescribed (but not rigid) curriculum, an ethical sense, a desire for service, and a profound interest in discovery of new and better treatments and diagnostic systems. Such a solid professional foundation will open the way for other types of psychologists to make their unique contributions in a receptive and responsible atmosphere.

Acceptance into practice of psychologists with generic or other than clinical specialty training in clinical positions will blur the meaning of the specialty. This will weaken a prime requirement for a profession: a disciplined and recognizable training program. And evaluation of clinical training programs should not be limited to the general level of psychological instruction in psychology departments.

There are ways in which the clinical aspect of our specialty has been too influential in orthogenetic evolutionary pressure. In becoming too clinical, the psychologist can lose emphasis to the point of limited if any scientific rewards. We should not imitate other clinicians; we should be psychologists. The frustrations of these overly clinical psychologists I have described seem to have determined a denial of the special field. If they devote themselves to becoming earnest and responsible clinicians while injecting more science into their work, they may still launch a satisfying as well as respectable new profession; but it may be too early for one. The frustrations I have indicated are punishing, and the scientific aspects of daily clinical work are minimal.

The scientific role, the ivory tower heritage, is gaining ascendancy. I have tried to show why this is true and to indicate my feeling that research and broad training must continue to hold a strong place. In sharp contrast, however, there is no doubt that the public that supports us will not shift its allegiance to us from social work and psychiatry without demanding a real and inexorable service contribution that we have implicitly promised. We have talked about this; we always dodge the direct action (3). We evolved on the impetus of service need. This need is growing: need for workers to man clinics and to apply tests and other scientifically derived procedures. Unless clinical psychology produces more workers to meet the need for direct service, produces a practical outcome and someone to practice in routine clinical work apart from scientific and research endeavors, then our culture will withdraw some of our present support and the prestige role of the clinical researcher and scientist will be partly lost (1). Such losses could leave the clinician stranded and empty of effective functions. He will perhaps also have to compete with a new, vigorous, and truly professional group.

Some psychologists would like to develop an ancillary psychological profession, like nurses for example. Such persons would be cheaper to hire and might be selected so they uncomplainingly fill the public need, leaving the real clinical psychologist to be the scientist and interpreter of data laid in front of him. But this technician group might achieve control of the applied techniques (psychometrics) that distinguish the higher level psychologist from his professional competitors. Then, too, ancillary staff sometimes rebel, and this solution may be old-fashioned because the new group would soon also demand more years of training and a special recognition.

I hope that my discussion of this topic of the factors that operate on the clinical psychologist will help to predict what will become of his species. On all hands one can see behavioral signs of the frustrations I have described. Psychologists who are abstracted enough can get a good deal of amusement watching the clinical psychologist try to hold both the service and academic research roles: trying to keep the lucrative, wise, and prestigeful role of clinical doctor, yet dodging the drudgery of clinical responsibility; trying to skim the cream of patients and the best of the role of the psychiatrist, without getting involved in the dependence on private patient fees; trying to be a scientist, yet seeking respect as a profession.

What other positive suggestions can be made? My own feeling is that we are leaving a professional field before we really are established in it. We are reneging on our promissory note. We are, rather, issuing a new one. It promises that, if the public will support all of us, we will do research and then hand to the clinicians the practical products. But what clinicians? I would have us continue M.A. and Ph.D. (or Psy.D.?) programs with preliminary but definite structure both in required courses and especially in didactic and applied experience with ill patients. The only way professional psychologists can hold to a responsible place is by partial separation from the academic, basic science psychologists; otherwise the present sabotage of the profession will continue. Presently we have very few nonacademic and nonresearch leaders. I do not want these leaders to be completely free of teaching, research, and administration; but I want them to be more than 80% in real clinical work with ill patients.

I would hope that such professionals would be able to revive the respectability of testing and diagnosis and the more applied aspects of psychology. One effective and appropriate way to accomplish this is to apply consistently, in all clinical settings, the primary observational and methodological techniques of psychology to the crucial problems of evaluation of personality pathology—this in contrast to loose formulations and clinical jargon even though these are the current mode. I am distressed that some practicing psychologists have argued that they yield to such nonsense because the chief of service wants it and doles out prestige for it. With a vigorous clinical approach, students would not feel inferior when they admitted to a desire for a mainly service job; and the present severe slump in the morale of clinicians would be stemmed.

There will be other positive moves that occur to some clinicians. My suggestion has sometimes seemed to be a lost cause. I hope that others of you who have been trying to be scientific clinical psychologists, not psychiatrists or social workers or administrators or teachers, will display courage in conviction and will speak up in active support of a new profession. Psychiatry, a service profession, is so strong on that commitment that it is handicapped. We, however, could find our own prestige and satisfactions in psychological service.

If I have seemed too cynical and destructive, I plead that it is important to all of us to see our problems and the sources of our behavior in order to build more solidly our own futures and the future of our common profession. I deeply believe that we are now entering a decade of special decision. We must not merely criticize ourselves in masochistic passivity. Applying our own solidly founded psychological principles, we must sharply and impassionately interpret the personal motivations of the evolving clinicians in terms of the needs and requirements of our culture.

REFERENCES

1. AMERICAN PSYCHOLOGICAL ASSOCIATION, Education and Training Board. Anticipations of developments during the next decade which will influence psychology. *Amer. Psychologist,* 1956, *11,* 686–688.
2. RAIMY, V. C. (Ed.) *Training in Clinical Psychology.* New York: Prentice-Hall, 1950.
3. STROTHER, C. R. (Ed.) *Psychology and Mental Health.* Washington, D.C.: APA, 1956.

Clinical Psychology and the Search for Identity* [1]

SOL L. GARFIELD

IT IS A truism that one is influenced greatly by his own experience and that one's views and perceptions are significantly colored by such experience. I mention this at the outset, not only to caution you, perhaps needlessly, that what I say will be influenced by my own professional experience over the past 20 years, but also, because many of the problems and difficulties within clinical psychology are related to the accelerated professional development of clinical psychology during the postwar period. Having been immersed in this development ourselves, we tend at times to lose persepective and to be unduly influenced by the shifting forces and events around us. However, it should be possible for us to try to analyze, with or without a psychological frame of reference, some of the developments which have occurred and which appear to be sources of conflict today. In what follows, I have at least attempted such an analysis in the hope of reaching a better understanding of some of the problems which give us concern.

It is apparent that there is a certain amount of unrest, excitement and dissatisfaction within clinical psychology at the present time. Some of these trends are by no means new, and one is impressed with the fact that clinical psychologists appear to be a particularly introspective, soul-searching, and self-critical group. One might even say, in a more negative way, that they have the appearance of being chronically dissatisfied. I believe that there are underlying reasons for such feelings, which deserve discussion. However, whatever one's view, it is evident that clinical psychologists are deeply concerned about their professional role in society, the social demands

---

* From the *American Psychologist,* 1966, *21,* 353–362.

[1] Presidential Address presented to Division 12 at American Psychological Association, Chicago, September 1965.

placed upon them for professional services, the dynamic state of the society in which we live, the conflicts between the scientific and professional aspects of psychology, and the implications of such matters for graduate training in our field. Clinical psychology is in many respects an unusual and unique field. Being a part of the broader field of psychology and deriving from it, it has of necessity been influenced by the values and developments within psychology proper. At the same time, as a result of significant social forces and needs growing out of the Second World War, it has worked closely and has been influenced by other disciplines which are involved with the treatment and understanding of emotionally disturbed individuals. In a sense, one can say that clinical psychology has had a part in each of two worlds—the academic-scientific and the clinical-professional. This has been both a source of uniqueness and enrichment, as well as a source of divisiveness and discontent.

Before delving into the current situation, and in order to obtain some perspective on what has transpired, it is worthwhile to take a very brief look at some of our previous history. From a somewhat modest beginning in this country, psychology showed a slow but steady growth in the approximately 50 years preceding 1940. As of 1940 there were less than 3,000 members in the American Psychological Association, and most of psychology was decidedly academic in its emphasis and tenor. Since 1940, there has been a tremendous growth spurt in psychology as reflected in the size of our association and in the number of doctorates awarded. In the decade 1951–60 our membership more than doubled (Hilgard, 1962), and as Brayfield (1964) has recently pointed out, two-thirds of all the doctorates awarded in psychology in the past 50 years were granted in the last 10 years. This rate of growth in psychology at one point was such as to lead to Boring's dire prediction (quoted in Sanford, 1954, p. 125) that if the rate of increase in psychology continued, by 2100 A.D. everyone in the United States would be a psychologist—a truly terrifying prospect. The rate of growth in the APA during the period from 1920 to 1950 also far exceeded that of other professional and scientific organizations (Clark, 1957). The APA increased over eighteenfold during this 30-year period as contrasted with the sevenfold increase of the Federation of Societies for Experimental Biology in second place, and as contrasted with the sixfold increase of an ancillary profession with initials similar to our own.

It is apparent, therefore, that we have grown rapidly and the small, somewhat intimate APA existing prior to World War II has been replaced by something closer to a three-ring circus. Apart from the rapid rise in sheer numbers, a change in organizational structure and in the interest and activity patterns of psychologists has also taken place. The rise in clinical psychology has been particularly notable. In a sample survey by Sanford (1955) of division preference, not division membership, slightly over one-third of the APA members queried indicated a primary interest in the clinical area. This trend has continued, and with it, a change in the composition of the APA membership. Tryon (1963), for example, has recently pointed out that the applied or professional divisions within APA have grown more rapidly in the period from 1948 to 1960 than have the more academic divisions. In this connection, we can also note that the membership of the Division of Clinical Psychology today approximates that of the entire APA in 1940. Most of these developments are of fairly recent vintage and I need not elaborate. My point of emphasis here is that we have experienced a period of rapid and significant change in psychology in a relatively short time, a fact which I believe is of some importance in understanding some of our problems today.

Of more immediate concern to us, perhaps, have been the rapid and significant changes which have occurred within clinical psychology. In less than 20 years we have witnessed and experienced the following: increased professionalization and concern with professional problems, increased demands for our services with accompanying social rewards, an emphasis on state certification and licensing, the setting up of formal training programs in clinical psychology, a broadening of professional roles, an increase in private practice, a decline in traditional clinical testing, a marked emphasis on psychotherapy, increased disharmony between the science and profession of psychology, and some evidences of dissatisfaction among those in the profession. There are undoubtedly others, but this list is long enough to indicate some of our growth and development since the war.

The fact that there appear to be several manifestations of dissatisfaction among clinical psychologists is a rather surprising finding when viewed in the light of the rapid growth and ostensible accomplishments which have taken place these past few years. At a time when, to paraphrase someone else's statement, so many have had it so good, it is indeed startling to encounter such apparent unrest, critical self-appraisal, feelings of rejection, hostility, and similar patterns—all of them indicative of less than adequate adjustment. While this, of course, is by no means true of all clinical psychologists, or even of a majority of them, it does appear to be true of a sizeable portion and to be symptomatic of underlying difficulties. Let me just mention a few happenings which justify my statement.

The energy and attention devoted to discussions of role models for clinical psychologists, to problems of identity, to conflicts with other professional groups, to critical self-appraisal, and to symposia and conferences on training is striking. While I have not made any comparable survey of other professions in this regard, it is my own impression that we are at least unique in this respect, if in no other way. This past year, for example, formal conferences on a state level pertaining to training in clinical psychology have been held in Michigan, Minnesota, and Wisconsin. Conferences of this type on a national level appear to be held every 4 or 5 years. The national involvement in the training conference just completed was at an unusually high level. All of these certainly bespeak of some type of lack of satisfaction and continued need for self-appraisal.

Another finding of interest is the follow-up of the Veterans Administration Assessment Study reported by Kelly and Goldberg (1959). In this study, carried out 10 years after the initial assessment research of 1947–1948, the individuals evaluated were asked about their satisfaction with their vocational choice of clinical psychologist. Forty percent of the sample expressed dissatisfaction and indicated that on the basis of their experience, in retrospect, they would have chosen a career other than clinical psychology.

While we have no comparable data for other professions, this finding is certainly a negative and disquieting one. Perhaps, being from a different generation of students than those studied by Kelly and Goldberg, my own expectations and satisfactions were quite different, and I was both surprised and disturbed at this report. While a majority of us may be relatively content with our field, such evidence of discontent among a sizeable number of our colleagues cannot be dismissed lightly. It seems to suggest that their expectations about clinical psychology and their actual experiences were not congruent. How can one explain this as well as other manifestations of dissatisfaction?

Let me start by focusing on what I consider to underlie or be at the heart of current discontent and confusion. This centers around the scientist-practitioner model for clinical psychology and the requirement of the Ph.D. degree as the basic professional requisite. It seems to me that all subsequent developments—such as the emphasis on psychotherapy, the increase in private practice, the growing schism between the scientific and professional aspects of clinical psychology, and the accompanying diffuseness and confusion with reference to professional identity—are interlocked with these earlier decisions as far as current concerns are involved.

The scientist-practitioner model was seen by the participants at the Boulder Conference as a unique one, and one which differentiated the profession of clinical psychology from most others, and by implication, ordinary professions. The point of view was expressed as follows:

the development of the profession of clinical psychology constitutes something of an educational experiment, in that clinical psychologists are being trained both as scientists and as practitioners. Most professions base their practices on one or more sciences and train their future members in a separate professional school. In contrast, clinical psychologists are trained concurrently in both the theoretical (scientific) and applied (clinical) aspects of psychology. This training occurs not in professional schools but in the graduate schools of our colleges and universities (Raimy, 1950, p. V).

There is little question in my mind that this noble objective has not yet been attained, and that many of our problems bear at least some relationship to this model. Let me state clearly, however, that I am not criticizing the Boulder model as a model, but rather that in trying to adapt training and practice to this model we have been, to put it mildly, less than optimally successful. While it may sound obvious and redundant, I want to say here that clinical psychology was clearly seen at that time as a specialty *within psychology* and as *deriving from psychology*. In the postwar planning, it was decided, therefore, to require the highest degree within psychology for the new clinical psychologist. This was, of course, the Ph.D. degree, a traditional degree emphasizing research competence and conferred by the graduate schools in our universities. The clinical or professional aspects of the training were added to or superimposed upon this traditional academic and research training. If the psychology departments were to train clinical psychologists, it was to be at the highest academic level available to them. The theme was, also, that the individuals to be trained in these programs were to be *psychologists first* and *clinicians second*. Furthermore, the specific training in diagnostic and therapeutic techniques was to be given along with training in the basic areas of psychology and in research methodology. Most people, apparently, were happy with this kind of training objective. The clinical psychologist was to be trained to perform diagnostic, therapeutic, and research functions, and the latter was to be his unique contribution in relation to his professional colleagues.

As we have already noted, in the relatively short time since the Boulder Conference, surprising and unanticipated changes in professional activities and settings have occurred, and these have had a profound impact on the field. The problem is admittedly complex and I can merely highlight some aspects of it here. For the sake of illustration let me focus on the areas of psychotherapy and private practice, where the degree of change and the amount of stress has probably been greatest.

One can start by discussing the relationship of psychotherapy to psychology. In the past (pre-1940), this was not a significant area of psychology nor a truly important function of the clinical psychologist. Even in most postwar training programs, instruction in psychotherapy clearly has constituted only a small part of the total program. The field of counseling, however, in a variety of forms, has had a more generically close tie to psychology and has existed in educational institutions for some time. Psychotherapy qua psychotherapy, on the other hand, has been more closely tied to psychiatry and has been an important part of psychology only in recent years. Thus, psychotherapy is the most recent of the psychologist's functions, does not have the historical tie to psychology that psychological tests and research have had, and has been more prominently identified with professions outside of psychology. The interesting thing that has occurred, however, is that many clinical psychologists have become increasingly preoccupied with the practice of psychotherapy, an activity not particularly or exclusively identified with psychology or emphasized in the graduate training programs, and have for practical purposes forsaken the more traditional and psychologically identified activities of testing and research. The reasons for this somewhat surprising state of affairs are undoubtedly varied, and I shall offer some possible hypotheses about it shortly. The facts, however, are clear as manifested, for example, in the survey by Lowell Kelly (1961). A large number of clinical psychologists spend most of their time in the practice of psychotherapy, and are generally concerned with activities pertaining to psychotherapy. I believe that this particular development with its related role and value implications plays a significant part in the current dissatisfaction, among practitioners and academicians alike, but for different reasons. Problems of professional identification are intimately tied in with this matter.

It is my thesis that the clinical psychologist who becomes primarily a psychotherapist, and this is particularly true of the private practitioner of psychotherapy, tends to lose his identification with the field of psychology. Such an individual tends to perform, or to see himself, as a practicing psychotherapist or psychoanalyst, and these terms are not synonymous with the term psychologist. Furthermore, it seems to me, at least, that many such individuals, outside of specific professional concerns, look for models, reading materials, journals, meetings, and even associations outside of psychology proper, and tend to be critical, not only of their past training which ill-prepared them to be practicing psychotherapists, but also of the field which holds values so divergent from theirs. From such an individual's point of view, there would appear to be ample justification for his feelings. The university and other psychologists do not appear to share his value system and he is critical of theirs. On the other hand, there may also be, as I hypothesize, some feelings of loss and some problem of identity on the part of the psychologist who becomes essentially a psychotherapist.

It appears that a number of events have interacted in helping to bring this situation about. While the participants at Boulder, and academic psychologists generally, saw the new clinical psychologist as having primary loyalties and identification with the field of psychology, with an emphasis on research competence, those who became practitioners either had or developed a different perception of things. Many of them were more interested in becoming clinical practitioners than scientists and some were more concerned with the model of the psychiatrist than with that of their mentors. Since, whether because of interest, status, or other value, psychotherapy became the activity which was highly prized and with private practice emerging as a new type of professional role, the divergences between "old" and "new" models of clinical psychologists increased.

Interest in diagnostic and assessment work, which has long been linked with psychology, has also diminished. There are undoubtedly a number of reasons for this, some of which may have been its limited use by others, the considerable negative findings in the literature, the lower status accorded diagnostic testing, and the fact that it was done at the request of others. Another factor involved in this estrangement appears to have been the role conflict with psychiatrists, which I believe was resolved in many instances by identification with the aggressor.

Another aspect, in more recent years particularly, relates to the confusion concerning what clinical psychology is all about and the discrepancy between the expectations of the clinical student and the clinical faculty in the university. Here there is a problem which is quite current today. At least a number of people who apply for graduate work in clinical psychology are interested in becoming psychotherapists or practitioners and are not interested in research.

Having been on both sides of the university fence, I can sympathize with such students who have no interest in research and only want to be practitioners, mainly psychotherapists. They go through the motions of a Ph.D. program and endure it if they are successful, only because they see it as a means to an end. Many are disappointed in the doctoral programs and have confused ideas as to what such programs entail, or more basically, of what clinical psychology consists. Some of this is the result of selective perception on the part of students, but it exists anyway. Many of these people want to be practitioners of some kind. Some want to avoid medical school as the path to psychotherapy and see the Ph.D. program as the lesser of two evils. Some, in the New York area, for example, feel they must have a doctor's degree to practice psychotherapy or psychoanalysis privately. Many of these people are not admitted to doctoral programs, but some are. For a number of those who enter our graduate schools the Ph.D. program is seen as an obstacle course to suffer through as a means of later doing what they want. There is no need to elaborate upon this situation further. The personal discomfort and the tremendous waste of human time and energy involved in such instances, on the part of faculty and students alike, is appalling—particularly in the light of current social needs and manpower shortages.

It is relatively easy to see why such persons are dissatisfied with clinical psychology as they experience it during their training and try to escape from it after receiving the Ph.D. degree. However, there is a more serious aspect of this problem with reference to students who are not so strongly committed to psychotherapy, who see themselves as clinical psychologists, and want to identify with the clinical psychologist as their model. Unfortunately, they are not given an integrated model with which to identify but are confronted instead by two apparently conflicting models—the scientific-research model and the clinical-practitioner model. As I see it, the Boulder model is really not available to them and in its place are two conflicting value systems, the academic and the professional. The clinical psychology student may gain some impression of this conflict within the university psychology department itself, but most likely it intrudes itself when he goes out to obtain practicum and internship experience. Instead of an integrated model of a scientist-practitioner, the student perceives an "either-or" choice.

At present we may find a situation which basically forces a student to see a split between research and practice and to align himself accordingly in terms of his own personal needs. In one course, or at the practicum center, clinical techniques are taught as if there were little question concerning their efficacy and validity. In another course, the student is confronted with an array of research data which may seriously undermine his faith in these techniques. The student also learns that it is not wise to raise certain kinds of questions, depending on the situation. This kind of dissonance is far from soothing, and to resolve it most students tend to identify with *either* the research *or* the practitioner model, and to blot out or defend one against the other. Both groups tend to have some problems in the area of identity, to a greater or lesser degree, since one group does not really behave like psychologists, and the other does not behave like clinicians.

Many of our current difficulties in self-concept and self-identity stem from limitations in the primary training centers for clinical psychologists, the universities. This is where the future clinical psychologist usually has his first contact with representatives of our field. Sooner or later, confusions and conflicts as to professional role models emerge and cause concern. Let us look at some of them; obviously, they will vary for different situations.

In many instances the students' professors will be talking about what clinical psychologists do, but not doing these things themselves. When the student makes contact with practicum or internship agencies, he is faced with models which differ markedly from the clinical psychology model at the university. There also appear to be different value systems and different ways of looking at problems. In addition, relationships to other disciplines take on greater significance. This is all reasonably familiar to most of you and I need not elaborate on it here. This experience, however, is decidedly important for the problem of professional identity and self-worth. There are clear dissonances here in terms of who or what is a clinical psychologist, as well as related problems over one's importance and independence. Some products of this program appear to have been decidedly traumatized by their experiences if one makes a clinical evaluation of their current personality and behavior. In some instances, there is evident very strong hostility to such diverse groups as academic clinical psychologists and psychiatrists—as if both of these groups somehow challenge or threaten their sense of personal worth. It is interesting to speculate here. A group of clinical psychologists are severely critical of their former teachers, fellow clinical psychologists with whom apparently they have little in common professionally, but appear to show the same response to psychiatrists, members of a different profession, with whom they share many similarities of practice. This behavior I would diagnose not as an unresolved double Oedipus complex, but as a case of confused identity, severe. I am quite willing to speculate further and say that much of the dissatisfaction manifested by private practitioners in our field is related to the identity problem in a significant way. While they are critical of psychiatrists, the latter represent much more of a realistic model to them than psychologists not in practice. Yet, they have been trained as psychologists, even though they do not believe that most psychologists really approve of them or think highly of them. They are caught here and in the more populated areas have banded together for mutual support and a feeling of identity.

Similar conflicts exist among clinical psychologists in academia. They, too, have some inadequacy feelings about really being clinical psychologists, and are quick to react to second-class status in medical settings. However, they get their support from the larger psychological as well as academic community and perhaps the identity problem is not as severe. However, to the extent that the dominant values they share may be those of the university and not of the clinic, their identity does not provide a sufficient or adequate model for all students.

The student in training is thus exposed to differing models which, calling themselves clinical psychologists, appear to do different things, value things differently, think differently, and even to be very critical of each other. Most students are alert to such happenings and the most perceptive are aware of what is valued in the appropriate setting. This is apparent also in what activities are emphasized at the different settings. Research, diagnostic testing, and psychotherapy are taught or emphasized differentially. Projective techniques may be very critically evaluated in the university, to the point where the student gets the impression they are really of little value, yet they may be highly touted at the internship center.

The student when faced with such a situation is forced to identify with one or the other of the models available to him. Some, for a variety of reasons, identify with their academic mentors and choose an academic career in clinical psychology. Others turn against what they perceive as the academic and nonclinical model, and identify more with their internship and practicum supervisors. Still others find neither model really satisfactory, and go into private practice, presumably based on a different model.

Thus, as I see it, the clinical psychologist has really had severe problems of identity and along with it some doubts about his own self-worth. To put it very succinctly, he has been a doctor who is not really a doctor, and a scientist who really is not scientific. Furthermore, as some have pointed out, he has had to function with techniques which are of doubtful social and scientific value. Is it any wonder then that some, if not many, clinical psychologists have had feelings of low self-esteem and have developed all sorts of peculiar defensive mechanisms? I believe that this type of problem lies at the core of much of the discontent in clinical psychology and is at least a partial explanation for the dissatisfaction, constant self-analysis, sibling rivalry, paranoid distortion, guilt, etc., apparent among clinical psychologists. I wonder if the astronomers show the same kinds of patterns.

There are other aspects to this problem. I wonder if a psychologist really justifies his training as a psychologist if he is engaged solely as a practicing psychotherapist. From the social point of view this is a tragic waste of training efforts devoted to the Ph.D. program, both on the part of the student and the university. The same holds true for a physician who devotes all of his time to psychotherapy or psychoanalysis. His medical training is really wasted. However, my main concern here is with psychologists. Let me make perfectly clear here that I do not mean at all that psychologists should have no concern with psychotherapy or the modification of behavior. On the contrary, I am disappointed that psychologists, particularly practicing psychologists, have contributed so little to a better understanding of what is involved in modifying personality and behavior and in contributing to newer and more efficient ways of helping people with problems of adjustment. The biggest sin of the clinical psychologist is that he has only done what others have done and has failed to bring his psychological skills and knowledge to the problem of improving practice in this area or in evaluating contemporary practice. This is indeed strong criticism, but I do believe it is germane to our problems. We have been content to emulate others and in so doing have lost our uniqueness and our real identity. In the May 1965 issue of the *American Psychologist,* for example, there is a letter which suggests that all psychologists "support my purpose which is to improve the quality of nonmedical training in psychotherapy as to provide no basis in fact for the claim of the medical profession to superiority in this field [Blanck, 1965, p. 367]." This is a "me too" philosophy. It is much easier to follow the crowd and do what is esteemed at the time, than to be creative or original. I am always struck by the fact that Behavior Therapy, something which is derived from psychology, had to be given its impetus by of all people—a psychiatrist. Even then, most of us are willing to reject it without even trying it, because it goes against traditional points of view, rather than because it has limited research data to support it.

Well, what about this state of affairs? To me, it points up the current ambiguity in our field and the accompanying identity problem in clinical psychology—a problem at the heart of our difficulties today. It leads me to ask if we can define our own field, our unique characteristics and our particular contribution to the world about us? If not, we most likely will present a confused image to others as well as to ourselves and our students. It is time for us to be clear as to what clinical psychology is, what its values are, and the kinds of goals toward which we strive. In our development thus far we have been unduly influenced, led, and tempted by forces and agents outside of our own profession and science. While we should always be sensitive to the needs of the society in which we live and the potential contribution which we can make to the betterment of its citizens, we must also clearly assume the responsibility which is ours for the guidance and development of our own field.

I have spoken rather bluntly but I do not feel we should try to push the current dissatisfaction within clinical psychology under the rug. It exists and I doubt that it will go away by itself if we ignore it. If we do nothing else, we must at least own up to it and, more hopefully, see what alternatives are open to us. As I see the situation now, we have at least three main courses open to us. We can try to ignore or blot out the realities around us and go about things as we have in the past. This style of life can be termed either living dangerously or living within oneself in blissful unawareness. We can attempt to meet the demands for better trained practitioners and follow the lead of the Clark Committee (APA, 1965) and others in attempting to set up primarily professional programs of training. With such a decision we make a radical break with our own historic past and attempt a new type of training and the creation of a new type of psychologist—if you want, a real professional, trained for his work. This would mean, I believe, the giving up of the unique scientist-practitioner model sketched out at Boulder and clearly separating the training of the scientists and professionals in psychology. The third alternative, however, is to insist on not throwing in the sponge at this time. Rather, it calls for an attempt to analyze why the scientist-practitioner model has not been more successful, and to see what modifications can be made to improve our efforts toward the goal of making it a truly viable model.

These are the main alternatives open to us at the present time. Since I believe the first alternative, the do nothing one, is basically not constructive, I will dwell mainly on the other two and their implications for clinical psychology. During the past few years, like most of you, I have been concerned about what modifications are required to improve training programs in our field and to help make the clinical psychologist more adequate in facing the demands which society places on us. With the discussions and recommendations concerning a new degree for professional training in clinical psychology reaching such a crescendo of late, I have given considerable thought to these proposals. I must confess that I have reacted with fluctuating but intense ambivalence. In spite of my own indoctrination as a Ph.D., I could readily see the shortcomings in the traditional training programs and the appeal of a program to train individuals for professional careers. Another related thought was that clinical programs in psychology were being criticized for not turning out the kind of professionally trained individuals that they were never really set up to train. If so, then why not specifically devise a program to do what many, at least by implication, say they want done. When one follows this line of thought, it is not difficult to come up with more than one professional model, and, if one is concerned with training psychotherapists, it becomes readily apparent that psychologists have no exclusive claim to the training of such persons. In fact, an interdisciplinary model of training psychotherapists exclusively has been suggested at a recent conference, (Holt, 1963) and much can be said for this model. However, such a solution also poses some problems for clinical psychology, for if psychotherapy training is to be done elsewhere, where does clinical psychology fit into this new scheme of things? What roles and functions will distinguish our field from others? Will the clinical aspects of our field gradually become divorced from the scientific? Thus, the matter of a professional degree is not merely a matter of training in a professional department or setting versus that in an academic department, as Tryon (1963) and some academic people may see it, but rather, what is the unique role and contribution of the clinical psychologist to be?

My own resolution of this conflict leads me back to a reconsideration of the Boulder model, which can be viewed as a distinctively psychological model. Until recently, I had favored a multiplicity of models for clinical psychology, with different programs of training for the respective models. However, in thinking further about what has transpired in recent years, I have come to the conclusion that there must be some basic unifying thread underlying and integrating our field, something which is unique to clinical psychology. The Boulder model does provide such a theme, the scientist-practitioner, and I am loath to give it up without a further test of its efficacy. For the moment let us put aside questions of whether this model has worked or can ever work. Let us look at its implications for the identity of the clinical psychologist.

If one is asked to differentiate the clinical psychologist from other workers in the fields of personality adjustment and mental health what characteristics come to mind? The two which most clearly are unique to the clinical psychologist are his use of psychological tests and his research training. These are the aspects which also provide the link to the broader field of psychology. However, as we have noted, diagnostic testing has lost its attractiveness for clinical psychologists and something which is uniquely psychological is relegated mainly to students or to other workers. In contrast, psychotherapy, the primary activity of most clinical psychologists, is not a unique function of psychologists and tends to confuse the problem of identity. The remaining function, research, has also, unfortunately, been seen as undesirable or "nonclinical" by clinical psychologists. One of the unique features of the clinical psychologist's training has apparently had little carry-over on what he does after he leaves the university. This, to me, has been a real failure on the part of our past training programs. Not only have many clinical psychologists shown an amazing passivity in this area, but many have clearly developed a strong phobic response where research is concerned. If we had purposely trained students to exhibit avoidance responses whenever the word research was mentioned, we probably could not have done a much better job than we have done in the past.

We are thus confronted with a situation where we have been rather unsuccessful in attaining our training objectives. We have sought to turn out a scientist-practitioner and we have turned out instead scientists and practitioners, neither of whom have been too satisfied with their training. In addition, we find that those activities and functions which have long been identified with psychology tend to be rejected by a large number of clinical psychologists, and, conversely, that there is a preoccupation with activities which are not the sole or unique province of psychology. This state of affairs conceivably may be interpreted as indicating that the Boulder model is an unrealistic or unobtainable one. However, it is also likely that current training programs have not been successful in achieving this goal, and that it has been the implementation of the model which has been at fault, and not necessarily the model itself.

Because of time, I will pass over problems pertaining to diagnostic training. There is little question that we need to take a serious look at this area and do some drastic overhauling. However, I prefer to say a few words about the research function and research training since these appear to be of fundamental significance for the problem at hand.

If research is to be a unique and important function of the clinical psychologist, both the training and the research itself must be meaningful and related to significant problems of adjustment.

Undoubtedly, the research training and the dissertation requirement in most doctoral programs do little to foster in clinical students a real regard for the importance of research and its relation to the advancement of their field. Research is seen as something in opposition to clinical practice rather than as being intimately related to it. For a field which needs research as badly as clinical psychology, this is a real social and professional tragedy. Yet, at the same time we must face the realities of the situation. If we are to change the nature of things, we will have to greatly modify our research training and our whole view of research. While it is easy to blame our experimental colleagues for emphasizing a certain type of research model, based to a certain extent on the physical sciences, it is up to us to provide a better model and to try to implement it in our graduate programs. Clinical psychology is certainly at a rudimentary stage of development, and the experimental model is certainly not the sole appropriate one. We need a lot more naturalistic and observational types of research on matters of clinical importance before we can proceed to research which is more precise and in which we can always state our hypotheses explicitly in advance. It is essential, however, that the research training of the student be intimately related to his clinical training, that there be interaction and integration between these two aspects of the field, and that there be no void or schism between them. The latter, in part, accounts for the unhappy state of affairs existing today. In fact, it is worth looking into this matter a bit more.

I feel strongly that the university clinical faculties in psychology must show some real leadership in helping to make clinical psychology *both* psychological and clinical. We must try to implement some of the ideas which are currently being discussed. We need to have as a minimum a truly viable psychological service center as part of every university clinical program in which clinical and related groups of psychologists can be trained—in both practice and in research. Hopefully, and necessarily, such centers should make significant contributions to the practice of our field. We have made surprisingly little contribution to new ideas or new techniques in our field of endeavor. In spite of drastic changes and innovations in other fields in the past 15 years, clinical psychology has advanced painfully little in this regard. Perhaps, because of our newness, we have been overly preoccupied with matters of status and public regard. Perhaps, also, we have kept our eyes on the wrong models to emulate. However, it is time for us now to take a new look at ourselves and to chart a new course.

If we are to have a meaningful and socially desirable identity we will have to train clinical psychologists who are able to tackle and solve significant problems, to devise new techniques, to function in new ways and to go beyond the tried and not so true. Without question, much of the dissatisfaction and turbulence current today is a reflection of the relative crudity and ineffectiveness of our diagnostic and therapeutic techniques (Meehl, 1960). As has been pointed out by many of us, the values of our techniques leave much to be desired, yet we go on training as if this were not the case. A great deal of the dissatisfaction and low status associated with diagnostic work is undoubtedly related to their lack of utility; yet we find it difficult to really face up to this problem. Instead, clinical psychologists become psychotherapists and administrators and reserve the available diagnostic work for clinical trainees, lest they lose this valuable experience. Nor is the flight to psychotherapy a solution. Even if psychotherapy were a completely effective and socially desirable activity, training programs in clinical psychology would not be justified on this basis alone. As I have indicated elsewhere (Garfield, 1964), current clinical psychology training programs were not set up to train psychotherapists nor is psychotherapy synonymous with clinical psychology. If training psychotherapists is one's objective, it is my opinion that it could be done far better in settings other than a graduate department of psychology, and in less time. I realize that this statement may be upsetting to some of our members who function primarily as psychotherapists, but I doubt that they would contest the validity of my statement. However, I do not believe that training psychotherapists in the conventional sense should be the function of graduate departments of psychology. Their concerns are somewhat different. Furthermore, such training does not meet the full range of social needs in terms of psychological problems and, as George Kelly (1964) and Hobbs (1964) have indicated, may well be training for obsolescence. The clinical psychologist should be a person who is not limited or identified with a particular technique, but one capable of devising methods, of adapting methods and of evaluating methods. Such an individual can be a practitioner fully as much as can the psychotherapist, but his model and his identity will be that of a psychologist.

If Hobbs (1964) is correct in his view of what he has termed the "Third Revolution," then we must plan intelligently for our future roles and responsibilities. If prevention, education, environmental modification, and group approaches in the area of emotional and social disturbance have more social relevance for our area of work than do current one-to-one models of therapy, we must modify our training programs and our professional models accordingly. We must anticipate needed changes and not always follow belatedly. In this kind of situation, we must train persons equipped to solve problems and to apply research knowledge and methods to such problems.

To me, the most pressing need in clinical psychology pertains to a reorganization of training, practice, and research in our approved university settings. This is essential for helping to provide a sound identity for clinical psychology and for eventually allowing us to make a worthwhile contribution to problems of personality maladjustment and change. Let me emphasize here that the motives back of such changes are constructive ones rather than simply refusing to play a secondary role in medical or other types of settings. Psychologists by virtue of their unique training have worthwhile skills which they can contribute to a variety of settings. However, there must be a type of institution or setting which is clearly psychological in nature, which provides an important service to the community, and which helps provide a basic sense of identity. While the center I envisage is similar to that advocated by George Albee (1964) I want to make certain emphases which, perhaps, differ in some respects from those mentioned by him. Albee reacts to limitations imposed on psychologists who work in medical settings and emphasizes the need for independence in terms of practicum and other needs. The points I would emphasize are, not merely to have one's own clinical facility, but more importantly, the need for a setting whereby research and practice are intimately related and tied together. The psychological center would not only emphasize both research and practice, but would demonstrate the mutual interaction and reciprocal relationship of the two. Problems encountered in practical work with clients would lead to the formulation of hypotheses or questions to be evaluated and explored through research. Research findings, on the other hand, would have a definite impact on what is being done in practice—not as is the case today where there is a marked hiatus between research findings and practical work with clients. In fact, as far as practical impact goes, much of the research currently published might just as well not have been done. In the utopian center I envisage, things would be drastically different. Clinical observations and inferences would lead to formulations which would be subject to research evaluation. Such research would have an exciting quality to it, for it would be related to problems generated out of the clinical psychologist's practice and would be expected to have some impact on that practice. Instead of an emphasis on different theoretical orientations and verbal disputes between different points of view, we might get some differences resolved by clear-cut research findings. As it is today, negative or challenging findings of any kind tend to be argued or rationalized away.

Another positive outcome of this type of psychological center is that it would provide a real model to receive a fair test. I believe, perhaps too idealistically, that such a venture has a reasonable chance of success. In spite of our relative youth, I believe we have gone through enough experiential living in the past 15 years to profit from that experience. We do not have to prove our clinical capabilities over and over again in relation to psychiatry, nor do we have to compete with or try to emulate the psychiatrist. We have lost out in some ways to other social scientists by pushing aside our research role in institutional settings, but with our combined research and clinical skills we should be able to make important contributions in this area. The opportunities are all around us if we have the vision and determination to strive for a unique role in the extremely important area of human adjustment. It is for us to decide what paths clinical psychology should take. We have a choice between being a unique socially sensitive research-oriented profession, or grabbing at chance opportunities to model ourselves after others. The choice is ours.

REFERENCES

ALBEE, G. A declaration of independence for psychology. President's message. *Ohio Psychologist*, 1964, *10*, No. 4.
AMERICAN PSYCHOLOGICAL ASSOCIATION, Committee on the Scientific and Professional Aims of Psychology. Committee on the Scientific and Professional Aims of Psychology: Preliminary report. *American Psychologist*, 1965, *20*, 95–100.

BLANCK, G. Riposte. *American Psychologist*, 1965, *20*, 367.

BRAYFIELD, A. H. Report of the Executive Officer: 1964. *American Psychologist*, 1964, *19*, 883–895.

CLARK, K. E. *America's Psychologists*. Washington, D.C.: American Psychological Association, 1957.

GARFIELD, S. L. President's column. *American Psychological Association, Division of Clinical Psychology Newsletter*, 1964, *17*(4), 1–3.

HILGARD, E. R. *Introduction to Psychology*. (3rd ed.) New York: Harcourt, Brace & World, 1962.

HOBBS, N. Mental health's third revolution. *American Journal of Orthopsychiatry*, 1964, *34*, 822–833.

HOLT, R. R. New directions in the training of psychotherapists. *Journal of Nervous and Mental Disease*, 1963, *137*, 413–416.

KELLY, E. L. Clinical psychology–1960: Report of survey findings. *American Psychological Association, Division of Clinical Psychology Newsletter*, 1961, *14*(1), 1–11.

KELLY, E. L., & GOLDBERG, L. R. Correlates of later performance and specialization in psychology. *Psychological Monographs*, 1959, *73*(12, Whole No. 482).

KELLY, G. A. Training for professional obsolescence. Columbus: Ohio State University, 1964. (Mimeo)

MEEHL, P. E. The cognitive activity of the clinician. *American Psychologist*, 1960, *15*, 19–27.

RAIMY, V. (Ed.) *Training in Clinical Psychology*. New York: Prentice-Hall, 1950.

SANFORD, F. H. Across the Secretary's desk. *American Psychologist*, 1954, *9*, 125–128.

SANFORD, F. H. Annual report of the Executive Secretary: 1955. *American Psychologist*, 1955, *10*, 778–792.

TRYON, R. C. Psychology in flux: The academic-professional bipolarity. *American Psychologist*, 1963, *18*, 134–143.

....

Will Psychologists Study
Human Problems?*

NEVITT SANFORD

THIS PAPER STARTED out to be a letter to Joseph M. Bobbitt in his capacity as Associate Director of the new National Institute of Child Health and Human Development. For some time it had seemed to me that certain unfortunate trends in psychology and social science were being aided and abetted by our great fund-granting agencies. Or was it that unfortunate trends in these agencies were being furthered by the "establishment" in psychology? Probably a chicken-and-egg situation. At any rate, it seemed that the inauguration of the new Institute was a good occasion for some analysis and criticism of the disciplines most directly concerned with research in psychological health and development. I warmed up to this subject, and went far enough in criticism so that it seemed I ought to undertake the more difficult task of offering some constructive suggestions.

And so my letter to Bobbitt has grown into an article, the main burden of which is that the new Institute—and other institutes and agencies—ought to encourage psychologists to study problems that people really worry about rather than only problems formulated on the basis of reading the professional journals.

If fund-granting agencies such as the new Institute were to insist that psychologists confront these human problems directly, they would be forced to examine longer sections of behavior, and larger areas of the person, than they usually attend to nowadays; they would have to deal with some really complex processes and, thus, they would be stimulated to devise methods for solving problems —rather than confining themselves, as they do today, to problems to which existing methods are suited.

This would be good for psychology, and I for one am as much

* From the *American Psychologist*, 1965, *20*, 192–202.

concerned about advancing this science as I am about finding a solution to any immediate problem.

Psychology is really in the doldrums right now. It is fragmented, overspecialized, method centered, and dull. I can rarely find in the journals anything that I am tempted to read. And when I do read psychological papers, as I must as an editorial consultant, I become very unhappy; I am annoyed by the fact that they all have been forced into the same mold, in research design and style of reporting, and I am appalled by the degree to which an inflation of jargon and professional baggage has been substituted for psychological insight and sensitivity.

I used to think, when I first noted the trend—10 years ago—that the authors' psychological knowledgeability had simply been edited out in the interests of saving space. I am now convinced that the trouble lies much deeper. The psychologists who are filling up the journals today just do not have sensitivity to human experience, and the fault lies in their training—which is an expression of what academic psychology has become.

We have produced a whole generation of research psychologists who never had occasion to look closely at any one person, let alone themselves, who have never imagined what it might be like to be a subject in one of their experiments, who, indeed, have long since lost sight of the fact that their experimental subjects are, after all, people. (Let us leave the rats out of it for the moment.) They can define variables, state hypotheses, design experiments, manipulate data statistically, get publishable results—and miss the whole point of the thing. Reading their papers you get a strange sense of the unreality of it all; the authors' conceptions of variables and processes seem a bit off; and then you realize that the authors have never looked at human experience, they went straight from the textbook or journal to the laboratory, and thence into print—and thence into the business of getting research grants.

The plain fact is that our young psychological researchers do not know what goes on in human beings, and their work shows it. Not only is it dull, which psychology should never be, but it is often wrong, for that context of processes-in-the-person which they have been trained to ignore is usually doing more to determine what happens in the situation under study than the variables that have been "isolated experimentally."

What has happened is that the revolution in psychology that occurred during World War II, and in the 5 years thereafter, has been over for some time and we are in the midst of the reaction. Or perhaps one might better say that normal operating procedures have been restored, that it is only in times of crisis that the academic disciplines are brought into contact with real life and shaken out of their professional preoccupations.

The revolution reached its high-water mark in 1949 when Erik Erikson was appointed professor at Berkeley. Two years later this would not have been possible; nor has such a thing since been possible in any psychology department in the country. (The appointments at Harvard are special and do not really count. Harvard is special, too, in that it is the only place that can afford to make mistakes.)

The critique is not of the experimental approach in psychology or of general psychology as a discipline; it is of a state of affairs in which the advocates of a particular kind of psychology—psychology-without-a-person—have been able to gain and maintain power through putting across the idea that they are the representatives in psychology of *true science*.

It is quite possible that nothing can be done about the state of affairs I describe. Maybe we are just playthings of social forces that no one can control. The issues underlying the situation are ones that have divided psychologists for a long time. I believe, however, that there is a constructive alternative to the prevailing orientation, one that might be called a "human-problems" approach. It is an approach that has a highly respectable past, but today it is staunchly opposed and falls outside the main current of contemporary work in psychology. It has many silent supporters, but few spokesmen.

THE KIND OF APPROACH NEEDED

Psychology and social science have, of course, always been oriented to action, in the sense that they have proceeded on the assumption that their theories and empirical knowledge would eventually be applied. Psychology, when it has thought seriously about itself, has included among its aims "to promote human welfare." Sociology, traditionally, has been concerned with the solution of social problems and with "building a better society." The National Institute of

Mental Health, which has supported so much research in biology, psychology, and the newer social sciences, has been guided by the principle that such research should be "mental health relevant," but in practice any fundamental work in these fields has been considered to have this characteristic.

Yet there is no denying that at the present time there exists a wide gap between research and practice. Psychology participates fully in the trend toward specialization and disciplinary professionalism that dominates in the universities today. The discipline is still much concerned to establish itself as a science, but the psychologists' naive conception of science has led them to adopt the more superficial characteristics of the physical sciences. This has made it difficult for them to study genuine human problems, since quantification, precision of measurement, elegance of experimental design, and general laws are so much more difficult to achieve once one goes beyond simple part processes.

There is, of course, a rationale for all this. It is not without some reason that the National Institute of Mental Health regards the so-called "pure science" of these disciplines as relevant to mental health. Science has always made progress through specialization. It can be argued, and it is argued, that findings concerning simple and isolated processes will eventually add up to systematic knowledge that can then be applied to human problems.

There are two things to be said about this. One is that the "adding up" function is rather neglected today, and the other is that many of these findings just do not add up. Concerning the first, the accent today is on the production of knowledge rather than on its organization. There are few attempts at systematization of the sort that would put particular facts in perspective and show their significance. More than that, there seem to be few attempts to organize knowledge in such a way that its relevance to practice or to policy becomes apparent. A college president might examine a large number of issues of educational or psychological journals without coming across anything that struck him as relevant to his purposes or helpful in the solution of his problems. It is not that all this material is irrelevant, but rather that the task of organizing and interpreting it so that it might be useful is so largely neglected. Scientists write for each other; and when they are looking for a problem to investigate, they turn to their professional journals rather than ask such questions as what might be troubling the college presidents.

When I say that the study of simple, isolated processes does not add up to an understanding of more complex ones, I am assuming that human and social processes are organized on different levels, and that processes on higher (more complex) levels have a character of their own, are just as "real" as processes on lower levels, and must be studied directly. It is just as "scientific" to study, say, self-esteem in its relations to other factors of equal complexity as it is to study the manifold conditioned responses into which self-esteem might be analyzed; it is just as scientific to study conditioned responses as it is to study by physiological methods the nerve processes that underlie them. The student of conditioning who was somewhat contemptuous of the vague globalism of the students of such personality needs as self-esteem could be regarded in the same way by students of the action of the nervous system. I assume, further, that there is *interaction* between processes on different levels. Just as complex phenomena are to be explained in part in terms of the activities of constituent processes, so simple processes have to be understood as partly determined by the larger structures in which they have place. Truth may be discovered by abstracting parts from the whole and studying them intensively, but the whole truth can never be discovered in this way. It is the whole truth, and particularly the truth about wholes, that is needed for practice. Thus it is that one has to be concerned about a trend in science that seems to put all the accent on the study of abstracted part functions. The main reason for this trend is that it is difficult to study complex processes by existing approved methods. In psychology it seems that theory making itself is often guided by consideration of what can be attacked by such methods rather than by an intellectual involvement with the problems of life. The kind of theory that is needed for the understanding of human problems is different from that which guides most laboratory research or is generated from it. Thus, instead of specialized personality theory and specialized social theory, a human-problems approach calls for a more general personality-social theory, a theory that is not formal or mechanistic but dynamic, not elementaristic but holistic, not narrow and specialized but comprehensive, not concrete and tangible but on a level of abstraction that is appropriate to the problem at hand. Each of these aspects of a human-problems approach may be taken up in turn.

Personality-Social Aspects

It seems clear enough that for an effective approach to human problems we must have an integration of personality theory and social theory. This is not as easy as might first appear. Most sociologists seem to get along quite well without giving much attention to the individual personality, and probably the great majority of clinical practitioners rely on an "individual-psychodynamic" approach that gives little attention to social and cultural factors. There is even a certain amount of interdisciplinary rivalry here: In discussions of problems such as prejudice or delinquency there is a tendency to oppose personality factors and social factors and argue about which is more important. But progress toward integration is being made. Certainly personality theory is far more "social" today than it was 25 years ago, and there is evidence, I think, that when sociologists note signs that their psychological colleagues are seeing the light they are willing to go halfway toward rapprochement. What is needed is more knowledge of the articulation of personality systems and social systems. This requires more, rather than less, attention to the relatively autonomous personality structures, and more searching analysis of social structures in terms that are psychologically relevant. The student of personality must, of course, focus on the internal structuring of personality, but he must grant that the hypothetical personality subsystems are not fully understood unless their situational relationships are specified.

Consider authoritarianism and how it might be changed. I assume that there are social organizations that can bring out the authoritarianism in almost anybody; but I would also assume that when it came to changing a particular organization the difficulty—and the strategy—would depend on how much authoritarianism in personality was found in people who occupied the key positions. To put this idea in more general terms: In order to induce change in personality it may sometimes be necessary first to change the role structure in the organization in which the individual lives or works. By the same token, since we deal with a dynamic interaction between personality and social system, it may sometimes be necessary to change certain personalities in order to change the social system. Individuals use their social roles for the expression of their personality needs; hence a change in organizational role structure will be resisted by individuals in the same way that they resist change in internal adaptive devices that have been found to be more or less satisfying. Thus a practicing social scientist needs to be familiar with personality dynamics.

Dynamic Aspects

A personality, or an organized social group, seems best conceived as a system of interacting forces, a going concern in which energy is distributed among constituent parts and between the system (or its subsystems) and its environment. Dynamic organization refers to the way in which these forces or units of energy interact. Personalities and social systems also exhibit formal organization. They may be examined with attention to such overall features as number of different parts or the connectedness of parts, or with attention to such formal relationships among parts as similarity, proximity, or inclusion. In general, the analysis of systems into states, conditions, or arrangements prepares the way for explanation in terms of dynamic theory.

Dynamic theory is essential when it comes to consideration of how a system might be changed. The question here, typically, is how to bring force to bear upon a particular subsystem that one wishes to modify. One might think first of bringing to bear upon the subsystem in question a potent set of environmental stimuli, and this might indeed be effective sometimes. It usually turns out, however, that the particular subsystem is really being determined by other subsystems and by processes of the whole system. The problem, then, is to find out what within the larger system is determining of what, and then to get a purchase on the master processes. To take an example from the field of personality: An individual's prejudice toward minority groups may be due to a nagging but unrecognized sense of weakness in himself; in such a case it would do no good to give him correct information about minority groups; there would be no change in his prejudice until a way had been found to modify his sense of weakness. In an organization it might be generally recognized that a change in one of its processes would increase production without loss in other essential values, but this would not mean that the change would now take place as a matter of course— whoever wished to promote it would still have to reckon with the implicit values of various segments of the power structure.

All this is not to deny the importance of information or of the mechanisms by which it is acquired. It is to say that in dynamic theory information is instrumental to purpose. Just as in an organization the gathering, storing, and communication of information is put in the service of the organization's explicit and implicit functions, so in the individual perception and learning are organized in the interest of strivings. We should not expect learned factual content to be retained for long without becoming integrated with the individual's purposes. But how such integration occurs is a complex question; it could hardly be answered unless individuals were carefully observed over relatively long periods of time—hence, it receives little attention from psychologists.

Programed learning of academic material affords a nice example of some of the difficulties created when more or less general laws, derived from the study of abstracted part processes, are applied in life situations, without anyone remembering to put the part process back into the living context where it belongs. If the psychologist fragments the person conceptually in the interests of research, many educators, by taking over bodily and applying directly the laboratory findings, seem about to fragment their students for keeps. The advent of the teaching machine, which could be a great boon to education, seems so far to have played into the hands of those educators who believe that the learning of factual content *is* education, that this learning is neatly separated from everything else that might be going on in the student, and that these other things do not matter much anyway. The real educational problem is not "how may students most efficiently learn material well enough so that they can pass examinations at a high level"; the real problem is "how to make academic material meaningful to them, so that it will play some part in the building up in them of the qualities of an educated person." How does the learning of factual material contribute to the development of such qualities as the ability to think well, self-understanding, sensitivity to ethical issues, intellectual integrity? This is the key question for educational psychology.

Holism

The essential idea was introduced above in our discussion of the neglect of complex processes; particular phenomena such as "a perception" or a "conditioned response" are almost always in part determined by—their very nature depends upon—the larger organismic patterns and purposes within which they have a place.

The implications of this are great, and I would like to carry my argument further.

The first point to be made is that few psychologists care to deny, on principle, the holistic premise. It seems to be almost universally understood and agreed that how a stimulus is perceived depends on the context in which it exists at the moment, that whether or not an idea will be assimilated by a cognitive system depends on the degree of that idea's consistency with ideas that are already present there, that the meaning of a particular act depends on its place in a larger pattern of striving. It can be said with perfect safety that all personality theories are holistic in the sense that they are concerned with the relations of particular processes to larger personality functions.

What, then, is the argument about? It is not so much about high theory as it is about what is the best strategy for research. The basic complaint against holistic theory is that it does not lend itself to testing by empirical methods. The very term "whole" suggests something that cannot be analyzed, and American psychologists have been taught to be wary of anything "global." This argument would have force—complete force—if it were true that the study of part-whole relationships were impossible. But to confirm that this is not true one has only to point to the work of Klein (1951) on the relations of perception to the ego control system, of Rogers and his associates (Rogers & Dymond, 1959) on the relations of various attitudes and beliefs to the individual's self-concept, or to the results of Witkin, Lewis, Hertzman, Machover, Meissner, and Wapner (1954) on sex difference in perception. The whole research undertaking that issued in *The Authoritarian Personality* (Adorno, Frenkel-Brunswik, Levinson, & Sanford, 1950) was carried forward in accordance with a holistic orientation and, indeed, would have been impossible without holistic theory. The F scale for measuring authoritarianism in personality was developed by a process of going back and forth from observed behavior to hypothetical inner structure. The coherence of overt behavior patterns led to the concept of an inner structure of personality, i.e., authoritarianism, and then this concept was used to predict other patterns of behavior.

It cannot, of course, be claimed that research carried out in accordance with the holistic orientation will soon achieve the standards of precision and elegance that are often attained in laboratory experiments involving a few simple variables. Such research can be improved in these respects, but it may never match the best laboratory experiments; it will have to aim at levels of rigor that are appropriate to the task at hand. It cannot be claimed, either, that this kind of research will be other than difficult and expensive. But the criticism of the current strategy of abstracting part functions for experimental study is more serious: It is that because of its very nature it is bound to fall short of the truth. It is not only that it avoids the big problems; it fails to achieve its own chosen goal, which is to establish general laws of behavior. But the main characteristic of such "laws" is their lack of generality. They break down as soon as a new variable is introduced into the picture. And since in real life new variables, or variables not taken into account in the laboratory experiment, are always in the picture, such laws are most limited in their applicability.

One can sometimes carry over into a life situation all the conditions that obtain in the laboratory and show that the general laws still hold. This has been done, for example, in the case of the teaching machine, which enables a student to learn material in just the way that laboratory subjects do. But this involves the dangers suggested above. Unless the educators, and their consultants, are very much aware of the limited role of content learning in education, of its embeddedness in a large context of other processes, the tendency is to transform life into a laboratory experiment. B. F. Skinner, the leading pioneer in the development of teaching machines, is himself fully aware of this danger—unlike many educators and many of his disciples. And yet he is deeply concerned with practice and cannot resist becoming involved with it. He says that his strategy of research is the slow but sure building up of a science from simple beginnings, and that so far he and his colleagues have attacked only the simple problems; but this does not prevent him from remaking school rooms and designing new cultures.

The above is the main argument for holism as the best road to knowledge; there is as strong an argument from the point of view of practice. If parts really are determined by the wholes to which they belong, and one wishes to modify a part, then clearly his best course is to bring influence to bear upon the whole. Thus it is that in the psychotherapy of Carl Rogers (1959) the whole thrust is toward modifying the self-concept, because an inappropriate self-concept is believed to be determining of numerous specific unfortunate attitudes and patterns of overt behavior. The same would be true of a social institution such as a school or college. Practices with respect to grading, course requirements, the organization of teaching, and so on, are usually integral to the whole system and are not to be changed until after there has been some modification in the general character of the institution. This is far from being a hopeless prospect. Just as one may influence an individual's self-concept as readily as one of its constituent attitudes, so one might initiate a process of change in an institution's general climate with no more difficulty than would be involved in changing one of its most specific part functions. Success would depend upon knowledge of the individual's or the institution's dynamics. By the same token, a holistic approach to individual or social change involves for the change agent a considerable responsibility: He should not seek change in whole structures unless he was prepared for change in numerous particulars.

I have put the case for holism as strongly as I can; yet I do not see how we can do without the intensive study of abstracted part functions. The student of personality, after all, engages in this activity when he undertakes to explain the functioning of social groups. Here he might well be inclined to favor analysis in terms of the personality types of the group's members, but if he is a holist he would not be surprised or put off if a social theorist reminded him that there are things about personality that do not become apparent until the individual is seen in the context of the social group.

At a time when the holistic orientation seems rather neglected in psychology and social science, it seems proper to accent it as is done here. If we must abstract parts from wholes let us be fully aware of the fact that we *are abstracting,* and let us devote as much energy to finding out how special bits of knowledge fit into the larger picture as we do to analyzing wholes in the conventional scientific way.

Comprehensiveness

The holistic orientation requires that we consider in what respects living systems function as units. It says nothing about the size or complexity of the unit. Such a unit might be the context of a perception, a pattern of striving that organizes particular acts, or the self that is expressed in numerous personality characteristics. The argument here is for bigger units; we must examine large areas of the person and of society, and long sections of behavior; and we must have theoretical models that permit us to do this.

The whole that helps to determine a particular personality characteristic may be the whole personality, and not merely the whole self or ego; hence, we need a theoretical model of the personality that permits us to deal with the relations of self to ego, and of these relatively large structures to others of like kind. Similarly for social structures. One may study, holistically, a department of an industrial organization or a classroom in a school, but for full understanding he would have to see the department or classroom in relation to the whole institution, and the institution in relation to the whole society.

Another argument for comprehensiveness is that the determination of human events is almost always complex. Multiple factors are involved, and it is the task of the scientist to find them. This always takes some imagination, but the right kind of theory can be a big help. Consider, for example, the phenomenon of compulsive drinking. A formula for this could be written out in terms of rewards and punishments, and in such a formulation the reproaches of the drinker's spouse might in some cases be put down on the side of punishment. But what about the case of a man who drinks in order to express hostility toward his wife and who welcomes her reproaches as signs that he is achieving his purpose? One could still describe what happens in stimulus-response terms, *after* discovering what the effective internal stimuli are. But in finding the stimuli the usual sort of learning theory and the knowledge that proceeds from laboratory tests of it would be of no help; the quest would have to be guided by theory and knowledge concerning the complex interplay of forces within the personality.

If we are to think comprehensively, it must be with the use of gross units of analysis. The psychotherapist, for example, faced with the task of making sense of vast quantities of verbal material has no alternative to using coarse categories for bringing it all together. And it is thus that when we wish to speak of elements which together make up the whole personality—elements defined with attention to the theoretical structure of the whole—we can do no better today than to use the Freudian concepts of id, superego, and ego.

Suppose—to glance at a relatively broad aspect of the social scene—one wished to compare the culture of San Francisco with that of Los Angeles, a matter that might be of great importance for some aspects of California governmental policy. It would hardly do to employ the highly elaborated schemes and finely calibrated instruments that are used in research on small groups. The investigator who had something less than a lifetime to spend on this undertaking would decide upon a few gross categories that seemed to him important, and then content himself with rough estimates of them.

Most scientists, probably, would dislike the loss of rigor involved in this and would prefer to let George do it. And George, of course, has been very active. Decisions in big and important social matters are still based mainly on the observations and judgments of practical men. No doubt this will always be so to some extent since in practical matters there is a place for wisdom and judgments of value as well as for scientific knowledge. Still, scientists often feel free to criticize the day-to-day decisions that affect us all, and to complain that they are not consulted. This is an admission of their obligation to study complex problems and to show how their findings are relevant to practice. They may do this without being any the less scientific, in the best sense of the word, than the laboratory man. All they have to lose are the chains of respectability. Their procedure should be to suit their instruments to the task at hand, and to make sure that the gross categories used are consistent with what is known at lower levels and lend themselves to reduction and systematic treatment.

LEVEL OF ABSTRACTION

When men are confronted with practical problems, their natural tendency is to focus on the concrete and particular. The psychotherapist, faced with the task of taking action on short notice, has to deal with what is happening to a particular patient in the situation of the moment; he cannot stop to translate his thoughts into the terms of a general theoretical system. The test specialist who wishes to develop an instrument for predicting some practically important pattern of overt behavior does not need abstract concepts to stand for general dispositions of personality; he can go far with a set of concrete test items that correlate with the behavior in which he is interested. And the business man or the administrator of an organization is likely to see his problems as particular, local, and pressing; he seeks solutions through manipulating plainly observable features of the immediate situation.

This kind of orientation to practical problems is a far cry from the most characteristic work of the scientist. The scientist interested in psychopathology must use terms for describing a patient that are sufficiently abstract so that one patient may be compared with others, and with nonpatients. The myriad specific acts of patients must be ordered to a conceptual scheme, so that future observations may be systematic, and general relationships among patients' processes may be established. As for organizations, one might say that we have hardly begun the scientific study of them until we have derived a set of abstract concepts—such as role, communication, power—that apply to organizations generally, so that we can carry over what we learn from one organization to the study of others.

If one uses abstract concepts he must, of course, be able to go back to the concrete, showing that a given concept applies in a particular case; or, to take it the other way around, it must be possible to show that a given concrete phenomenon may reasonably be ordered to the abstract concept. Where everything under consideration is open to direct observation this task is not difficult. "Response," for example, is a highly abstract psychological concept; yet, since it refers to something observable it is not difficult, usually, to get agreement that a given phenomenon is indeed a response. "Unconscious wish," on the other hand, is an abstract concept that stands for processes behind behavior: By definition it is something inside the person that expresses itself in various ways; hence, it is very difficult to show that a given observable phenomenon is a special case of an unconscious wish. We deal here with a hypothetical construct, something conceived or "dreamed up" by the psychologist not to categorize his observations but to make sense of them.

Strictly speaking, no elements or features of personality are observable with perfect directness; all are *inferred* from behavioral indices. But there is wide variation in the degree of directness or explicitness with which the inferences may be made. The kind of theory that is needed for the study of human problems must necessarily make free use of concepts whose ties to what is observable are highly indirect.

This kind of theory does not go unchallenged by those scientists who consider that the essence of the scientific approach is accuracy of observation and precision of measurement. These "hardheaded" scientists have something in common with the hardheaded men of affairs: Both prefer to deal with the concrete and tangible, with "the facts," with what they can get their hands on; hypothetical constructs smack of mysticism or "untried theory." This orientation gets the practical man into trouble because it leads to too narrow a definition of his problem and cuts off inquiry into the more complex, less observable, patterns of events which may have largely determined his difficulty of the moment. The situation is similar for the scientist who places observability at the top of his hierarchy of values. The highest levels of observability and precision of measurement are attained in the laboratory experiment; but the psychologist who restricts himself to this mode of investigation denies himself the opportunity to study the whole personality. There are aspects of personality that cannot be experimented upon in the usual laboratory situation: For example, there are aspects of the person that become apparent only when he is observed in numerous varied situations, and there are aspects whose meaning cannot be detected unless they are seen in broad context. Also, at the present time it is impossible or unfeasible to arouse in a laboratory situation motives and feelings that equal in quality and intensity some that are common in everyday life. In these circumstances it is natural for the convinced experimentalist not only to limit himself to problems for which his method is suited, but actually to conceive of personality as made up of elements, e.g., measurable performances, that he can get hold of, as it were. He often defeats his own purposes, as we have seen, for those performances owe something of their nature to factors that have been excluded from consideration.

The issue of observable versus hypothetical constructs is an old one in psychology. The early psychology of personality, which stemmed mainly from the clinic, made free use of hypothetical constructs, and this practice was severely criticized by academic psychologists who were eager to establish their discipline as a science. For the latter, objectivity was the watchword, and when Bridgman's "operationism" appeared on the scene in 1927 they embraced it wholeheartedly. It became something of a fashion in psychology to reject, as outside of science, concepts that could not be "defined operationally," that is, in terms of the steps taken to obtain an objective index of a given concept. During the years since the late 1920s, the struggle between the operationists and the traditional personality theorists has continued. The personality theorists have been largely vindicated, but they have been forced to give some ground. Today it is pretty generally recognized that there are practically no theoretical statements that can be completely and directly verified by observation, and that hypothetical constructs are not only necessary to intellectual activity but have led to the best success in predicting and explaining behavior. Modern operationism does not require that every concept be defined in terms of operations; it does require that every concept be connectable, however indirectly, with some kind of observable phenomenon. Personality theorists, while perfectly free to use hypothetical concepts, have had to proceed with more attention to conceptual clarity, to objective indicators of their concepts, and—most important—to the question of just how their theoretical formulations might be proved or disproved by observation.

I am arguing that abstract theory is not only necessary to the development of a science of personality and social systems but also most useful in practice. Personality-social theory that is dynamic, holistic, and comprehensive, as practice demands, must be on a high level of abstraction. It is mainly through its use of hypothetical constructs that science gets beyond common sense, and it is in getting beyond common sense that its greatest usefulness lies. To revert to the example of prejudice: Most of what psychologists and social scientists have said about the situational, social, and economic determinants of prejudice conform well with what everybody knew already; to show that prejudice in some of its aspects springs from a hypothetical deep-lying structure of personality is to go beyond the depth of the man in the street. At the same time it is to state a proposition whose implications for practice are very different from those that flow from the conventional wisdom.

My argument rests most heavily upon a conception of the nature of practical problems and of the role of science in efforts to solve them. We must inquire further into these matters. If we look at the history of psychology, it appears that there was a time when this science was far more concerned with practical problems than it is today, and that the results were not always to the good. For example, the early very practical concern with psychological tests led to many misapplications while contributing little to the advancement of psychology as a science. Again, the experiments of Thorndike and Woodworth (1901a, 1901b, 1901c) on "transfer of training" were carried on in an educational setting, with practice very much in mind. Their major conclusion, that learning was specific, that what was learned in one area of content or skill was not transferred to others, was immediately and very generally applied in the schools. This led to the introduction of all kinds of technical subjects into the schools, the proliferation of courses, the fragmentation of the curriculum. If children had not gone on transferring their training anyway, and if teachers had not continued to use their common sense, the results might have been even more serious. Experiences of this kind led the universities, in time, to become exceedingly wary of practice or "service," which were seen as restrictions upon the scientist's freedom to be guided solely by his curiosity and to look for answers anywhere that he pleased. Hence the present accent on pure science, and the relegation of members of the professional schools to second-class citizenship.

I am arguing that the pendulum has now swung too far in the other direction, that psychology and social science have become too far removed from practice. Many early applications were premature, and science has gained from its period of withdrawal into "purity"; now it can afford to become involved with practice again, and in doing so it will fulfill its obligations and derive benefit for itself.

We have to go at it in a different way from before, however. For one thing, we have to consider that a practical concern involves the setting of goals, and this raises the question of who is to do this setting. When individuals or organizations look to science for help, they are usually focused narrowly upon a problem that seems very pressing, and they often have an overrealistic conception of what they desire. Often in such cases the most useful thing a scientist can do is to bring about a reconsideration of the goal. Psychologists, for example, have been asked to devise tests that will predict success in college and, this being something they are good at, they have gone about it with extraordinary singleness of purpose—and this before the question of what is success was satisfactorily answered. Where grades have been regarded as the only practicable criteria of success the testing has gone forward, usually, without anyone's asking what grades have to do with becoming educated or what success in college, measured in this way, has to do with success in life.

For the scientist to include participation in goal setting within his conception of his role is to interfere in no way with his pursuit of knowledge. On the contrary, this is to open the way for scientific inquiry into complex matters. By insisting that practical problems are complex, interwoven with other problems, and tied to long-range human and social goals the scientist puts himself in a position to ask questions of general scientific interest. He may now adopt the simple rule that no problem is worthy of his attention unless it can be regarded as a special case of something more general, unless it can be phrased in such terms and attached in such a way as to promise some addition to systematic knowledge. It is thus that he may resist pressure to produce results at once and avoid involvement in local, ad hoc, or fragmentary studies, often called "practical," that contribute nothing to science and do little for the individual or group seeking help.

In the domain of public affairs, where the concern is with such problems as what to do about culturally deprived people or about youthful drinking, there is little reason, save insufficient public enlightenment, for conflict between an interest in solving problems and an interest in advancing social science. Support for both of these kinds of activity comes, ultimately, from the same source—that is, the people, expressing themselves through public agencies. Here the ideal is to build the research function into the planned social actions, and to state research problems in terms of how to induce desired effects. This is to adopt for social and human problems the model of clinical medicine, in which inquiry and action are two aspects of the same humanistic enterprise.

Choice of Problems

A human-problems approach not only calls for a different theoretical orientation, it implies a different basis for choosing problems. I would like to see the new Institute include something of the following in its program:

1. Accent problems defined in terms of their human significance rather than in the terms of particular scientific disciplines. Study of these will require interdisciplinary theory and multidisciplinary research teams. It may work if the starting point is a human problem and not a disciplinary question or issue. And let us get away for the moment from the familiar psychiatric categories. I have in mind such problem areas as transitional stages, developmental crises, commitment (premature or delayed), institutional dependence, pleasure and play, problem drinking, aging.

2. Look at these problems in the perspective of long-range goals for the individual. If we want people to give up or get over some sort of problematic behavior we have to think of suitable alternatives

to that behavior. Think about this for a while and we are bound to come to considerations of what is good for people and of what they might well become. Why not? There are good philosophical as well as practical reasons for this.

3. To think about long-range goals and how they might be reached we have to use a developmental perspective. We have to consider present events with attention to their future consequences. Otherwise we can have no part in the planning of institutional arrangements for the development of young people. Nor can we have anything sensible to say about when is the best time to introduce young people to particular ideas or experiences.

4. If we adopt a developmental perspective there is no way to avoid attention to the whole life cycle. We cannot leave this whole area to Erik Erikson—and Charlotte Buhler. We have to have longitudinal studies, or suitable substitutes for them. At the least we must have studies of lives.

5. But study the conditions and processes of developmental change —in general, at any age. Assume that such changes can occur at any age. It is a matter of the right conditions being present. I say development in general—so I am interested in general laws. I mean organismic laws, which state relationships between part processes and the larger personal contexts in which they are imbedded.

6. This means study the general psychology of personality— particularly the general psychology of personality development. We have to conceive of structures in the person and we have to have theory to explain how these structures are modified through experience. Studies of structures—experimental studies or others—may of course be appropriately investigated in isolation, but there should be awareness of the fact that they *are* being studied in isolation and must eventually be related to persons.

7. Look at various kinds of social settings in which developmental changes occur, particularly settings that have been designed to modify people in some desired way: schools, training programs, correctional institutions, hospitals, psychotherapeutic programs, summer camps, etc. Or, look at development in unnatural environments, forms of rigid institutionalization, for example, which result in regressive changes or fixations. Let all these settings be described and analyzed in sociological terms, but keep the focus of attention upon developmental change in individuals.

8. Give special attention to youth, but be flexible in defining its

boundaries, and of course do not neglect its relation to earlier and later periods. Youth is a neglected area as compared with childhood and old age. It is not so much behavior of youth as development in youth that has been neglected. The theoretical bias has been that little or no development occurs during this period.

The study of development in youth is bound to force a confrontation of theoretical issues. It should lead to the production of new theory concerning the interaction of social and personality variables. If we assume that personality goes on developing, after the age of, say, 16, after the young person has been brought very much under the influence of factors outside the home, then we have to formulate such factors and conceive the ways in which they do their work. Classical personality theory has little to say on this subject—but it can be appropriately modified.

I have listed here special interests of my own. If the new Institute were to show that it really intends to support work of this kind, a great many other psychologists would take heart, believing that their interests would be served also. Proposals would come in from people who have not been heard from in Washington for some time; and new kinds of proposals would come in from scientists who saw a chance to do what they knew was important to the solution of human problems rather than what could be supported.

REFERENCES

ADORNO, T. W., FRENKEL-BRUNSWIK, ELSE, LEVINSON, D. J., & SANFORD, N. *The Authoritarian Personality.* New York: Harper, 1950.

BRIDGMAN, P. W. *The Logic of Modern Physics.* New York: Macmillan, 1927.

KLEIN, G. S. The personal world through perception. In R. R. Blake & G. V. Ramsey (Eds.), *Perception: An Approach to Personality.* New York: Ronald Press, 1951. Pp. 328–355.

ROGERS, C. R. A theory of therapy, personality, and interpersonal relationships, as developed in the client-centered framework. In S. Koch (Ed.), *Psychology: A Study of a Science.* Vol. 3. New York: McGraw-Hill, 1959. Pp. 184–256.

ROGERS, C. R., & DYMOND, R. (Eds.) *Psychotherapy and Personality Change.* Chicago: Univer. Chicago Press, 1954.

THORNDIKE, E. L. & WOODWORTH, R. S. The influence of improvement in one mental function upon the efficiency of other functions. I. *Psychological Review*, 1901, *8*, 247–261. (a)

THORNDIKE, E. L., & WOODWORTH, R. S. The influence of improvement in one mental function upon the efficiency of other functions. II. The estimation of magnitudes. *Psychological Review,* 1901, *8,* 384–395. (b)

THORNDIKE, E. L., & WOODWORTH, R. S. The influence of improvement in one mental function upon the efficiency of other functions. III. Functions involving attention, observation and discrimination. *Psychological Review,* 1901, *8,* 553–564. (c)

WITKIN, H. A., LEWIS, H. B., HERTZMAN, M., MACHOVER, K., MEISSNER, PEARL B., & WAPNER, S. *Personality through Perception: An Experimental and Clinical Study.* New York: Harper, 1954.

■■

The Prevention of Mental Illness*

NEVITT SANFORD

IN THE LITERATURE of clinical psychology and psychiatry, "prevention" has had an ambiguous and shifting position. Prevention is often said to be the ultimate aim of research—in psychiatry, in clinical psychology, and in various areas of social science—and it is evoked as a justification for practices in training, including training for psychotherapy; but it is treated virtually as an afterthought in textbooks and treatises on psychiatry and abnormal psychology.

The final report of the Joint Commission on Mental Illness and Health (*1*) is of two minds about prevention. Four of the seven published studies of the Commission (excluding the final report) have mainly to do with prevention, in the largest sense of the term, and these are faithfully summarized in the final report, but the recommendations of the Commission have little to do with prevention. Instead, the "core problem" is said to be major mental illness— psychosis and other forms of chronic illness— and the mental hygiene movement is criticized for neglecting this problem in favor of an interest in prevention. But the mental hygiene movement seems not to have been altogether cowed by this criticism, as witness the rejoinder of Dr. René Dubos (*2*) of the Rockefeller Foundation:

> The Final Report of the Joint Commission on Mental Health and Mental Illness states that humane treatment and rehabilitation of the mentally ill is the great unfinished business of the mental health movement. But the great unfinished business really is to do something about the social, psychological and other circumstances leading to this condition.

The educated public in North America has, since the early years of this century, been consistently interested in prevention and consistently neglectful of the mentally ill in hospitals, as *Action for Mental Health* (*1*) correctly points out. But this public has tended to follow the specialists, adopting whatever ideology of upbringing or

* From the *Bulletin of the Menninger Clinic*, 1966, *30*, 1–22.

early treatment the psychiatrists or psychologists advocated during a particular period and doing what it could to look after the mental health of itself and its children. For their part, the mental health specialists have tended to serve the interest of this public more than those of the less privileged segments of the population, from which most patients in mental hospitals come. The mental health specialists themselves have participated in the "diversion of attention from the core problem."

HISTORY

We deal here with conflicts of value and interest that can be understood only in the light of what we know about the culture and social structure of the United States—and about certain events of the last fifty or sixty years. This brief account of the mental hygiene movement may well start with the founding of the National Committee on Mental Hygiene in 1909. This was largely a result of the writing and activity of Clifford Beers, whose book, *A Mind That Found Itself* (3), was published in 1908. Beers was out to reform the mental hospitals, but the leaders whom he aroused—men such as William James and Adolph Meyer—were more interested in prevention of mental disease.

Beers was a catalyst. The soil for the flowering of a mental hygiene movement had already been prepared. Some writers, for example, Seeley (4), traced the origins of the mental health movement to the breaking up of the settled order of the Middle Ages. When the church lost its position as the sole authority on questions of virtue and the good life, a power vacuum was created into which the mental health movement, along with a variety of competitors, could move. Other writers, for example, Rickman (5), are content to begin their accounts of the movement with Darwin and his contemporaries, who shattered belief in the fixity of the species and revolutionized ideas of human potentialities. By the time of Beers' writing it was understood that children could develop beyond their parents, and the "new psychology" had revealed some of the mechanisms by which the environment had its effects. Hence there was a general loss of faith in the traditional bases for the rearing of children, and growth of the belief that parents and the community should provide an environment favorable to the child's welfare. Hence the early mental hygiene movement in the United States inspired the establishment of child guidance clinics and programs of education for parents and the public.

Psychiatric experience during World War I provided fresh impetus to the movement. Not only was there some success in the early identification and treatment of potential psychiatric cases among soldiers, but also knowledge of the "war neuroses" led to increasing acceptance of the theory of the psychogenesis of mental disorders. During the 1920s there was a vast increase in the number of outpatient services, child guidance clinics, and programs of public education. All these activities were pervaded with a general air of optimism.

Meanwhile, in Europe, psychoanalysis, with its heavy accent on childhood events as determinants of neurosis, led to much concern about the applications of psychoanalytic principles to education. Freud (6) himself was not very optimistic about the possibilities in this area, believing as he did that neurosis is inevitable in highly civilized societies. Rather, he seems to have put his faith in what nowadays is called "secondary prevention," envisioning large numbers of psychoanalytically trained "secular pastoral workers" who would apply themselves to the early treatment of neurosis. He permitted himself this tongue-in-cheek remark:

Perhaps once more an American may hit on the idea of spending a little money to get the 'social workers' [1] of his country trained analytically and to turn them into a band of helpers for combating the neuroses of civilization (p. 250).

But some of Freud's followers—for example, Siegfried Bernfeld, August Aichhorn, and Anna Freud (of the Vienna group)—were very much interested in the preventive possibilities of psychoanalytic knowledge and wrote extensively on child training and education. Psychoanalysts of the English school—notably Melanie Klein, Susan Isaacs, John Rickman, and Ella Sharpe—soon joined in the discussion, differing in important respects from the Vienna group (5), (7). By the mid-1930s there had begun in the United States the outpouring of more or less popular psychoanalytically-oriented literature for parents and educators that has been a feature of the American scene ever since.

During the time when Freud was developing his ideas and starting

[1] In English in the original.

his psychoanalytic movement, socialism was very much in the air. The Russian Revolution was having its impact on European intellectuals, including some of Freud's followers. There were "socially-oriented" psychoanalysts almost from the start. Most of these, it seems, kept their psychoanalysis and their socialism in separate compartments; but some, perhaps most notably Alfred Adler, tried to integrate their psychological and their social theories. Adler wrote and lectured widely on education for cooperation and social responsibility, and founded, in Vienna in 1931, an Individual Psychology Experimental School, which was closed in 1934 "for political reasons." (*8*), (*9*) Adler developed a psychology that differed fundamentally from Freud's and the two men went their separate ways.

The decade of the 1930s was a period of great ferment in American psychology and psychiatry. The Great Depression drew attention to the importance of broad economic and social processes in the determination of behavior. The assimilation of European ideas, which had been very gradual, was enormously speeded up by the great influx of psychologists, psychiatrists, and psychoanalysts—refugees from the Nazi oppression. All the great European systems of psychological thought, and a great variety of other ideas and points of view, were now strongly represented in this country. All received a hearing, but those that took root and flowered were those that could be most readily assimilated to trends in American culture. For example, this culture, traditionally, has accented self-improvement and adjustment rather than social change as the road to the good life. Hence the socially-oriented psychology of Adler, Horney (*10*), and Fromm (*11*), (*12*), though it could win many supporters, could never attain a dominating position in the mental health field. Freudian psychoanalysis, on the other hand, with its accent on individual psychodynamics, its appeal to the Puritan mentality, and its neutrality with respect to social questions—especially after it had found a home within American medicine—could attain to great power and influence. Again, the English school of psychoanalysis, with its emphasis on native factors, on the priority of aggression, and on the importance of the child's fantasies in the determination of neurosis, clashed with American optimism and empiricism and has never gained more than a foothold in this country. Freudian psychoanalysis, in contrast, proved more flexible. Accenting its environmentalist features—especially the role of the family in the determination of neurosis—sticking to medicine and embracing science and developing an "ego psychology" that was congenial to American academic psychology, it found the going relatively smooth.

The newly imported European ideas combined with trends of thought

already present in the United States to give the mental health movement
an enormous push forward in the 1930s and early 1940s. A psychodynamic
approach to the understanding and guidance of children became a part of
American culture, being the basis not only for a surge of popular literature
but for movie and radio and television programs. World War II led to
even further public interest in mental illness and health. Psychiatric
screening of recruits to the armed services, breakdowns in the services,
and the adjustment problems of the returning servicemen were very much
in the public eye, and after the war it was not difficult to persuade Congress to spend money for programs of service, training and research in the
field.

This climate, and the availability of public funds for training and
research—mainly through the National Institute of Mental Health
and the Veterans Administration—made possible a great leap forward in clinical psychology. During the decade after 1945 this field
of psychology made large gains in status, both within the universities
and on the national scene; several thousand Ph.D.s were turned out,
most of whom had had some training for psychotherapy. Psychotherapy, indeed, was the order of the day. The practice of psychotherapy, on the psychoanalytic model, had the highest prestige
among workers in the mental health professions and, since from the
point of view of the National Institute of Mental Health there could
never be enough psychiatrists and psychologists to meet the demand
for this service, social workers, counselors and ministers found it not
difficult to enter programs for training in this specialty.

During this period, the prevention of mental disease received
relatively little attention. There was, to be sure, some continuing
attention to the early diagnosis and treatment of disorders in children, and there is no doubt that the understanding of children was
broadened and deepened as compared with what it was before 1930;
but apparently the main trends of activity in psychiatry and clinical
psychology were borne on the assumption that true prevention was
to be achieved in the new generation through giving enough psychotherapy and enough knowledge of psychodynamics to parents and
educators.

It was during this same period that the concept of "positive mental health" began to loom large in clinical psychology—a prelude to
the present concern with creativity. Efforts to learn something of
the determinants of superior personality functioning were begun by
Murray and his associates (*13*) in the early 1930s, were carried

forward by the OSS assessment teams during World War II (*14*), and were continued in several centers after 1945. This trend was combined with the older concerns of some psychologists and psychiatrists with developmental tasks and the goals of psychotherapy in much new writing about the "positive"—writing that reached a kind of culmination in Jahoda's report (*15*) for the Joint Commission on Mental Illness and Health. Although highly relevant to prevention in its most basic sense, this writing did not result in many suggestions for programs of action aimed at changing the social environment of the developing individual. Psychotherapy still seemed to be generally regarded as the means *par excellence* for attaining to the highest levels of development.

In the years since 1950, many of the assumptions and practices of psychodynamically-oriented clinical psychologists and psychiatrists have been challenged, mainly by social scientists and public health specialists newly arrived on the mental illness-mental health scene.

As early as 1938, Kingsley Davis (*16*) argued that the mental hygiene movement in the United States was promoting under the guise of science the prevalent, middle-class values of our society— indeed that it defined mental health in terms of conformity with these values—and that because of its "psychologistic" bias, it failed to investigate the social and cultural determinants of behavior and tended to regard social norms as universal human traits. This line of argument has been put forward by sociologists and anthropologists ever since, but it was not until some of these social scientists actually entered the mental health field and conducted empirical investigations—most often at the invitation of psychiatrists—that their thrusts began finding their marks among exponents of traditional psychodynamic psychotherapy.

Meanwhile specialists in public health, having gained control over the communicable diseases, which were the first concern of community health departments, have turned from a primary concern with mortality to concern with reducing rates of morbidity. In recent years, health departments have been engaged in programs, such as those having to do with maternal and child care and the control of syphilis, which have significant implications for mental health. In some of the newer and current programs, such as those in the fields of alcoholism and chronic disease, the mental illness or health factor has been large. And since the passage of the National Health Act of 1946, an increasing number of specialists in public health have been interested in assuming greater responsibilities for problems in the field of mental illness.

Since public health programs arise out of community needs and consist of actions within the community, it was natural enough that public health workers should make common cause with social scientists. Thus by the mid-1950s there was a convergence. Sociologists, anthropologists, and social psychologists, no longer content to limit themselves to their function of criticism, were now taking part in research and action programs in the health fields, accepting positions on the staffs of medical schools—most often in departments of psychiatry—and schools of public health, and finding kindred spirits among psychiatrists who saw mental illness as a community problem. Public health specialists, meanwhile, were moving into the mental health field, finding collaborators among social scientists and adopting social science techniques, while sticking to the basic public health strategies.

These developments were also in some part the fruits of the "culture and personality" movement, which had persisted since its origins in the early 1930s; of the steadily growing influence of British social psychiatry; and of the new chemotherapy, which, by reducing acute disturbance among hospital patients to a mimimum, permitted sociological and sociopsychological experimentation on ward and hospital organization and the changing of staff attitudes toward patients.

In 1962 a committee of the Harvard Medical School (*17*) was able to list, for the years 1953–1960, over 1000 publications in the fields of community mental health and social psychiatry, many of them being reports of large-scale empirical studies. The entry of social scientists and public health specialists into the field of mental health brought not only new conceptions and strategies of prevention but also a shift in values and ideology: there was now a new emphasis upon the underprivileged, the acutely ill, the deviant, and the "mass" of people—in short, upon what used to be called the "socially significant."

It would be surprising, in the light of this history, if there were anything like unanimity in outlook on prevention among all the workers now active in the field. Owing to their different backgrounds and training, and to their memberships in different intellectual traditions, mental health specialists today approach the problem of prevention with different theories of personality development and of social process, different conceptions of mental illness and different views respecting its determinants, different orientations to value and, accordingly, different strategies of prevention. In the most general terms, the big difference is between those who focus on the individual and those who focus on social processes. The former see the determinants of mental disease as residing primarily in the individual, having there been set in motion very early in the individual's life, if not before that; and, consistent with this, they see prevention mainly as a matter of reaching the troubled child as early as possible or, better, of reaching parents so that they will start their children off right. The latter see mental illness mainly as a function of processes in society, and prevention mainly as a matter of intervention in these processes. The remainder of this paper is concerned with the reconciliation of these views.

THE PUBLIC HEALTH APPROACH

The public health approach to prevention focuses upon a community or population rather than upon individuals, and attempts to reduce the rate of mental illness by modifying factors believed to be affecting large segments of that community. The approach has grown out of the conviction, formed on the basis of public health experience, that no disease has ever been controlled by early diagnosis and treatment, and that mental disease will be no exception (18), (19). This is partly a matter of logistics; with mental disease, as with others, there can never be enough therapists to provide more than a drop in the bucket. Partly, also, this is a deduction from a theory of causation; all diseases, and perhaps particularly mental diseases, have multiple causes, some of which arise out of processes in the environment. Hence not all causative factors can be touched by treatment or other actions directed to individuals. It also follows from this view of causation that it is impossible to predict that, unless specific preventive steps are taken, a particular individual will develop a disease.

This line of reasoning holds even for organic diseases of which the causes are known. Just as the eradication of malaria was achieved by modifications of the environment, so the control of syphilis will eventually be achieved not merely by treating infected individuals but by actions designed to change behavior and attitudes throughout the whole community.

It is not necessary to know how a disease is caused in order to take effective preventive action. A famous example in the public health literature concerns the control of a cholera epidemic in London by the removal of a public water pump. This was long before there was any knowledge of infection by microorganisms. Someone noticed that the frequency of cases varied with the proximity to this pump, and so its removal seemed a good action and was—eventually —a sensationally effective one. Again, Bowlby and his associates (20), (21) did not need to prove that a two-year-old child's separation from his mother for periods of two weeks or longer is a cause of psychopathology in later years. His thesis was persuasive enough so that the British Ministry of Health issued a directive permitting and encouraging mothers to visit their children in hospitals for unlimited amounts of time. This administrative action might or might not prevent any specific mental disease, but it might lead to a reduction in the rate of mental illness in general; and in any case, it seemed a humane thing to do.

Most characteristic of the public health approach, perhaps, is the idea of intervention at some point in a system—some interruption of the course of events—with a view to changing the system in such a way as to reduce the rate of mental illness. Consider, for example, a school system. From the point of view of individual psychodynamics, the proper approach to the prevention of mental illness in childhood would consist in actions such as hiring mentally healthy teachers, teaching them about mental illness and health in children, and training them to recognize signs of disturbance in children and to give psychological first aid. A spokesman for the sociological approach would express grave doubt that these measures would reduce the rate of mental illness among the children in that school system; he would suspect that the causes of their disturbances lay not only in the personality structures that they brought to school with them but also in the school system itself, and that the problematic behavior of teachers and other school personnel sprang not so much from *their* neuroses as from the situation in which they worked. Accordingly, he would also suspect that proper preventive action would consist in efforts to change the system as a whole, so that everybody in it was happier, in less conflict, and more productive. A teacher of the writer's acquaintance is sure that a large step in this direction could be taken, in the system in which she works, by allowing school principals academic tenure.

SOCIAL-PSYCHOLOGICAL THEORY

The public health approach can go quite a long way on the basis of knowledge or hypotheses about the correlations of broad social factors, such as unemployment or bad housing, with mental illness, and on the basis of theory of social structures. Action for mental health would consist in removing or reducing the harmful or hazardous factors, or in intervening at some point in the social structure—an organization, institution, or community—in such a way as to make for favorable change. Actions of these kinds, however, always involve, at least implicitly, psychological assumptions or theories about how people in general will react to an environmental condition, how they are organized as personalities, and how they develop from birth onward.

The British Ministry of Health, in encouraging mothers to visit their children in the hospital, must have assumed that both mothers and children would be happier and less anxious if this were done, and that doctors and nurses could adapt themselves to this change in routine without too much disturbance of their work. When large-scale social actions are based on wrong psychological assumptions, the result can be damaging to large numbers of individuals. In Poland, for some years after World War II, the official word was "We have no delinquency because we have socialism"—this at a time when the police were all but overwhelmed by masses of disturbed and delinquent children, the products of broken homes, poverty, neglect, and general social disorganization. This was not merely official hypocrisy, but an expression of the belief that a far-reaching change in the organization of society would immediately and automatically bring far-reaching changes in people, including children. Again, in England during the same period, large numbers of families were moved from bombed-out areas of the East End of London to clean and comfortable but rather sterile housing estates in the suburbs around the city. The assumption seems to have been made that these former slum dwellers would immediately begin living like middle-class people. They did not. The women, especially, missed their family and community networks and were unhappy because the kitchen, having become modern and small, could no longer be the center of family life. Many of these people returned to the true communities from whence they came.

In this last instance, more appropriate action would have had to be based on knowledge of culture, and of a particular subculture, as well as on knowledge of the psychological laws according to which cultural values are acquired. Nowadays in this country specialists who would improve mental health by changing environments are very alert to cultural factors. This has been favored by public health experience and, of course, it has been further promoted by the entrance of anthropologists and sociologists into the mental health field. For that matter, it is doubtful that anywhere in the Western world today anyone interested in mental illness or health would seek to apply so doctrinaire a version of socialism as the Polish officials did or so class-bound a version of the good life as did the British planners of the housing estates. In Mexico, for example, when people are moved by the thousands into new housing developments, there is the closest attention to the requirements of family life and to what favors psychological as well as physical well-being.

PERSONALITY THEORY

The public health approach also makes assumptions about the elements of personality and their organization in individuals. The idea of susceptibility to disease or to kinds of diseases and the idea of resistance must have reference to more or less enduring structures in people, structures which are built up over time and which stand ready to help determine what will happen when stimuli arrive. The public health specialist or the social scientist may or may not believe, with most personality theorists, that personality functions as a unit and that mental illness or mental health is a condition of the whole person. He may believe—and this with good reason—that problematic or deviant behavior can be a response to a momentary stimulus and is open to change without alteration in the structure of the person; but to take preventive actions aimed at particular conditions without giving attention to the complexity of personality, particularly to the interactions of its constituent processes, is to court trouble. Such an action might affect a particular condition in the predicted way but still do more harm than good if there is no theory to suggest other consequences of that action. For example, the segregation and exposure to special educational procedures of slow learners or the gifted in school might result in more appropriate learning of content by children of these two groups, but might lead to a kind of labeling and to a kind of self-conception that would be most unfortunate from the point of view of mental health.

It may also be suggested that attention to personality theory, which deals with the complexity of processes inside the person, is a good safeguard against the extreme forms of collectivism which sometimes animate social planners. The frame of mind that permits enthusiasts for social action to concentrate on the group without attention to what goes on inside people appears to be close to that which can contemplate sacrificing individuals for the good of the group.

Today, most specialists who would reduce rates of mental illness by modifying the social environment are aware of these considerations. They are also aware of the great difficulties in the way of persuading people to take measures to protect their health. Smoking, drinking too much, indulging indiscriminately in sexual relations, driving without seat belts may be bad for the health, but people do not seem to be at the point of changing their ways. Effective actions in areas of this kind will require at least as much knowledge of human motivation as knowledge of social processes.

Public health workers and social scientists who work in the mental health field also have their theories and assumptions about personality development but, as suggested above, their notions tend to run counter to the general position of classical psychodynamic—typically Freudian psychoanalytic—theory. What is this theory? Most essential is the notion that personality exists in time and exhibits continuity over time. As with all living things, early events have lasting consequences; other things being equal, damage to the growing organism will be the more far-reaching in its consequences the earlier in the individual life that it occurs. Major features of the personality are formed in childhood, and childhood is the time when events that are most significant for the genesis of mental illness occur. This last follows from the fact—according to psychoanalytic theory—that childhood is preeminently the time for repression. Then the ego is relatively weak, while emotional strains are great. Hence the child commonly adapts to strains with the use of unconscious mechanisms, and these, which are not open to modification through ordinary experience, become the basis of vulnerability to future strains; when these are met in a maladaptive way, pathology snowballs.

A mental health worker who takes this view of the matter naturally wishes to educate or otherwise intervene with parents so that the maladaptive reactions will not occur in the first place; or if, as seems likely, some such reactions are inevitable, then the thing to do is reach the child as early as possible, using special techniques to modify his unconscious adaptive devices and to help make other more adequate devices available to him.

What is wrong with this picture, from the point of view of the social scientist or the public health specialist? One thing that is wrong—so runs the argument—is that the individual psychodynamic approach, after years of work and the expenditure of huge sums of money, has not succeeded in reducing rates of admission to mental hospitals. At least there is no evidence that this is the case. This may be because the early treatment was ineffective; children seen in child guidance clinics went on to become hospital patients anyway. More likely it is because people who are treated in child guidance clinics, or who are treated privately as children, and people who fill the mental hospitals are drawn from different populations (22). As is well known from the work of Hollingshead and Redlich (23) and others (24), the highest rates of admission to mental hospitals are found in the lowest economic stratum of society, while there is a strong tendency, pointed to by Albee (25), for child guidance clinics, and outpatient clinics generally, to turn away people who have the most serious problems. These last, typically, are individuals from the lower economic classes; it is they, rather than individuals who can "benefit from psychotherapy," who from the start are more likely to be destined for the mental hospital. Hence the argument, often forcibly put by social scientists, that the most highly trained specialists in the mental health field, that is, the psychoanalytically oriented psychotherapists, are devoting themselves to the least ill members of the population affected by mental illness—and are training and otherwise encouraging more people to do the same thing.

This kind of critique often attributes wrong practices by psychiatrists, clinical psychologists, and social workers to the domination of the mental health field by psychodynamic theories, mainly those of the Freudian variety. There is a strong implication that practice is wrong because the theory is wrong, and that everybody—particularly the mentally ill—would be better off if Freud had not saddled us with his theories about the determination of neurosis in childhood.

This may be doubted. Criticism of mental health practice is one thing; criticism of psychodynamic theories is something else. Various psychological theories besides the psychodynamic ones focus on individuals rather than on the mass of people, and the way mental health services in this country are organized would seem to depend more on the kind of society we are than on the kind of psychological theory favored by psychiatrists during a particular period.

The rewards for performing two-person psychotherapy with people who are not very sick—and particularly with people who can pay— are, by American standards, great compared with those for using other kinds of methods with very sick people in public institutions. These rewards are not primarily status and money, though these no doubt have their place; most important is the satisfaction of seeing an individual "improve" or benefit otherwise as a result of therapeutic efforts. This satisfaction is of the same kind as that experienced by devoted teachers or counselors of individuals; to observe a favorable change in the "statistics" for a population is not a substitute for it. We should expect what we in fact find— that the professionals of various theoretical points of view, including modern behavioristic ones, prefer to practice individual psychotherapy, and that the role is often chosen before there is commitment to a theoretical position.

No doubt there is interaction between theory and practice. People who are trained for the practice of psychoanalysis, or for psychoanalytically oriented psychotherapy, naturally tend to interpret Freudian theories in ways that lend support to what they do; and their practice often cuts them off from experiences that might broaden their horizons. When they are thus led to overgeneralize from their clinical experience, or to overaccent the role of childhood traumata in personality functioning, they become easy targets for the sociological critics. But these critics, if they are to attack Freudian psychodynamic theories effectively, must do more than suggest that belief in these theories has led to the poor allocation of our mental health resources.

These critics have, of course, done more. They have attacked the theories directly—both the theory of determination of neurosis in early childhood and the theory of personality change that underlies psychoanalytic psychotherapies.

With respect to the determination of mental illness, the social scientists critical of psychoanalysis have argued that broad social and economic factors such as social disorganization, unemployment, and bad housing may be more important than emotional crises arising in the context of relationships within the family. But this does not seem to touch the psychodynamic theories themselves, for however much one may be struck by bad cultural and social conditions and feel moved to change them, an explication of their role in psychopathology would still have to make clear the ways in which they affect the individual personality. And here the role of the family as mediator and the role of psychodynamic mechanisms of input and adaptation seem as important as ever.

Nor does the social scientist's accent upon events occurring later in the individual's life, rather than upon the events of childhood, lead to any great shaking of the psychodynamic position. It is possible for the psychoanalyst to agree readily that "later events are important, too," for nothing has happened to threaten his view that in every neurotic or psychotic breakdown there was a predisposition laid down in early childhood. This view is not contradicted by evidence that such a breakdown would not have occurred but for severe strains arising in adult life. The psychoanalyst would say that people with neurotic or psychotic predispositions commonly find modes of life that serve their defensive needs or offer enough support so that a more or less adequate existence is possible. Breakdowns come when supports are withdrawn or when radical change in the individual's situation renders his defensive operations ineffective. This seems to have happened to thousands of young men when they were inducted into the armed services during World War II.

This is not to say that there are not environmentally determined strains of such severity or of such a character as to cause prolonged emotional disturbance, malfunctioning, or deviant behavior in anyone—regardless of predisposition or resistance. The psychoanalyst would say simply that these disturbances are not manifestations of neurosis in his sense of the term; and the fact that this is so, he would argue, helps to explain why so many people with severe psychological problems get well without benefit of professional help.

Sophisticated critics of psychodynamic theory have warned their colleagues in social science, who have thought they had psychoanalysis on the run, not to throw out the baby with the bath water. It may be suggested to enthusiastic social and situational determinists that they approach this whole baby-bath complex with caution. We are dealing here with differences in emphasis upon one or another aspect of what should be a total theory of causation. In particular cases there will always be a question of whether the situational or the predispositional factors were crucially important, and the psychoanalysts will often turn out to be right.

The psychodynamic theories, then, remain pretty much intact—so far—but when it comes to the question of what to do, the social scientists and the public health specialists have made a point. No psychodynamicist can deny the importance of precipitating factors in mental disease, or of situational events in emotional disturbance. There are enough unnecessary strains and enough failures in support in the lives of enough people in this country to keep an army of preventers busy. And since the strains and lacks of support affect millions, it seems clear that actions that might modify these conditions in whole communities have a better chance of reducing rates of mental illness than does psychotherapy with its very limited applicability.

The second major line of argument against psychoanalysis and the psychodynamic theory has to do with the nature of personality and the processes of personality change. Once again it seems well to separate arguments about practice from arguments about theory. Many psychologists, psychiatrists, and psychoanalysts, in addition to social scientists and public health specialists, have long been aware of the practical limitations of psychotherapy and have sought substitutes for it. The success of such substitutes as group psychotherapy or even the therapeutic community does not necessarily imply any criticism of the theory, nor does the fact that various kinds of psychotherapy besides psychoanalytic ones bring benefits to patients. Actions that induce changes in people and the explanation of those changes are two different things.

The same consideration holds generally for activities designed to effect changes in behavior without pretending to modify the structures of the personality. Certain types of alcoholism, for example, can be regarded as symptoms of underlying disturbances in the personality. Action which leads to the exchange of alcoholism for some other symptom but involves no change in personality might be a great benefit both to the alcoholic patient and to people around him.

The crucial theoretical question is: "How central or all-determining, within the personality, are the unconscious structures laid down in early childhood?" There is a tendency sometimes found among psychoanalysts, and often attributed to them by their critics, to suppose that personality formation is a matter of building unconscious defenses against instincts, and that personality development is a matter of undoing, or having undone, these defenses and of contriving better ones. Some psychoanalysts and some psychologists sympathetic to psychoanalysis (26–28), as well as numerous writers of quite different persuasions (29–31) have argued and assembled evidence to show that this is not the whole story. There are parts of the personality that do not become involved in the child's unconscious complexes, and always there are parts of the personality not dominated by unconscious processes but open to modification through ordinary experience. Significantly, the best evidence for this view has been contributed not by psychotherapists, who focus on neurotic structures, but by investigators who have seen neurotic or mentally ill people in various settings other than psychotherapy. Most impressive has been evidence from work in mental hospitals that even the most seriously ill patients are still capable of functioning in organized groups and of responding to stimuli which in normal people raise or lower self-respect (32), (33).

The point is of enormous significance, both for the care of the mentally ill and for prevention. It means that much can be done for people in trouble, outside as well as inside mental hospitals, by less highly trained professionals and even by nonprofessionals, for, on this view of the matter, benefit to troubled people does not flow entirely from changes in their unconscious structure or even from psychological understanding of them. And where the concern is with the education and upbringing of children, it means that one makes no mistake when he devotes effort to the development of those parts of the personality that are free or relatively free of involvement with unconscious processes. It does *not* mean that those who have responsibility for troubled children can ignore the unconscious processes determining their symptoms; for although such children can respond to efforts to develop the unimpaired parts of their personalities, some of them will, if not understood, insist on acting out their unconscious motives in ways irreparably destructive to themselves or others. One may hope that with respect to facilities for troubled children we will not always have to choose between those which adhere to rigid stereotypes of Freudian categories and those inspired by a blind optimism concerning what can be achieved by providing a favorable environment.

The final issue concerns the possibilities of modifying unconscious structures of the personality by means other than psychotherapy or its equivalents. The writer has argued elsewhere (*34*), on the basis of observations of college students, that in individuals with symptoms based on underlying neurotic structures developments in the unimpaired parts of the personality may so change the relationships between what is conscious and what is unconscious that the latter fades into relative insignificance. And the writer has also argued (*35*) that unconscious processes are not necessarily cut off from direct influence by social stimuli. The traditional and well-substantiated psychodynamic view is that unconscious processes have a heavy determining effect upon cognition; there is reason to believe that the determination may also be the other way around. This is a frontier area for research—although those who have no truck with concepts of the unconscious will not be intrigued by it.

Once again, this kind of liberalization of the psychodynamic view is consistent with the "new thinking" that supports the activities of social scientists and public health specialists who would reduce rates of mental illness by modifying the social environment. Some supporters of the "new thought" seem to have come by their liberal views too easily. It will be up to clinical psychologists to see to it that the practical orientation, and particularly the practical success, of the new breed of mental health workers does not impair investigation into the nature of personality organization and functioning. In the long run, knowledge of these matters will be essential if preventive work is to reach a high level of effectiveness.

ORIENTATION TO VALUE

All programs of preventive action have to be guided by values, that is, values over and above the simple faith that mental illness is bad. This follows from the fact that pathological conditions are not isolated in the person (a change in them might induce desirable or undesirable changes in other areas of the person) and from the consideration that actions deemed necessary to prevent an unhealthy condition may affect a person in various ways, some good and some bad.

The mental health specialist faces this issue as soon as he says, as he must, that he wants to be sure his preventive actions do not do more harm than good. The evaluation in such a case cannot possibly be limited to the single dimension of increased or decreased "mental health," for it is unthinkable that all virtues, all desiderata of human development, can be brought under the mental illness-mental health rubric. To be convinced of this one has only to ask what should a person who has achieved mental health do with himself, or whether one would be willing to give up our ideals of individualism in order to eliminate psychological strains and thus to reduce rates of mental illness. It would be hard to imagine circumstances in which the goal of reducing or preventing mental illness should take precedence over humanity, or justice, or the fullest possible development of the individual's potential.

Critics of the efforts by psychologists to formulate positive goals for people—too often, unfortunately, under the banner of "positive mental health"—early critics such as Kingsley Davis (*16*) and late ones such as Elaine Cumming (*36*)—do not belabor the psychologists so much for having values as for having the wrong values, that is to say values which these sociologists would not put very high on *their* hierarchy. Fundamentally, it seems, writers such as these want more "social conscience" and less "social desirability" or, more seriously, more attention to the welfare of people in general and less to what might be ideal for particular individuals.

In the literature on positive mental health, two conceptions of positive mental health may be differentiated. First, there is the conception of something, over and above freedom from illness, that stands as resistance to, or relative immunity from, mental illness. There would seem to be a place for this conception, and for research that could specify what such a condition might be. The criticism that positive mental health is indefinable would seem not to apply with any great force here, for to define resistance, and to specify it experimentally, would seem to be no more difficult than to define and to specify susceptibility to illness. The second conception embodies a set of ideals referring to what a person might become. This conception might easily come into conflict with the first one, for it may turn out that qualities, such as insensitivity for example, which contribute to resistance to illness, do not fit into conceptions of the ideal.

Particular conceptions of this second kind are always easy to criticize. Frequently they can be shown to be culture-bound or class-bound, or expressions of particular historical periods. But the search for ideals must go on, and there is no reason why psychologists and social scientists should not take part in the quest. If these scientists are to assist in the designing of plans for the upbringing and education of children and youth, they must be guided by open-ended conceptions of what people can become. They need commit themselves only tentatively to particular systems of value, while continuing their efforts to improve thinking about values—by showing how values are arrived at and what will be the consequences of particular values. Perhaps they can make their greatest contribution by urging —and this flows directly from knowledge they now have—that where human beings are concerned, ends and means cannot be separated. In a humanistic approach to prevention, means as well as ends are humanistic. This is to say that long-range programs of discipline or deprivation aimed at the ultimate inculcation of some virtue cannot be supported. What is good for people in the long run is, by and large, good for them *now*. Actions that aim to develop people or to build resistance to mental illness can be evaluated in the momentary situation without waiting for long-range consequences.

Such evaluation would take into account the motives, feelings and behavior of the "helping" parent or professional as well as the immediate effects of their actions upon the object of their concern. If the helpers are well motivated and their actions have good effects upon *them*, the chances are that the other will be benefited.

CONCLUSION

Despite all that has been said about social actions to prevent mental disorder, the fact remains that there are and there will be in the future people in trouble who need the help of the individual clinician. Indeed there are at the present time far more such people than all available psychotherapists could possibly take care of. We cannot turn away from those who present themselves to us for help just because our helping them would not seem to contribute much to the total effort to reduce mental disorder.

On the other hand, the clinical psychologist should be well aware of the fact that times are changing. It seems not unlikely that the present generation of psychotherapists will be the last to devote themselves primarily to the private practice of psychotherapy. But lest this picture be overdrawn, let us remember that psychotherapy still has, and should have, a highly important place in the training and in the work of the clinical psychologist. To perform psychotherapy or to take responsibility for individuals in trouble is still the best way to learn about people. It is not only the best way for the individual psychologist to acquire knowledge of the functioning of the person as a whole, but it remains a major source of hypotheses for subsequent testing by rigorous methods. Moreover, experience designed to give the individual insight into his own functioning is still an invaluable part of preparation for psychological work in various settings. This means that an important function of the most highly trained mental health specialist—that is, the psychoanalytic psychotherapist—will continue to be the training of, and consultation with, other specialists and the advancement of knowledge through observations from his special vantage point.

In order to realize the benefits of this special training, the psychoanalytic psychotherapist must work in other settings besides that of the two-person therapeutic one. If he is to make his full contribution to the prevention of mental illness, he must work in various fields—educational, industrial, medical, correction, and social welfare—in which service to the vulnerable is offered and in which developmental crises occur. Although in the foreseeable future there will be a place for individual diagnosis and treatment, the clinical psychologist who would be maximally useful must broaden his horizons in order to utilize his special knowledge of people in settings where actions for human welfare are carried out.

REFERENCES

1. Joint Commission on Mental Illness and Health. *Action for Mental Health.* New York: Basic Books, 1961.
2. Dubos, R. Paper read at National Association for Mental Health, Miami, 1962.
3. Beers, C. *A Mind That Found Itself.* Garden City, N.Y.: Doubleday, 1921.
4. Seeley, J. R. Social values, the mental health movement, and mental health. *Ann. Amer. Acad. Polit. Soc. Sci.,* 1953, *286,* 15–24.
5. Rickman, J. *On the Bringing Up of Children.* London: Routledge, 1938.
6. Freud, S. The question of lay analysis. In *Standard Edition of Freud's Collected Works.* Vol. XX. London: Hogarth Press, 1959. Pp. 176–258.
7. Isaacs, Susan. *Social Development in Young Children.* London: Routledge, 1933.
8. Adler, A. *The Education of Children.* New York: Greenberg, 1930.
9. Ansbacher, H. L., & Ansbacher, R. R. (Eds.) *The Individual Psychology of Alfred Adler.* New York: Basic Books, 1956.

10. HORNEY, KAREN. *New Ways in Psychoanalysis*. New York: Norton, 1939.
11. FROMM, E. *The Fear of Freedom*. London: Routledge, 1942.
12. FROMM, E. *Man For Himself*. New York: Holt, 1947.
13. MURRAY, H. A. et al. *Explorations in Personality*. New York: Oxford Univer. Press, 1938.
14. OSS ASSESSMENT STAFF. *Assessment of Men*. New York: Holt, 1948.
15. JAHODA, MARIE. *Current Concepts of Positive Mental Health*. New York: Basic Books, 1958.
16. DAVIS, K. Mental hygiene and the class structure. *Psychiatry,* 1938, *1,* 55–65.
17. HARVARD MEDICAL SCHOOL AND PSYCHIATRIC SERVICE. *Community Mental Health and Social Psychiatry*. Cambridge, Mass.: Harvard University, 1962.
18. MCGAVRAN, E. G. Facing reality in public health. In *Key Issues in the Prevention of Alcoholism: A Report of the Northeast Conference*. Harrisburg: Pennsylvania Department of Health, 1963.
19. LEMKAU, P. V. Mental hygiene. In S. Arieti (Ed.), *American Handbook of Psychiatry*. Vol. II. New York: Basic Books, 1959. Pp. 1948–1959.
20. BOWLBY, J. *Maternal Care and Mental Health*. Geneva: WHO, 1951.
21. BOWLBY, J., AINSWORTH, MARY, BOSTON, MARY, & ROSENBLUTH, DINA. The effects of mother-child separation. *Brit. J. med. Psychol.,* 1956, *29,* 211–247.
22. FORSTENZER, H. M. Problems in relating community programs to state hospitals. *Amer. J. Publ. Hlth.,* 1961, *51,* 1152–1157.
23. HOLLINGSHEAD, A. B. & REDLICH, F. C. Social stratification and psychiatric disorders. *Amer. Sociol. Rev.,* 1953, *18,* 163–169.
24. ROSE, A., & STUB, H. Summary of studies on the incidence of mental disorders. In A. Rose (Ed.), *Mental Health and Mental Disorder*. New York: Norton, 1955. Pp. 87–116.
25. ALBEE, G. W. *Mental Health Manpower Trends*. New York: Basic Books, 1959.
26. HARTMANN, H., KRIS, E., & LOEWENSTEIN, R. M. Comments on the formation of psychic structure. *Psychoanal. Study of the Child,* 1947, *2,* 11–38.
27. SANFORD, N. What is a normal personality? In J. Katz, P. Nochlin, & R. Stover (Eds.), *Writers on Ethics*. Princeton, N.J.: Van Nostrand, 1962. Pp. 615–629.
28. WHITE, R. W. *Lives in Progress*. New York: Dryden, 1952.
29. MASLOW, A. H. *Motivation and Personality*. New York: Harper & Row, 1954.
30. ALLPORT, G. W. *Pattern and Growth in Personality*. New York: Holt, 1961.

31. KELLY, G. *The Psychology of Personal Constructs.* Vol. 1. New York: Norton, 1953.
32. GREENBLATT, M., LEVINSON, D. J., & WILLIAMS, R. H. (Eds.) *The Patient and the Mental Hospital.* Glencoe, Ill.: Free Press, 1957.
33. MILBANK MEMORIAL FUND. *An Approach to the Prevention of Disability from Chronic Psychosis.* New York: Milbank Fund, 1958.
34. SANFORD, N. Ends and means in higher education. In *Current Issues in Higher Education.* Washington, D.C.: Assn. for Higher Education, 1962. Pp. 10–20.
35. SANFORD, N. Surface and depth in the individual personality. *Psychol. Rev.,* 1956, *63,* 349–359.
36. CUMMING, ELAINE. Pathways to prevention. In *Key Issues in the Prevention of Alcoholism: A Report of the Northeast Conference.* Harrisburg: Pennsylvania Department of Health, 1963.

....

Personality Measurement and the Ethics of Assessment*[1]

SAMUEL MESSICK

PSYCHOLOGICAL TESTING IN general and personality measurement in particular have been severely criticized in recent years on charges that vary all the way from "tests are inaccurate" to "tests are anti-Democratic and subvert American values [Amrine, 1963, p. 266]." For example, four of the major criticisms, which were recently discussed and rebutted by Ebel (1964), include the views that (a) tests dictate permanent status and hence undermine self-esteem and limit motivation; (b) tests decrease diversity of talent by focusing attention on narrowly conceived, easily measurable attainments; (c) the widespread use of tests gives the tester potential control over educational and industrial practice, as well as over the destinies of individuals; and (d) tests foster impersonal and mechanistic evaluations and decisions at the expense of individual freedom of choice. In addition, testing, particularly personality testing, has been branded an unwarranted invasion of privacy, an "indirect inquisition into your most personal affairs." [2]

These charges do not stem only from disgruntled parents dissatisfied with their youngsters' low test scores but apparently reflect a significant segment of public opinion as expressed by journalists, teachers, deans, and United States Senators. Thus, it would seem that psychologists who use assessment, particularly personality assessment, in the pursuit of their science or in the practice of their

* From the *American Psychologist*, 1965, *20*, 136–142.

[1] The author wishes to thank Junius Davis and Silvan Tomkins for the benefit of several clarifying discussions on the problem of self-regulation in psychological assessment, and to thank Sydell Carlton, William Coffman, Fred Damarin, Salvatore Maddi, and David Rosenhan for their helpful comments on the manuscript.

[2] Barry Goldwater, quoted in Amrine (1964, p. 216).

profession have run afoul of powerful social forces that view themselves as operating to protect the public interest. We can anticipate that this public hostility to psychological testing may be funneled through institutional and legislative channels and that attempts may be made to control the application of personality assessment and to limit the areas of acceptable inquiry. In order to avoid these external controls and to maintain the autonomy of psychology as a science and a profession, it is argued by some that we should seize the initiative by moving toward self-regulation.

But self-regulation of psychological assessment is no simple matter, not only because the normative standards and values that should govern such regulation are manifold, but primarily because many of these norms and values are in conflict. This problem of a conflict of commitment in the assessment of personality and its implications for the regulative process will be developed later.

SELF-REGULATION OR PUBLIC RELATIONS?

Before accepting the immediate need for further regulation, however, we should briefly consider whether the charges brought forward warrant this action and what such a decision might imply. Except for some specific (and sometimes cogent) critiques of selected test items, most of the criticisms of psychological testing have been in the form of blanket indictments that fail to distinguish the different uses a test may serve. One of the major criticisms is quite simply that some tests are poor. Although this is lamentably often true, it is also the case that many tests are poor for some purposes and quite adequate for others. A second major criticism is that tests are often misused—that they are frequently employed for inappropriate purposes or, when appropriate, are often applied in misleading or ineffective ways. The first charge impugns the adequacy of tests, the second the adequacy of testing practice. Taken together, along with the complaint that tests invade privacy, they provide a capsule summary of the points made by various test critics (Lyman, 1963). Since psychology has already established both psychometric standards for evaluating the adequacy of a test and ethical standards for guiding test use, and since some of the recent criticisms have been extravagant and unfair, we might ponder whether the immediate need is for further self-restriction (as opposed to renewed affirmation of existing principles) or for improved public relations. Further efforts at public education on the nature of tests and the motives of the testers, following the excellent beginnings of Chauncey and Dobbin (1963), Ebel (1964), Hathaway (1964), and Wolfle (1963), would seem called for.

THE DILEMMA OF REGULATION

I do not mean to imply that our present test standards and ethical principles are perfect or even sufficient. On the contrary, I feel they should be revised periodically to take account of improved methods and changing norms. Indeed, in light of the recent controversy, they may currently need considerable clarification in the area of test use. The point is not that we should refuse to implement further self-regulation, but rather that we should be cautious and insist that any changes in our ethical standards be based upon their intrinsic merits and not upon external pressures. We should be especially careful not to let it be inferred that any change in our standards for psychological assessment necessarily reflects a general admission of past guilt. A few unethical practices may have occurred, to be sure, along with many inadequacies of omission and commission, but the majority of recent criticisms seem to have been incurred at least as much through the misconceptions and restricted purview of our critics as through the incompetence and ethical lapses of our colleagues.

For the most part, the unethical and inadequate practices that have unfortunately occurred in recent applications of psychological assessment have already been condemned in the "Technical Recommendations for Psychological Tests and Diagnostic Techniques" (APA, 1954) and in the *Ethical Standards of Psychologists* (APA, 1953). Other reprehensible tactics that have not been previously anticipated could also readily be covered at any point by recommending elaborations to these codes of acceptable practice. The problem, then, in the regulation of much of assessment practice is not in the statement of principles about which most of the profession could agree—this has already been done or could easily be done on many issues. The problem lies in the formulation of a workable control procedure for enforcing the accepted principles. The present paper will not be concerned with this type of problem in self-regulation, i.e., where the guiding principles are generally accepted and the major concern lies in formulating an adequate control mechanism. Rather, I will direct attention to those situations where serious differences of opinion exist as to which principles deserve ultimate allegiance and where attempts to resolve these differences founder upon conflicts of commitment having much of value on both sides.

Such conflicts of commitment in the area of personality assessment pose a dilemma for psychology similar to one discussed by Gouldner (1962) in his brilliant analysis of Weber's doctrine of a value-free social science. Gouldner points out that the expression of value differences in the German universities of Weber's day threatened to provoke the state into censoring the universities, thereby jeopardizing their autonomy. Partly in an effort to avoid the impending external control and to free social scientists to go on with their work, Weber proposed the principle that sociology should be value free. Gouldner (1962) counters that

one might as reasonably argue to the contrary, holding that one limitation of freedom is no excuse for another. Granting the reality of efforts to inhibit unpopular views in the University, it seems odd to prescribe self-suppression as a way of avoiding external suppression. Suicide does not seem a reasonable way to avoid being murdered. It appears, however, that Weber was so intent on safeguarding the autonomy of the university and the autonomy of politics, that he was willing to pay almost any price to do so, even if this led the university to detach itself from one of the basic intellectual traditions of the west—the dialectical exploration of the fundamental purposes of human life [p. 203].

These are extravagant phrases, perhaps, to invoke in connection with our dilemma in assessment, but a similar danger may be present, even if not clear. Psychological assessment is pursued for many purposes, and the norms and values guiding these pursuits are sometimes in conflict. Self-regulation in the face of value conflicts must be determined by policy decisions, with all of their inherent dangers of fallibility and possible arbitrariness. In considering the nature of these value conflicts and some of their implications for regulation and policy making in the field of testing, we will next discuss some of the major uses of assessment and the relativity of both test properties and ethical requirements to the purpose and context of the measurement.

USES OF ASSESSMENT

Relativity of Test Properties to Assessment Purposes

The two major criticisms discussed earlier, that some tests are poor in quality and that tests are often misused, parallel two major questions that arise in evaluating the appropriateness of a particular test administration: (*a*) Is the test any good as a measure of the characteristic it purports to assess? (*b*) Should the test be used for its present purpose? The first question is a scientific one and may be answered by evaluating the test's reliability, construct validity, and empirical criterion validity against standards of psychometric adequacy (Campbell, 1960; Campbell & Fiske, 1959; Cronbach & Meehl, 1955; Loevinger, 1957). The second question is partly an ethical one, and the answer may require a justification of the proposed use of the test in terms of social values (Messick, 1964).

Answers to the second question are clearly a function of the purposes of the testing and the intended uses of the test information, but it is not as widely appreciated that for personality tests the properties evaluated in the first question are also relative to the purposes and circumstances of the testing. We commonly recognize that a test has as many empirical validities as there are criteria with which it has been correlated. In addition, however, since the motives and defenses of the respondents intervene, a test may also exhibit different proportions of reliable variance and even measure different constructs under different testing circumstances. The psychometric properties of a test on a particular occasion are a function of the psychological processes used in responding, and these processes, being determined in part by the conceptions and needs of the respondents, often entail mechanisms of self-deception and deliberate facades (Messick, 1964). Thus, a test may measure one thing in the context of scientific inquiry in a research laboratory, but radically different things if administered for diagnostic guidance in a clinic or for personal evaluation in college or industry. Furthermore, even ethical limitations upon the manner of gathering private information vary widely for these different testing purposes (Cronbach, 1960).

Assessment for Diagnosis and Guidance

In counseling and psychotherapy, assessment is undertaken for the benefit of the individual client, to clarify his condition and to help him make better personal decisions. The APA (1963) Ethical Standards include the following statements on client relationship and welfare:

The psychologist informs his prospective client of the important aspects of the potential relationship that might affect the client's decision to enter the relationship [Principle 8, p. 58].

The psychologist who asks that an individual reveal personal information in the course of interviewing, testing, or evaluation, or who allows such information to be divulged to him, does so only after making certain that the responsible person is fully aware of the purposes of the interview, testing, or evaluation and of the ways in which the information may be used [Principle 7d, p. 57].

In line with these precepts, Cronbach (1960) points out that even though the client comes freely into the clinic or guidance office seeking help, he can still be offered the warning that some of the tests and questions to be used are indirect and may reveal things that he is not prepared to unveil. "The psychologist is not 'invading privacy,'" according to Cronbach (1960), "where he is freely admitted and where he has a genuine need for the information obtained [p. 460]." But the two parts of this statement may sometimes conflict. What if the psychologist is not freely admitted but he does feel a genuine need for the information in his concern for the client's welfare? Although such information might not be very useful anyway in counseling the client (Cronbach, 1960), it could be quite critical in the clinical setting. As long as the patient does not terminate the relationship (so his continued presence might be interpreted by the psychologist as tacit approval), does the psychologist have license to circumvent defensive resistance? Under these circumstances, is it our obligation to respect privacy absolutely or not to invade it offensively or for trivial purposes? And what would be the standards for regulating this distinction?

Assessment for Selection

In academic and industrial selection, assessment is in the service of an institution rather than of the individual. Test information is gathered to help the institution make a decision about the individual's acceptability or placement. (Such information, incidentally, may also guide the individual's personal decisions, as in his choice of a college, but that has little relevance here.) Personal information pertinent to institutional policy is often required whether the applicant wishes to reveal it or not. In so doing, the issue of invasion of privacy is usually sidestepped, at least for private institutions: The individual does not have to apply for this job or for admission to this college if he does not want to. If he does apply, he should be willing to conform to the policies of the institution, at least as long as they do not violate any widely held public principles. The institutional psychologist is especially open to conflicts in his commitment to the individual applicant and to his institution, particularly in his attempts to implement institutional policies through an assessment program. He has an obligation to the institution to see that its selection decisions are based upon optimally valid and economical assessment procedures. But he also has an obligation to protect the dignity of the individual applicant by ensuring that the assessment experience is not unduly offensive. By what norms, however, do we judge the infringement of one obligation upon the other?

Assessment for Research

In personality research, assessment is frequently undertaken to obtain measures of psychological variables in order to study their interrelations and their interactions with experimental treatments. The test information is gathered neither for the benefit of the individual nor for the benefit of an institution, but rather for the advancement of science. Considerably more leeway is usually afforded psychologists in research settings with regard to the problem of invasion of privacy, since the subjects can be assured that the information is being obtained for scientific purposes only and will be revealed in no way that could be identified with them personally or that could affect their position. Cronbach (1960) states that

No ethical objection can be raised to the use of subtle techniques and even misleading instructions when the information so obtained will be used entirely for research purposes, the subject's identity being concealed in any report [p. 461].

But what of the subjects who demur anyway, in spite of our efforts to build a reputation for trustworthiness in this regard? Perhaps they do not wish to have certain things revealed even to themselves and hesitate to confront the questions. If they are members of a captive population, another conflict of commitment arises—this time between our obligation to protect the subject from undue exposure to stress and our obligation to avoid biasing our scientific investigations by relying exclusively upon volunteer samples. Nor would our agreement to use only volunteers as subjects in research avoid this conflict completely. Their consent to participate would be meaningful in this context only if it were based upon a realistic appraisal of their prospective experience, and again our concern about biasing the data usually prevents us from providing the appropriate specific information in advance. On these issues, the APA (1953) Ethical Standards state that

Only when a problem is significant and can be investigated in no other way is the psychologist justified in exposing research subjects to emotional stress [Principle 4.31-1, p. 122].

The psychologist is justified in withholding information from or giving misinformation to research subjects only when in his judgment this is clearly required by his research problem and when the provisions of the above principle regarding the protection of the subjects are adhered to [Principle 4.31-2, p. 122].

But by what criteria do we judge when the potential significance of a research problem offsets possible threats to the subject's welfare or justifies misleading him, either to obtain his cooperation or to study his behavior?

CONFLICTS OF COMMITMENT AND THE REGULATIVE PROCESS

We have seen that personality tests, and even personality testers, operate differently under different testing circumstances. The properties of a test vary as a function of the purposes of the testing and the intended uses of the test information. Psychologists' evaluations of the appropriateness of a test in a particular instance are dependent upon the uses to which the test is to be put. Absolute evaluations—that a test is good for all purposes or poor for all purposes—do not occur, at least on the positive side. We have complained that our critics, in their monolithic charges that tests are poor and that privacy is being invaded, have not made their criticisms appropriately relative to the purposes of the testing. Now, as we appraise the desirability of further self-regulation in assessment, we should insist that psychology not make the same error.

Absolute rules forbidding the use of these tests or those questions because they delve into contents beyond the bounds of decent inquiry would be an intolerable limitation both to scientific freedom and to professional freedom. It makes a difference why the information is being sought! Thus, in our consideration of possible ethical bases for self-regulation in assessment, it seems imperative that we go beyond ethical absolutism (or what Weber has called the "ethics of ultimate ends") and espouse an "ethics of responsibility," in which pragmatic evaluations of the consequences of alternative actions form the basis for particular ethical decisions. In Weber's words:

> The matter does not appear to me to be so desperate if one does not ask too exclusively . . . "Who is morally right and who is morally wrong?" But if one rather asks: "Given the existing conflict, how can I solve it with the least internal and external damage for all concerned?" [Gerth & Mills, 1946, p. 9]

In this sense, then, we need continual assessments of ethics as the basis for an ethics of assessment.

This recommendation provides a general precept that self-regulation in assessment should be relative to the intended uses of the test and to the circumstances of testing; it does not offer much help, however, in specifying the nature of an adequate regulative process. Ordinarily, regulation involves the setting up of standards or norms and attempting, by careful monitoring and the use of correction procedures, to keep certain performances in line with these standards. The situation becomes more complicated when, as in psychological assessment, the norms are manifold, disparate, and relative. In addition, some provision must be made for adjusting the standards themselves, since some norms, particularly those that embody our aspirations and not just our minimum requirements, frequently change with the efforts made to attain them. Yet, even in the face of disparate and changing standards, the regulative enterprise, however intricate it may become, is still relatively straightforward, as long as the various norms can be organized into a hierarchy with clear orders of precedence and with all norms ultimately subordinate to a single guiding principle (Vickers, 1964). The problem for self-regulation in psychological assessment, however, lies precisely in the lack of such a hierarchy: Competing norms are frequently not ordered but instead reflect dissonant values.

As I have tried to indicate for several areas of application, we face conflicts of commitment in personality assessment that are similar to the conflict of commitment in clinical research so brilliantly analyzed recently by Loevinger (1963). These conflicts are not determined solely by the fact that psychology is both a science and a profession, although that undoubtedly exacerbates the problem. In addition to clashes between scientific and professional commitments, value conflicts also arise within the science (e.g., Baumrind, 1964) and within the profession as well (e.g., Krasner, 1962; London, 1964; Rychlak, 1964). The primary source of the difficulty appears to reside in the fact that the object of the science and the user of the professional services is man, and "the psychologist believes in the dignity and worth of the individual human being [APA, 1963, p. 56]."

Unfortunately, it is the nature of value conflicts that they are not often resolved easily or even rationally. In the face of these conflicting norms, then, how might the self-regulation of psychological assessment proceed? One approach would be to emphasize the *self* in self-regulation and exhort individual psychologists to evaluate carefully the consequences of their actions. Each would be responsible for his own decisions and liable to sanctions if complaints were lodged against him. But on what basis would the complaints be adjudicated? In order to avoid anarchy and to provide at least some rough standards for evaluating conduct, it would seem necessary to add to such a system of strictly individual responsibility a set of general principles, such as our current Ethical Standards of Psychologists, with which nearly everyone could concur. But how might we provide precepts in advance to guide individual judgments in those critical areas where consensus is split, where values clash? One answer would be to eliminate the value conflicts by fiat, to take a vote to favor one side or the other, to establish *policy*. However, the circumvention of value conflicts by policy making is an extremely hazardous undertaking. As Loevinger (1963) puts it, these value dialogues are like "the battle of the sexes. . . . If either side wins, the cause is lost [p. 243]." It is discomforting to contemplate, but in the resolution of conflicts in values, even if by compromise, somebody (and occasionally everybody) gets hurt. As we might have learned from the history of medicine, risks may have to be taken to secure the scientific and professional advancement of the general welfare. It falls to the policy makers to decide when the benefits are worth the risks. An awesome obligation to be sure, but not the only one; there is yet another responsibility the policy makers must share.

THE IMPACT OF POLICY

Sir Geoffrey Vickers (1964) has recently pointed out that the policy-making process, as a response to conflicting and manifold demands arising from what he called "appreciating a situation," has two distinct consequences: one the intended regulative effect and the other a change in the evaluative context or atmosphere of the regulated domain. This change in atmosphere affects the way people look at things, the details they select for emphasis, the interpretations they favor, and it thereby helps to determine the values of the future. Vickers (1964) illustrated this long-range impact of policy with an account of a 1920 Supreme Court decision that upheld a conviction of sedition for the publication of pro-Bolshevik literature. Seven Justices voted in favor of the conviction, but one dissented. To the seven judges

the publication was an act of sedition; as such the law required that it should be suppressed and punished. To Justice Oliver Wendell Holmes it was an expression of opinion; as such it was absolutely protected under the constitution. . . . Holmes was more prone to see threats to the free speech of men; the others more prone to see threats to the stability of society. They were at issue not on what to do but on how to see; and unlike most of us, they knew it [Vickers, 1964, p. 470].

Vickers went on to point out that in 1920 Joseph McCarthy was a young man. He was not implying that this Supreme Court decision determined McCarthy's values in a direct way, but that it helped to create an atmosphere in which those values could flourish.

Overview

What can we distill from all of this for our problem of self-regulation in psychological assessment? To begin with, there is the recognition that, apart from obvious faults on both sides, much of the recent controversy about testing represents a dialogue between conflicting values. These value conflicts exist not only between the testers and the critics but within psychology as well: "The psychologist believes in the dignity and worth of the individual human being," and at the same time "he is committed to increasing man's understanding of himself and others [APA, 1963, p. 56]." The implementation of self-regulation in psychological assessment would seem to require that some of these conflicts of commitment be resolved by policy decisions. The policy makers, however, are faced with both a dilemma and a responsibility. They face a dilemma because they must attempt to decide what the behavior at issue "really" is. Is it sedition or the free expression of opinion? Is it invasion of privacy or a legitimate inquiry for advancing individual or general welfare? And there are no *correct* answers; there are only opinions as to what some *good* answers might be (Vickers, 1964). They face a responsibility because a policy decision to favor one side or the other, or to compromise the issue, may create an atmosphere in psychology that would bias scientific and professional values of the future. Therefore, if the pressures of reality lead us to establish further policy-based self-regulation in psychological assessment, it would seem imperative to include at the same time formal provisions for its continuing reappraisal. Many may consider such a precaution to be a time-consuming annoyance, but since "policy sits above conscience," [3] its rule should not be extended unquestioned beyond the tenure of necessity. The intention here is not to subvert the utility of policy as a regulative principle, but to moderate its impact on the atmosphere of the regulated domain and, above all, to keep the dialogue open.

References

AMERICAN PSYCHOLOGICAL ASSOCIATION. *Ethical Standards of Psychologists.* Washington, D.C.: APA, 1953.
AMERICAN PSYCHOLOGICAL ASSOCIATION. Technical recommendations for

[3] William Shakespeare, *Timon of Athens,* Act III, Scene 2, Line 95.

332   PERSPECTIVES IN CLINICAL PSYCHOLOGY

psychological tests and diagnostic techniques. *Psychological Bulletin,* 1954, *51* (2, Part 2).

AMERICAN PSYCHOLOGICAL ASSOCIATION. Ethical standards of psychologists. *American Psychologist,* 1963, *18,* 56–60.

AMRINE, M. Psychology in the news. *American Psychologist,* 1963, *18,* 265–267.

AMRINE, M. Psychology in the news. *American Psychologist,* 1964, *19,* 216–218.

BAUMRIND, DIANA. Some thoughts on ethics of research: After reading Milgram's "Behavioral study of obedience." *American Psychologist,* 1964, *19,* 421–423.

CAMPBELL, D. T. Recommendations for APA test standards regarding construct, trait, or discriminant validity. *American Psychologist,* 1960, *15,* 546–553.

CAMPBELL, D. T., & FISKE, D. W. Convergent and discriminant validation by the multitrait-multimethod matrix. *Psychological Bulletin,* 1959, *56,* 81–105.

CHAUNCEY, H., & DOBBIN, J. E. *Testing: Its Place in Education Today.* New York: Harper & Row, 1963.

CRONBACH, L. J. *Essentials of Psychological Testing.* (2nd ed.) New York: Harper, 1960.

CRONBACH, L. J., & MEEHL, P. E. Construct validity in psychological tests. *Psychological Bulletin,* 1955, *52,* 281–302.

EBEL, R. L. The social consequences of educational testing. In *Proceedings of the 1963 Invitational Conference on Testing Problems.* Princeton, N.J.: Educational Testing Service, 1964.

GERTH, H. H., & MILLS, C. W. *From Max Weber: Essays in Sociology.* New York: Oxford Univer. Press, 1946. (Reprinted: Galaxy, 1958.)

GOULDNER, A. W. Anti-minotaur: The myth of a value-free sociology. *Social Problems,* 1962, *9,* 199–213.

HATHAWAY, S. R. MMPI: Professional use by professional people. *American Psychologist,* 1964, *19,* 204–210.

KRASNER, L. Behavior control and social responsibility. *American Psychologist,* 1962, *17,* 199–204.

LOEVINGER, JANE. Objective tests as instruments of psychological theory. *Psychological Reports,* 1957, *3,* 635–694.

LOEVINGER, JANE. Conflict of commitment in clinical research. *American Psychologist,* 1963, *18,* 241–251.

LONDON, P. *The Modes and Morals of Psychotherapy.* New York: Holt, Rinehart & Winston, 1964.

LYMAN, H. B. Review of M. L. Gross, *The Brain Watchers,* and B. Hoffman, *The Tyranny of Testing. Journal of the Association of College Admissions Counselors,* 1963, *8,* 31–32.

MESSICK, S. Personality measurement and college performance. In *Proceedings of the 1963 Invitational Conference on Testing Problems*. Princeton, N.J.: Educational Testing Service, 1964.

RYCHLAK, J. F. Control and prediction and the clinician. *American Psychologist*, 1964, *19*, 186–190.

VICKERS, G. The psychology of policy making and social change. *British Journal of Psychiatry*, 1964, *110*, 465–477.

WOLFLE, D. Educational tests. *Science*, 1963, *142*, 1529.